BEST SEAT
in the House

BEST SEAT
in the House

Untold Stories of:

DiMaggio
Mantle
& Foreman
Other Sports Legends

Dan Wheeler

DELSTAR™

Printed in the United States of America

Publisher's Cataloging-in-Publication
(Provided by Quality Books, Inc.)

Wheeler, Dan, 1954–
    Best seat in the house : untold stories of DiMaggio,
Mantle, Foreman & other sports legends / Dan Wheeler.—
1st ed.
    p. cm.
    ISBN 1-891686-21-6

    1. Athletes—Biography. 2. Sports—History—20th
century. I. Title.

GV697.A1W44 2001   796'092'2
                                             QB100-901584

06 05 04 03 02 01 00   10 9 8 7 6 5 4 3 2 1

Cover and book design: Ron Hughes

DelStar Books
3350 Palms Center Drive
Las Vegas, NV 89103
Phone: (702) 798-9000
Fax: (702) 597-2002
e-mail: DelStarBooks@aol.com

This book is dedicated to my mom, Marjorie Wheeler, who always taught me to believe that "with God all things are possible." I love you, Mom!

Contents

Foreword

By George Foreman

I had been out of professional boxing for eight years in 1985. I was leading a fairly quiet life that involved pastoring a church and running the George Foreman Youth and Community Center to help young boys get off the street. Most of the media had forgotten about George Foreman at that time, and that was fine with me.

One day my phone rang, and an enthusiastic gentleman told me he wanted to come down to Texas with a television crew to produce a documentary about my life. At first I was apprehensive. I wasn't convinced that my story would be told in an objective way. But this young man was persistent, and he wasn't going to take "no" for an answer. I had met some pretty tough opponents in the boxing ring over the years, but this guy was as tenacious as any I had ever met.

After several phone calls, I decided to "throw in the towel" and let him come down to Texas to tell my story.

The first day I met Dan Wheeler, I was impressed with his desire to do things right. He was a hard worker, and he made me work hard. He was able to get me to do things that I hadn't done in years. I'll never forget at the end of a long day of taping he said to me, "You know, George, it would be great to get a shot of you running down this long road in front of your ranch." I told him I would, but his crew had better get it right the first time because I was not in the best of shape, and I could only do it once. Fortunately, his cameraman got it right. Earlier in the day, Dan even got me to open up my old training gym on the ranch. I had hardly been inside since the day I walked away from boxing eight years earlier.

When I stepped into my old boxing ring that day, a strange feeling came over me. My mind was flooded with memories of a sport that had been good to me. For a brief moment, I even had the crazy thought that I could come back and win the Heavyweight Boxing Title of the world past the age of 40! Imagine that. Well, you never know what can happen to you when you walk down memory lane. And I should say that Dan was one of the few people in the world who actually believed that I could accomplish my crazy dream.

After four days of taping, Dan and his crew returned to Chicago. A few weeks later he sent me a copy of the documentary that he produced, entitled, *Winner by Decision: George Foreman.* Dan had delivered on his promise. He told my story in a way that was honest, fair, hard-hitting and even entertaining. That's the way that I have always tried to live my life (although I only hit hard in a boxing ring wearing thickly padded gloves). To this day, his documentary is the most thorough piece of television journalism that has ever been done on my life.

I lost touch with Dan over the next few years. I was pretty busy in the boxing ring, and he was busy producing television specials. Our paths crossed again years later, when I came to QVC with the George Foreman grill. To my surprise, he was a host for the world's premier electronic retailer. Recently, he told me that he had written a book about all of the great sports legends he has interviewed over the years. When he told me there was a chapter about me, I said, "Hey wait a minute! I'm not old enough to be a legend." He assured me that I am one of the youngest legends he has ever met.

Once again, Dan Wheeler has knocked me out with his fresh and inspiring writing style. He told my story in an honest and humorous way. If you know me, you know that I love to laugh. When you read this book you will laugh, too, and you'll probably cry. But I think you'll enjoy reading about the lives behind the legends of some of the biggest names in the history of sports. I feel honored to be in the company of many athletes that I have admired throughout my life.

So fire up your George Foreman grill; make yourself something tasty and enjoy sitting in the *Best Seat in the House!*

Sincerely,
George Foreman

P.S. If you find yourself inspired to follow your dreams after reading this book, go for it! It's never too late. After all, I was fortunate enough to recapture the Heavyweight Championship of the World at the grand old age of 45!

Introduction

Like most boys who grew up in America during the sixties, I dreamed that I would one day play in a World Series, Super Bowl or All-Star game. While I never got the chance to play in one, I have enjoyed watching them from some of the best seats in the stadiums. But the very best seat I've had is the one I have enjoyed over the years, sitting right next to the heroes of these games as I have interviewed them for QVC Sports and WCFC, TV-38, in Chicago. And now I'd like to let *you* sit in the *Best Seat in the House.*

I realize how fortunate I am. Not many people ever have the chance to meet a sports legend like Joe DiMaggio, Mickey Mantle or Nadia Comaneci. Most would be thrilled to meet some of today's superstar athletes like Ken Griffey, Jr., Scottie Pippen or Brett Favre. I have had the privilege not only to meet them, but also to spend time with them both in front of and away from the television camera. I've observed them under the glare of the lights, and also in more realistic situations away from the camera's "eye." QVC is carried by cable into 70 million homes in the United States, including Alaska, Hawaii, Puerto Rico and the Virgin Islands. Thousands of different products are presented in a variety of categories, 24 hours a day, 364 days a year—we take a break at Christmas. I am one of 22 hosts employed by QVC full-time. Each host specializes in a few categories. My main category is sports. I have had the opportunity to interview Olympic medalists, Hall of Famers and future Hall of Famers from every major sport. While most sportscasters conduct brief interviews that last from 30 seconds to 3 minutes, I have had the opportunity to sit down with these great athletes and interview them for an hour, two or even three hours at a time.

In the *Best Seat in the House*, you'll have the chance to sit in my chair for a while and find out which athletes are the easiest and which are the most difficult to interview. You'll experience some truly memorable moments in the pre-show meetings with the athletes and their agents. I'll also share some of the after-show conversations I have had with these legendary sports figures.

If you're the type of person who doesn't like to stay in one chair for too long, don't worry. I'll take you on the road with QVC Sports. You'll travel with me to baseball's All-Star Games, football's Super Bowls and even the 1996 Atlanta Centennial Olympic Games! Feel the pain and the excitement associated with baseball's spring training camps and football's pre-season conditioning. I want you to experience not only the game but also the entire "event." So, we'll attend the parties and the gala happenings that surround some of today's major sports contests. Can you imagine walking into a party that costs over a million dollars to throw? And then realize that the guy standing next to you is the legendary Walter Payton? Or imagine, after being greeted at the door by the Miami Dolphins cheerleaders, you look up and see some of the world's biggest celebrities. I relive these special moments with you in the pages that follow.

It's great to have a job that requires you to attend Super Bowls and All-Star Games. While I honestly believe I have one of the best jobs in the world, it is not all fun and games. You'll learn what it takes to conduct a knowledgeable sports interview, while also presenting licensed sports merchandise with producers and directors constantly talking to you through your earpiece. Trying to remain articulate and focused can be quite a challenge when product coordinators are continuously moving products on and off the set in front of you. These are some of the challenges I'll describe in this book. Keeping up with every player's statistics throughout every season is difficult enough when it's your full-time job, but I also have to be knowledgeable about electronics, collectibles, fitness equipment, jewelry, tools and all of the other product categories that I present regularly on QVC. While each area requires a great deal of preparation, when it comes to sports, I want to go the extra mile (or yard or inning, depending on your sport). So, we'll meet with the buyers, visit the library, go online, watch documentaries and talk to researchers and vendors as we prepare for a major QVC Sports Presentation.

One of the things that QVC Sports is known for is our ability to react instantly to major sports events. Within seconds of a game ending or a record being broken, QVC is on the air presenting the official championship merchandise. You'll feel the thrill of "controlled chaos" as we prepare to interrupt our regular programming with a QVC Sports Break In. While there is a great deal of excitement, there is always an equal amount of pressure. You'll feel your heart pounding as the red tally light on the camera in front of you flashes on.

Best Seat in the House offers you the chance to sit in my chair in the studio and the stadium. But it's not just a book about sports. It's about life. From my experiences over the years, I have learned that superstar athletes pay a price that is difficult for most people to understand. In many ways, they give up their right to things that you and I take for granted. However, I have discovered that the truly great athletes, the ones whom I would call "legends," are also truly special people. The same hard work and discipline that makes them winners in sports also helps them win at life.

For even more great untold sports stories, go to www.untoldsportsstories.com.

I hope this book entertains and educates you. But more importantly, I hope it inspires you to be the best team player that you can be, regardless of whether that team is a family, a company, a church or a civic group. So sit back, relax and have a seat in my chair. It's the one that I have occupied for the past eight years on QVC. I think you'll agree with me that it really is the *Best Seat in the House*.

Acknowledgments

I would like to thank the legendary team of people who helped me put this book together.

First of all, thanks to my good friend Mark Schneider, who called me up one day and said, "Hey, Wheels! You should write a book about all of the great athletes you've interviewed." My first response was, "No way. I don't have enough material to write a book." Then for some crazy reason, I just started writing.

Secondly, I would like to thank another dear friend and mentor named Joe Sugarman—one of the best in the world when it comes to direct marketing and sales. Joe really believed in me and, along with Mark Schneider, was instrumental in getting this book published.

Many thanks to my family, who watched me spend hour after hour at the computer as I hammered and chiseled this thing out. To my wife Beth and my daughters Kirstyn and Kelsey, thank you for your love and support. A special thank-you to Kirstyn for sharing your computer expertise with Dad.

I'd like to thank my friend Doug Brendel for recommending my tremendous editor, Jaxn Aronnax-Hill. Thank you, Jaxn, for spending countless hours both on the manuscript and on the phone with me. You're the best.

Ron Hughes did a masterful job of designing the cover of this book. Thanks for putting up with all of my ideas and suggestions.

A special thanks to Donna Bailey of Product Concepts Company for her tireless efforts getting out letters and manuscripts. Thanks, Donna!

To the staff at the Tanger Group, my hat goes off.

Thanks for your love and support. Working with you guys has been a "sweet" experience.

Lyn Chaffee deserves a big thank-you for using her talents in the field of typography to make this manuscript pleasing to the eye. Thanks also to Brooke Graves of Graves Editorial Service for expert proofreading and editorial advice.

I'd like to thank my friend Rich Ennis for the emergency use of his Go Video dual-deck VCR.

To Del Reddy, whom I have never met in person: Thank you for going out of your way to encourage me and thanks for just being a nice person. The Howes are fortunate to have you working with them.

Speaking of the Howes, I would like to thank Gordie and Colleen Howe and all of the true legends of sport with whom I have had the pleasure of working these many years. Thanks for the magical moments and the memories. I would like to especially thank boxing great George Foreman for the beautiful foreword.

Also, I'd like to give special thanks to Darren Daulton, Harry Kalas, and Thomas Kinkade for wholeheartedly endorsing this book.

To all of the wonderful people who work with me at QVC, thank you. It is hard to believe that so many talented people work at one company. Thanks for supporting me as a program host these many years. Without QVC, I would not have sat in the *Best Seat in the House.*

I would like to thank my sisters, Margie Lou, Mary Jane and Dawn, and all of their families, for supporting me all of these years even though you always thought that Mom liked me best.

To my mom, Marge Wheeler, I just want to say that without you I would be lost. You have been my biggest fan for

45 years. "Thank you" seems so inadequate when it comes to you. You are a Hall of Fame mother and friend. Thanks for your prayers and love.

To my father, the late Joseph D. Wheeler, "Dad, I miss you. Thanks for all of the encouragement."

Finally, all that I am or ever hope to be, I owe it all to the Lord Jesus Christ.

Chapter 1

Joe DiMaggio

I heard all the tributes, saw the amazing video, understood in my head that Joltin' Joe was gone ... but on March 8, 1999—the day we lost him—what was really on my heart was a March day seven years previous when I was nervously pacing the host lounge at the QVC Network, and all I could think was:

Today I am going to meet a legend. He has appeared on the cover of every major magazine. Songs have been written about him. The legendary writer, Ernest Hemingway, referred to him as "the great DiMaggio" in The Old Man and the Sea. *I have never been nervous about meeting anyone before. But then again, I have never had the chance to meet Joltin' Joe DiMaggio. Today my path will cross with greatness.*

Joe DiMaggio was scheduled to be my guest on a special three-hour edition of *Baseball Collectibles.* The show was scheduled to begin at 7:00 P.M. eastern time. DiMaggio had requested to meet me at 1:00 P.M. I figured this would be a 10-minute meeting in which he would go over the ground rules of the interview, but I was prepared.

The library had been my home for the three weeks preceding this meeting. I had read everything I could find about Joe DiMaggio. After all, this was the chance of a lifetime.

1

Joe was 78 years old and rarely granted interviews. Most sportscasters would give just about anything for the chance to sit down with the Yankee Clipper for even an hour—and here I had the opportunity to go one-on-one with Joltin' Joe for *three hours*. From my research, I knew that he was an intensely private person. It was difficult for him to simply go out and enjoy an afternoon at the ballpark. Fans mobbed him wherever he went. More than 40 years after he played in the Yankee pinstripes, he was still "larger than life." But Joe simply wanted to live his final years in peace.

When the phone rang in the host lounge, I knew it was time. Mr. DiMaggio was ready to meet me. On the way down to the green room, I anticipated his directives for what would be "in bounds" and "out of bounds." I was certain he did not want any questions about Marilyn Monroe or his son. I planned on sticking to the subject of baseball.

I walked into the green room and was greeted by a dignified-looking, silver-haired man dressed impeccably in a navy-blue suit. He asked me to take a seat right next to him on the couch. As I went to take my place, he introduced me to the gentleman with him, Barry Halper. Part owner of the New York Yankees at the time, Barry also possessed one of the most extensive collections of baseball memorabilia in the world. At the dry cleaner when you give them your ticket, they usually push a button and all of the clothes move around on a track system along the ceiling. I'm told that Barry Halper has one of those systems in his home. Instead of shirts, pants and blouses, he has "game worn" jerseys of legendary players such as Ruth, Gehrig, DiMaggio and others.

After the introductions, Joe looked at me and said, "Dan, let's talk baseball."

I responded, "Mr. DiMaggio, that is one of my favorite subjects."

We began sharing one story after another. Even stories I had read or heard elsewhere took on new life because I was sitting with the man about whom the stories were written and watching his expressions change as he recalled inning after inning of his career.

Of course, I referred to him as "Mr. DiMaggio" out of respect, but he insisted that I call him Joe. So Joe, Barry and I talked about baseball.

It was interesting to see that when Joe DiMaggio talked *everybody* listened. At one point, Barry broke into the conversation while I was talking. Joe looked at him sternly and said, "Barry, apologize to Dan for interrupting him." Barry looked at me sheepishly and apologized. "Now Dan, finish what you were saying before Barry so rudely interrupted you," Joe continued. Barry looked like a schoolboy who had just been reprimanded for talking in class . . . Joe had that kind of authority.

Joe told me about his first game in a Yankees uniform. He was sitting on the bench observing his new teammates when suddenly a man with a megaphone started walking around the field announcing that the highly touted Joe DiMaggio would be playing in his first major league game the next day. He was encouraging everybody at the stadium to come back because this 21-year-old kid was going to be sensational. Joe told me that he became very nervous every time he heard the guy make that announcement. He repeated it between every inning of the game. By the time the next day rolled around, he had butterflies in his stomach. They must have flown away by game time on the beautiful May afternoon in 1936 when Joe played his first game in pinstripes. He gave the fans plenty to cheer about as he stroked a triple and two singles.

He said the most exciting thing about it was that Babe Ruth came down into the locker room after the game to meet him. Babe was cordial and told Joe that he had a tremendous future ahead of him. After the great Bambino left, all of Joe's teammates told him that he had made quite an impression on the Babe. When Joe asked them why they said that, they replied that the fact that the Babe actually had called him by his first name was amazing. Apparently, Babe Ruth had a terrible memory for names, so he referred to most players as "kid." That afternoon he called the rookie sensation "Joe."

Before I knew it, an assistant producer came into the green room and informed me that I had 10 minutes until the show started. I looked at my watch in disbelief. I realized we had talked baseball for nearly six full hours! So much for the 10-minute meeting! Not once did Joe tell me what to ask or what not to ask him during the show. He just wanted to be comfortable with me before we did a three-hour "live" television show together. I think he also wanted to make sure that I knew my subject.

We simply moved our discussion in front of the television cameras and had the best *Baseball Collectibles* show in the history of QVC up until that time. Joe's autographed ball was presented for $399, and more than a thousand people dialed in to order it. We offered some beautiful autographed photos and other truly unique DiMaggio items, and it was all very popular. In fact, QVC's phone lines were jammed for the entire three hours!

At the 90-minute halfway point, we decided to give Joe a short break. A QVC page escorted him back into the green room. At that time, the green room looked over the main arena. The producer, broadcast coordinators, product information specialists and about 75 phone operators could all be seen through that window. Out of respect for Joe's privacy, memos had been issued at QVC during the previous week informing the employees that absolutely no one was to approach Mr. DiMaggio other than the producer, the page and myself. Everyone else was to leave Mr. DiMaggio alone. But as Joe was watching everyone at work, he suddenly asked the page if he could go out and say hello to the phone operators. The page was shocked, but she led Joe to the main arena. One by one the operators looked up from their terminals in disbelief as the great Joe DiMaggio made his way to every one of them, shaking their hands and chatting along the way. He made a lot of friends that day.

Back on the set, Joe shared a humorous story from 1938 that I'll never forget. It seems the Yankees had put out a lot of publicity announcing that Joe DiMaggio was coming to town for "contract talks" after the season had ended. This was an attempt to sell more tickets for the following season.

"Now in those days," Joe told me, "you didn't have an agent or a lawyer. 'Contract talks' meant that you walked into the owner's office, sat down, and he told you what your salary was going to be for the next season." Joe decided that he would take the initiative with the owner of the Yankees at the time, Colonel Jacob Ruppert. "As I sat down, I looked Mr. Ruppert in the eye and said, Mr. Ruppert, I think I'm worth $43,000 next year."

Ruppert almost hit the ceiling. He shouted back, "Young man, how long have you been with this ball club? Three years? Well, let me tell you something, Mr. DiMaggio, Lou Gehrig has been with this ball club for 13 years, and do you know how much money he makes?"

Joe replied, "No sir, I don't."

Ruppert immediately responded, "Well, I'll tell you. He makes $41,000 a year. Now, what do you think of that?"

Joe glanced down and then looked Ruppert directly in the eye and said, "Mr. Ruppert, I think he is *severely* underpaid!"

After I stopped laughing at that anecdote, I asked Joe if he got his $43,000. He said he didn't even come close.

In fact, he settled that year for a salary of $28,000. Just three seasons later, Joe went on his legendary 56-game hitting streak! That record still stands a full 12 games beyond Pete Rose's National League record of 44 games. In fact, Joe's 56-game streak is one record that most experts agree will never be broken.

We talked extensively about The Streak that night. Joe recalled that he was able to take things in stride until it reached the mid-thirties. At that point, the media was swarming around him before and after every single game. To make things worse, there was a dispute about the record Joe would have to break to hold clear title to the hitting streak crown. At first, the writers told him the all-time record was George Sisler's 41-game streak. But when Joe hit safely in his forty-first game, they announced that they had uncovered another record from 1897. Wee Willie Keeler, apparently, had hit safely in 44 games. Joe pressed on and finally passed 44, but The Streak didn't end there, and the pressure on Joe only grew worse.

He told me there were many nights when he didn't get a base hit until his final at-bat. "That kind of pressure really takes its toll on your nerves!" he exclaimed.

Joe's eyes narrowed as he told me about his eerie cab ride to the ballpark on July 17, 1941. "The cabby didn't say two words to me until we pulled up in front of the player's entrance to the stadium. After I paid him, he turned around, pointed his finger at me and with this wild expression on his face shouted, 'It's going to end tonight. It's over!'"

Joe said he thought the guy might be demon-possessed. But he was confident his bat could overcome any hex that might have been placed on him. Sure enough, Joe was swinging a good stick on that particular night, a game against the Cleveland Indians in Cleveland. In his first two trips to the plate, DiMaggio smashed hard ground balls down the third base line that normally would have been extra base hits. But the Indians' third baseman, Ken Keltner, made spectacular backhand catches on both. In the eighth inning, Joe came up one more time with the bases loaded and smashed yet another sizzler. This one was handled by the Indians' shortstop, Lou Boudreau.

Just like that, The Streak was over.

Joe told me he decided to walk alone all the way back to his hotel room that night after the game. After a long night of introspection, he came back the next day and went on another 16-game hitting streak. It's mind-boggling to realize that if Ken Keltner or Lou Boudreau had missed just one of those shots that night, Joe DiMaggio's hitting streak would have been 73 games! Think about that one.

When I asked Joe if he thought about what might have been, he became philosophical. He shared some wisdom that I'll never forget: "Baseball is a lot like life. You can't spend much time looking back or you miss your next turn at the plate!"

That wasn't the only memorable moment of our baseball collectibles program with Joe DiMaggio, which turned out to be a huge success. When we went off the air, sales for the show totaled over one million dollars.

After the show, we returned to the green room. I typically thank the guests and their agents or whomever else is with them, and then I make my way back to the host lounge. I figured Joe was exhausted after a very long day—I know I was. But he asked me if I wanted to stay and chat for a few more minutes. Well, there was no way I was going to miss a minute with Joe DiMaggio! I would have stayed and talked to him all night long if he had wanted to. We talked about baseball—and life—for another hour. Shortly after 11 P.M., Barry Halper told Joe that it was getting late, so we began to wrap things up.

I had been with Joe DiMaggio for 10 straight hours, and it was now time to say good-bye. As badly as I wanted to ask him for his autograph, I decided not to bother him. I went to shake his hand, and instead he gave me a big hug. He looked at me and said, "Dan, tonight I spent more time in front of a television camera than I have in the last five years put together! And, thanks to you, I thoroughly enjoyed every minute of it." I was thrilled with the compliment—but he went on to say something which I will treasure forever. "I want you to know that I was extremely impressed with your knowledge of the game and your interviewing skills. You are the best interviewer I have ever worked with. You know more about me than I do."

Joe may have said that just to be polite, but it meant the world to me, and so did his next gesture. He asked a representative from the Scoreboard Company for an American League baseball. (The Scoreboard Company supplied QVC with most of our sports memorabilia and guests at the time.) Joe took the ball and signed it, "To Dan, a super fan. Joe DiMaggio." That made me bold enough to ask him if he would mind writing a little something on my product information card for his baseball. He wrote, "Dan. Thanks for a great night talking baseball. Sincerely, Joe DiMaggio." That's a piece of baseball history no one else will ever have!

As I watched Joe, Barry Halper and the people from Scoreboard walk down the long hall that led away from the green room, I wondered if I would ever see the great DiMaggio in person again. Unfortunately, I never did.

When I arrived home that night, it was close to midnight. I was still "wired" from the show, so I woke up my wife, Beth, and we talked until about 3 A.M. I told her everything that had happened before and after the show.

The next morning the phone rang around 8:30 A.M. It was a woman from QVC's public relations department asking if I could possibly come in on my day off. Several sports writers from around the country wanted to interview me about what it was like to interview Joe DiMaggio! I told her I would come in around 10 A.M. For a couple of hours that day, sportswriters and radio reporters from around the country interviewed me over a speakerphone. Everyone wanted to know what it was like to spend a day with Joltin' Joe.

I'll never forget one newspaper columnist from New Jersey who was very excited about the show. He told me he had been flipping through the channels when he suddenly saw Joe DiMaggio on QVC. He said he couldn't believe his eyes. He watched the final two hours of the show. He then asked me, "What was it like? I mean, here was the great Joe DiMaggio talking to little Dan Wheeler."

I said, "I beg your pardon. *Who* was Joe DiMaggio talking to?"

He apologized and admitted that he was jealous. "I have tried, unsuccessfully, for 25 years to land an interview with DiMaggio. This is probably as close as I am going to get." The poor guy had to settle for interviewing me about what it was like to interview Joe DiMaggio.

The last time I caught a glimpse of Joe on television was the night that Cal Ripken, Jr. broke Lou Gehrig's record by playing in his 2,131st consecutive game. The fact that Joe was there, at the age of 81, spoke volumes about the significance of Cal's accomplishment. It was an especially fitting tribute since Joe had been a teammate of Gehrig's in 1938 and '39. In fact, Joe was standing directly behind Gehrig when Lou gave his farewell speech at Yankee Stadium on July 4, 1939.

Joe's farewell came much later. He underwent lung cancer surgery in October of 1998 and valiantly battled a series of complications for weeks afterward. He died shortly after midnight on March 8, 1999.

If ever there was a legend of the game of baseball, Joe DiMaggio was it. He was the class of the game. Joe had dignity and grace on and off the field. Among the boys of summer, he stood out as the man.

In his 13 seasons with the Yankees, he played for 10 pennant winners and 9 World Series Champions. That marks him as one of the greatest team players in the history of sports. He batted .325 for his career and smashed 361 home-runs. His teammate, Phil Rizzuto, told me that every season Joe hit 50 or more shots into deep left centerfield in Yankee Stadium that would have been homeruns in any other park. Yankee Stadium's left centerfield fence is 475 feet from home plate. It is often referred to as "cavernous." Phil marveled at the way Joe made everything look so easy. He recalled many times when a line drive would go whizzing over his head at shortstop and he'd turn around expecting it to be an extra base hit in the gap. "Sure enough. There would be Joe standing and waiting for it like he was waiting for a bus. He seemed to instinctively know where every hitter was going to put the ball," he told me.

Joe was the Most Valuable Player of the American League in 1939, 1941 and 1947. He was the AL batting champion in 1939 with a .381 average and in 1940 when he hit .352. He led the league in RBIs in 1941 and '48. He had the most homers in the league in 1937 and in 1948.

There were other records and there would have been even more had he not volunteered for the Army during World War II. As a result, he missed three seasons during the height of his career. Joe enlisted in the Army in 1943 at the age of 29. He served until 1946, when he returned to baseball at the age of 31. These were the prime years of his career, but Joe put his country first.

Joltin' Joe embodied the American dream. He was the son of Italian immigrant parents. He carried himself with dignity, grace and style. He represented the ideals of our country at a time when Americans needed a hero. His quiet strength and humility were a refreshing contrast to many of today's professional athletes. While some of today's superstars tend to lead with their mouths, Joe led with his actions. He was the type of hero that every dad wants his son to emulate.

The name *Joe DiMaggio* has become so synonymous with all that is good and noble that he is referenced regularly in films, books and music. In one famous song, for example, the question is asked, where has he gone? Although he has gone away in the physical sense, in many ways—if we are lucky—he will always be with us.

It's easy for me to understand the frustration that the reporter from New Jersey felt after he saw me on television with Joltin' Joe. The poor guy tried to land an interview with Joe DiMaggio throughout his entire career and never got the chance. I was fortunate. Spending a day with Joe was the highlight of my television career. After meeting the great DiMaggio, nobody else seems intimidating. He was the one and only person I have ever been nervous about meeting, and yet he made me feel as comfortable as if I were talking with an old friend.

While I always look forward to my next sports show, there was something about the one with Joe that reminds me of his 56-game hitting streak. It will most likely remain "untouchable." To this day, I consider the day I spent with Joe DiMaggio to be my shining moment in broadcasting. May he rest in peace.

Chapter 2

Mickey Mantle

When I was eight years old, my parents took a trip to New York City. I had the option of going with them or staying with my friend, Joel Kruggel, and receiving the ultimate present. I chose the latter. After dreaming about it for so long, I couldn't wait to finally get the chance to wear it. Believe me, I was thrilled when my parents returned home and presented me with my very own New York Yankees uniform with the big number seven on the back. I'll never forget standing in front of the mirror for about half an hour looking at myself as I wore the uniform of my childhood hero, Mickey Mantle. I never could have imagined back then that I would one day have the chance not only to meet him but also to interview him on several occasions.

The first time I met "the Mick" was in October of 1989. As a host with CVN, the electronic retailing channel which QVC purchased in 1990, I was sent along with Alan Skantz, another CVN host, to *Mickey Mantle's Restaurant and Sports Bar* in Manhattan. We were to co-host two, two-hour Baseball Collectibles shows live via satellite from his restaurant. Our guests were none other than Mickey Mantle and his two closest friends, Whitey Ford and the irrepressible Billy Martin. Alan and I were as excited as two eight-year-olds going to their first big-league game.

I arrived at LaGuardia Airport at 5:00 P.M. on a Friday. A car picked me up and the driver told me I might as well sit back and relax because I had picked the worst time of the week to go anywhere in Manhattan. To make matters worse, it was raining like cats and dogs (or Yankees and Dodgers in keeping with our baseball theme). The traffic was a nightmare and it took over two hours to get to the hotel—or I should say, *a* hotel. Leona Helmsley owned three hotels in New York City at the time. I gave the driver the name of the Helmsley Park Palace. When we arrived, I got out of the car and the driver handed me my luggage. After I paid him, I turned around and looked up at the name of the hotel. As I read the name, I realized he had brought me to the wrong Helmsley Hotel! When I turned around, he was gone. So, after spending two hours in bumper-to-bumper traffic, I had safely arrived at the wrong hotel! I then had the joy of trying to grab a cab during a Manhattan Friday evening rush hour in the rain. I finally made it to the correct Helmsley hotel around 8:15 P.M.

After a quick shower, I met Alan in the lobby, and we walked to *Mickey Mantle's Restaurant and Sports Bar*, which is located right across the street from Central Park. We did a "live hit" to promote the two shows that were scheduled for the next day. Since neither one of us had been in Manhattan for several years, we walked around that night just to check out the Big Apple.

The next morning, we quickly realized we weren't in Minnesota anymore. After looking at several breakfast menus, we settled for the most affordable one. Two eggs, bacon, toast and coffee were only $16.50. Oh my! No wonder people say you have to make a minimum of $100,000 a year to simply "eke out" a living in New York City!

The crew was busy putting the finishing touches on the set and the lighting when we arrived at the location. The main broadcast area was roped off and a crowd was already gathering almost two hours before the first show. Mickey, Billy and Whitey arrived about half an hour later. All three seemed to be in good spirits as they looked at some of the autographed photos we would be presenting. They shared the memories and the stories behind each photo. It was almost magical to listen to these three legends of the game reliving great moments in their careers and enjoying some fun time together.

I was scheduled to do an "opening tease" on the sidewalk in front of the restaurant. As I was rehearsing my lines and movements with the cameraman, I felt a tap on my shoulder. I turned around and the gentleman said, "Excuse me, what television station are you with?" I recognized my inquisitor as none other than O.J. Simpson. Standing next to O.J. was Irv Cross, another network sports anchor at the time. After I explained who I was and what we were doing, they asked if they could say hello to Mickey. We hurried them inside where they chatted for a few minutes with Mick, Whitey and Billy. I noticed them standing in the audience for the first 15 minutes of the show before they slipped out through the crowd.

The first show went extremely well, with the exception of Mickey ripping his earpiece out early in the show and asking, "How do you listen to that woman talk into your ear when you are trying to talk?" (He was referring to our producer and I'm inserting the word "woman" in place of the word Mickey actually used because I want this to be a book that the entire family can read.) Let's just say that Mickey was not pleased. Other than that incident, the first hour and a half went by without a hitch. Mickey, Whitey and Billy shared entertaining stories about each piece of memorabilia, and the crowd enjoyed the show. I should also mention that sales were strong.

During the last half-hour of the show, I noticed that Mickey was growing tired and irritable. He wasn't as upbeat or talkative as he had been in the early going. I know that some people become more outgoing and friendly when they drink—and Mickey had at least six mixed drinks during the two-hour show—but in his case, the drinks seemed to make him more withdrawn. Mickey's closest friends knew about his battle with alcohol, but I was seeing it for the first time. Obviously, I was in no position to advise him, and truthfully, it was great fun just to be in the presence of Mickey, Whitey and Billy together.

These three baseball legends and close friends shared one story after another. They frequently broke out into laughter. During shows like this I think to myself, "What am I doing here with these guys?" I realize how fortunate I am to have a job that affords me so many unique opportunities. My favorite story on this day was one that Mickey shared early in the show.

I've since heard this story told by others, but the way Mickey first told it to me was just hilarious. It seems he was taking Billy pheasant hunting during the off season back in the sixties. Mickey had a friend who had told him he was welcome to hunt on his farm outside of Commerce, Oklahoma, any time he wanted. As they pulled into the friend's driveway, Mickey told Billy to wait in the truck while he went in to make sure it would be all right. Mick's friend was glad to see him and told him to have a great time hunting with Billy on his farm. But he asked Mick if he would do him a favor. Mick said, "Of course," and asked what the favor was.

"Well, my mule is up in his years and he's blind and sick. I just can't bring myself to do it, would you mind putting him out of his misery?" the friend asked. Mick agreed to do the deed.

On the way to the truck, Mick decided he would

have a little fun pulling a practical joke on Billy. He got into the truck with an upset look on his face and slammed the door shut. "Well, can we hunt?" Billy inquired.

"No, he said we can't. And I'm mad. In fact, I'm so mad I'm gonna plug his mule!" Mickey replied. He then grabbed his gun and marched up to the mule, loaded his shotgun and fired the fatal shot. Immediately after he fired, he heard two more shots and turned around to find Billy standing there holding a smoking rifle.

"I went ahead and got two of his cows!" Billy said with a smile on his face. They never told us if Billy really shot the cows or not, but Mickey said he vowed right then and there never to try to pull a joke like that one on Billy Martin again.

We had a two-hour break before the afternoon show. About a half-hour before the second show was scheduled to begin, a man in the audience grabbed my arm as I walked by, and asked if I would please ask Mickey to sign his son's baseball. The boy was about nine years old and was wide-eyed with excitement. I told him I'd try, but that I couldn't promise he'd do it. Mickey was sitting with Whitey in a booth near the back of the broadcast area. I very politely asked Mickey if he would mind signing the boy's baseball. Mickey turned red with anger and let loose with a few expletives as he told me if he signed one he would be signing all day for everyone in his restaurant. I understood his reasoning, but I didn't understand why he seemed to fly off the handle over a simple autograph request. I took the ball back and handed it to the dad. I explained that Mickey couldn't sign it because if he signed one he would have to sign for everyone in the restaurant. I guess I stretched the truth when I told him that Mickey was really sorry. I just didn't want the kid's feelings to be hurt any more than they already were. I'll never forget the disappointment in that little boy's eyes.

The second show that day was a success, thanks to

Billy and Whitey, who remained warm, friendly and halfway sober. Mickey, on the other hand, became more sullen and withdrawn as time went by. Needless to say, Alan and I focused more on Billy and Whitey during the last hour of the show.

Billy Martin really impressed me that day. He had a genuine enthusiasm and zest for life. It was that "zest" that continually got him into trouble with Yankees owner George Steinbrenner. Of course, that's what led to his roller-coaster coaching career with the Yankees. But most experts agree that whether Billy was playing or coaching, he always had that extra spark on the field with his hustle and "never say die" attitude.

Early in the second show, I was presenting a "500 Homerun Club autographed baseball bat" near the front of Mickey's restaurant. I remember quoting the statistics of the players who had signed the bat (guys like Hank Aaron, Willie Mays, Frank Robinson, etc.). As I was attempting to wax eloquent about each of their accomplishments, I noticed Billy Martin acting the clown, standing right next to the camera directly in front of me, making gestures with his hands as if he were conducting an orchestra. At the same time, he would react to everything I said with dramatic facial expressions. As I quoted a statistic or shared a piece of trivia, Billy would raise his eyebrows as if he could hardly believe what I was saying, or give an overdone bouncing nod of affirmation with his head. The bat sold out, and I tossed it back to Alan, who was sitting in the back of the restaurant with Mickey and Whitey.

As I walked past the camera, Billy put his arm around my shoulder and said, "Dan, you have a gift. Your description of that bat was music to my ears. In fact, I was ready to order one myself." I'm sure Billy was trying to be sincere, but I knew he had slammed down a few mixed drinks by this point in the show. Let's just say he was in a very complimentary mood.

17

When the second show ended, Mickey, Whitey and Billy wasted no time exiting through the back door of the restaurant where a car was waiting to take them away. Alan and I stayed at the restaurant for about a half-hour and then decided to explore the Big Apple. We talked about the shows all night long. The next day we were still on a high from meeting our childhood heroes. We decided to scale the Empire State Building (by elevator, of course) and walk around the city one more time before boarding our plane back to Minneapolis.

A month and a half later, I was shocked when I heard on the news that Billy Martin had been killed in an accident at his home. He apparently drove his truck off of a cliff. America had lost a great ballplayer, coach and man. Mickey Mantle had lost his closest friend. Those people who knew Mickey the best said he was never the same after Billy died.

The next time I saw Mickey was two and a half years later, in 1992. We were scheduled for a three-hour show at the QVC studios in West Chester, Pennsylvania. There seemed to be a strong air of sadness around him. He was professional and sober, yet slightly aloof. Even though we discussed some of the same humorous stories that we did in New York, he seemed simply to go through the motions. The spark that I saw in his eyes in New York when he was with Billy and Whitey was gone. In a sense, he had lost both of them. Billy was gone, and he had not spoken with Whitey in over a year. It was rumored, in baseball circles, that Whitey had borrowed some money from Mickey and had fallen behind on the payback schedule.

During the summer of '93, I flew from Milwaukee, where I was vacationing with my family, to Baltimore to host a live, three-hour show from *Major League Baseball's Fanfest* at the Baltimore Convention Center. *The Fanfest* is like a mini *Disney World* for baseball fans. Both kids and adults have the chance to step into the batter's box and try to hit a Nolan

Ryan fastball, through the magic of video technology. Visitors can try to catch a Major League fly ball or see how fast they can run to first base. It's an exciting and fun-filled experience for fans of all ages. The special guests scheduled for the show were Rollie Fingers, the handlebar-mustachioed relief pitcher for the Oakland A's and the Milwaukee Brewers, Harmon Killebrew, who stands at number five on the all-time home-run list with 573 career round-trippers, and the incomparable Mickey Mantle. The athletes and products for this show were supplied by the Upper Deck Company, which is headquartered in Carlsbad, California. QVC host Jane Rudolph-Treacy filed entertaining and informative reports from various locations around *Fanfest,* and I hosted from a set that was built to resemble the bleacher seats at a Major League ballpark.

Mickey and the Upper Deck representatives scheduled a meeting one hour before the show to review the products and discuss the format. I was escorted to a private room where Mickey and the people from Upper Deck greeted me. It was immediately obvious to me that Mickey was on edge. Large crowds made him extremely nervous and irritable. Unfortunately, the convention center was absolutely packed on this particular night. Approximately 15 minutes before show time, four security guards arrived to escort Mickey and me to the set. As soon as we emerged into the main hall, a huge crowd erupted with chants for "the Mick." I was in awe of the attention this man still commanded over 25 years after retiring from baseball. People were reaching out trying desperately to touch him. As more people caught a glimpse of Mickey Mantle, bedlam erupted through the entire building. By the time we took our seats at the top of the bleachers, thousands of people had gathered around our staging area. A baseball musical revue was taking place on the stage next door to our set. The music was blasting. The noise level was deafening, making it impossible to hear any directions from the producer or director in my earpiece. In addition to that, the video monitors were located so far away that I couldn't see them. As a host, I depend on the monitors and the directions from the producer and director. Without these two key elements, I was "flying blind." I knew I was in for a very long night.

The best analogy that I can think of to describe what this show was like for me would be like a pilot trying to fly a plane without his instrument panel or the air traffic controller's instructions. I had to be careful of my every move and word for the entire three hours, since I was never quite certain when I was on camera or off. The noise level was so high that even though Mickey and I were sitting just two inches apart, we had to literally shout to hear each other. We desperately needed the headphones with the attached microphones that most sportscasters wear when they are covering a sports event in the middle of a noisy crowd. In fact, we have used them ever since at QVC when we are working in a location around lots of people.

As you can imagine, all of this only served to heighten Mickey's stress level. I thought we were doing a pretty good job of holding the show together, however, and our technical crew truly gave an all-star performance. Mickey was on for the first hour, Rollie Fingers and Harmon Killebrew divided the second hour and Mick came back for the third and final hour. All things considered, the show was a success. The representatives from the Upper Deck Company, however, let it be known that they were disappointed with the sales results. (I should point out that those two gentlemen are no longer with the Upper Deck Company.) When I said goodnight to Mickey, he seemed polite enough. It wasn't until two years later that I learned that Mickey had been mad as a hornet!

Two summers later, I was flying to the 1995 All-Star Game in Arlington, Texas, with my producer, Alan Massero. He asked if I had heard about the book entitled, *Baseball's Card*

Sharks. I said that I had heard about it but hadn't seen it. He pulled out a copy from his briefcase and said, "Here you go. You should read the first 10 pages." My eyes must have opened wide as I read. The book began with Mickey and me before the show at the *Fanfest* in Baltimore two years earlier. The writer talked about the crowd and the security as we made our way to the set. I was shocked when I read that when Mickey went back to the private room during the second hour of the show he was extremely upset. Apparently, he was complaining because I had asked him a couple of questions about Joe DiMaggio. The book said that this upset him because DiMaggio was under contract at the time with the Scoreboard Company out of Cherry Hill, New Jersey, and Mickey was signed with the Upper Deck Company for sports memorabilia.

Nobody had ever said anything to me about DiMaggio being a sore subject for Mickey. If I had thought this was a problem for him, I never would have mentioned Joe's name. However, I had discussed DiMaggio in previous shows with Mickey and it was never a problem.

Joe DiMaggio, obviously, is a big part of the Mickey Mantle story. Mickey's rookie season with the New York Yankees was 1951, Joe's last year in the pinstripes. DiMaggio was in centerfield and Mickey in right when Willie Mays hit the fateful line drive into right center. Casey Stengel, the manager of the Yankees at the time, had told Mick before the game to take anything he could get to because Joe's knee was bothering him. At the time, Mickey Mantle was considered the fastest ever to play the game. He had been timed running to first base in a blazing 3.3 seconds! So, Mick was on his horse going after that line drive when he suddenly heard DiMaggio call out, "I've got it." When Mick tried to put on the brakes, one of his spikes got caught on a drain cover in the outfield. His knee twisted sharply, and he fell to the ground in excruciating pain. In 1951, there was no arthroscopic surgery, and, as a result, Mickey played with pain his entire career.

People often speculate about what Mick could have achieved if he had been able to play pain-free. Perhaps in the back of his mind, he blamed DiMaggio for that injury. I also think that was the real reason Mickey was so angry during that show in Baltimore. Some 44 years after the accident, the mere mention of DiMaggio's name brought to the surface some deep-rooted anger. I had never seen him get upset before when we discussed Joltin' Joe. I believe his reaction had to be based on something much more involved than the fact that different memorabilia companies represented them. I also suspect that the writers of *Baseball's Card Sharks* may have greatly overstated Mickey's reaction.

The following October, Ted Williams appeared with me on a Baseball Collectibles show at QVC. Mickey called in from the World Series in Toronto and spoke with us during the show. Ted's face lit up when he realized it was Mickey on the phone. In fact, he was so excited that he was shouting during the phone conversation. I wondered if he thought he had to shout so Mickey could hear him all the way up in Toronto! It was a wonderful conversation between two of the greatest ballplayers of all time. Mickey was cordial and upbeat during that phone call, and it was quite apparent that Mickey held Ted Williams in high esteem. He praised Ted for Ted's tremendous ability at the plate and his amazing knowledge of hitting. In fact, Mickey admitted that while Ted had superb vision and patience, Mickey himself often was very impatient at the plate. Unlike Ted, Mickey was known frequently to swing at bad pitches thrown outside of the strike zone. In fact, he was one of the best "bad ball" hitters ever to play the game.

Although it is always troubling to realize that a childhood hero is as human as the rest of us—and to think that you may have offended a baseball great—I still felt it was a privilege to work with Mickey Mantle again. Just a few months after he went through the program at the Betty Ford Clinic he came back to QVC for a two-hour show. This time he was a very different person. I'll never forget the night.

The phone rang in the host lounge at QVC about an hour before the show. When I answered, the security guard on the line told me that Mickey was ready to see me in the green room. He then added that there was a slight problem. "Well, what's the problem?" I asked. He told me Mickey had been given the wrong time for the show, and that he was hot under the collar about it. Apparently, he told the guard that he would only stay for the first hour of the show. The guard recommended that I get down to the green room right away. After all that I had been through with Mickey Mantle over the years, this did not surprise me. I had learned a long time ago that when you work in live television you simply have to be flexible and go with the flow. I always try to work with a bad situation by steering things in a positive direction whenever possible.

When I entered QVC's green room, I had decided I was going to start steering. I immediately apologized to Mickey for any mixup with the time. I told him that we would be happy to have him as a guest for any amount of time he could give us. If he had to leave early, that was O.K. I said we would simply make the best of the situation. When I finished rattling this apology off like a fast-talk deejay, Mickey started laughing out loud. He then punched me on the shoulder and said, "Aw pard', I'm just playing a little practical joke on you. I'm here for the whole show!" The security guard was laughing along, and I stood there for a moment with a blank stare on my face. I was very surprised for two reasons. First of all, I had only heard Mickey call his closest friends "pard," which is a Mantle-ism for partner. Secondly, I knew he only pulled jokes on people he really liked. At the time, I didn't think I fell into either category.

Mickey seemed like he was truly happy that night. He told me that he felt like a new man since he had stopped drinking. He was finally at peace with himself. You could see it in his eyes.

Before the show, he asked if he could speak with me in private. I said, "Of course, Mick!" We went into the make-up area of QVC's green room and I pulled the door closed behind me. "What's up?" I asked.

He told me he owed me an apology for the way he had acted over the years. He asked for my forgiveness for his belligerence and his drinking. "I know I haven't made your job very easy at times, but I want you to know you have always acted professionally even when I didn't," he went on to say very soberly. The reason that he exploded when some-one asked him for his autograph, he explained, was that he felt unworthy. Mickey told me he could never understand why everyone wanted to make him a hero when deep down inside he knew he was an alcoholic. I told him that he *was* a hero, and I even started to defend him—but he wouldn't hear a word of it.

At one point, I reminded him that he was the clutch guy on the greatest team of all time in any sport, the World Champion New York Yankees. But he cut me off and said he was just a man with many problems. He didn't feel deserving of any hero status.

Mickey Mantle always considered himself to be the coal miner's son from Commerce, Oklahoma, who just hap-pened to be great at hitting a baseball. He told me he never got used to the fact that highly successful businessmen would often start crying when they were introduced to him at various functions. They were just so thrilled to meet him— but it made him feel extremely uncomfortable. Of course I understand how those businessmen felt. Mickey Mantle epit-omized the New York Yankee tradition. He was "Mr. Clutch."

He was the guy who always came through in the bottom of the ninth. I couldn't believe he was apologizing to me and asking for my forgiveness ... although I have to admit, it was considerate of him, considering our past misunderstandings.

Mickey and I had our best show ever that night on QVC. He spoke freely and honestly. That old spark was back in his eyes. He offered his knowledge and insight on every item we presented and on every player we discussed. I remember thinking that I had finally met the real Mickey Charles Mantle. I was glad the QVC audience had that chance as well. It was Mickey Mantle at his best, one last time.

After the show, we talked in the green room for quite a while. He was very tired and at one point lay down on the couch. I remember noticing that he appeared thinner than before. His once powerful forearms and legs looked as if they had begun to shrivel up. When I went home that night, I mentioned to Beth that Mickey didn't appear to be in the best of health. Later that year, we all learned that Mickey was in desperate need of a liver transplant. His dilemma raised the public consciousness to the overwhelming need for organ donors. He worked hard for the cause, and we all watched as he battled valiantly for his life after the operation.

In August of 1995, I was vacationing with my family in the Pocono Mountains of Pennsylvania. I turned on the television set in our room and saw video footage of Mickey Mantle hitting a homerun and jogging around the bases. I knew immediately that we had lost him. ESPN was carrying a wonderful tribute to his baseball career. I'll never forget sitting on the edge of the bed in that room and watching the television set with tears running down my face.

Later that week, I watched Mickey's funeral service on television. It was one of the most beautiful and moving services I have ever seen. Sportscaster Bob Costas delivered a powerful eulogy. He talked about the fact that although

Mickey Mantle had his flaws as a human being, he was still a hero to millions of baseball fans. He said, "God knows how much we need heroes." He then recalled the Mick coming to the plate late in the game and knocking it out of the park. The Reverend Bobby Richardson, who played second base for the Yankees during the Mantle era, gave the message. He told how Mickey had called him when he wanted to make things right with God. He said that Mickey had asked the Lord Jesus Christ to forgive him of his sins and to come into his heart. I knew then that Mickey Mantle had entered a Hall of Fame that is far greater than the one located in Cooperstown, New York.

It is true that Mickey Mantle had his share of personal problems. We all tend to put our sports heroes up on pedestals. We want them to be as good at the game of life as they are at their sport. Unfortunately, many are not.

Mickey was known in baseball for his ability to come through in the crucial moments of the game, "in the clutch." In fact, nobody delivered in the big games like the Mick. To this day, he still holds the record for the most career homeruns in the World Series with 18. When I look at the way Mickey turned his life around and the way he raised the public's awareness of problems like alcoholism and organ donation, I have to say that the Commerce Comet hit his most important homerun in the bottom of the ninth inning of his life.

I'll never forget you, Mickey! Thanks for being my hero and thanks for being my friend.

Chapter 3

Magic Johnson

My mailbox was one of the most exciting places on my college campus. I never knew what surprises I would find there. An occasional $10 bill from my dad, a letter from my girlfriend back home in Michigan or, best of all, a letter from Mom. I always had a little extra bounce in my step when I went to check my mail.

One spring day during my sophomore year, I noticed a letter in my box that seemed unusually thick. When I checked the return address, I recognized the name of one of my high school buddies. He was a guy I had played sports with, but he wasn't known for his literary prowess, so I was very curious as to what was inside. As I tore open the envelope, I realized that he had sent me a page from the sports section of my hometown newspaper. There was an article about the Benton Harbor Tigers' basketball team. The Tigers were a perennial powerhouse on the Michigan high school basketball scene. However, the article revealed that the mighty Tigers had been knocked out in the regional game of the Class A State Tournament. They had been beaten by Lansing Everett, a school that was not known for having outstanding basketball teams. In fact, Everett had dusted Benton Harbor by 20 points.

As I read the article, a certain name caught my eye. A sophomore had led the Lansing Everett team, scoring 36 points. I thought to myself, *Nobody scores 36 points against Benton Harbor, especially not a sophomore.* My friend had circled the name and wrote, "Who is this guy?" I looked closely at the name: Earvin Johnson, Jr. I thought this guy must work some kind of magic on the court.

By 1978, most of the country knew the name Earvin "Magic" Johnson. He led his Michigan State Spartans all the way to the final game of the NCAA tournament his sophomore year. In the spring of '79, the Spartans faced the Sycamores of Indiana State University in what was the most publicized NCAA Finals game ever. Everyone was anticipating the big match-up of superstars: Magic for the Spartans versus Larry Bird of the Sycamores. Everybody thought this game was going to be a nail-biter, but Magic and his Spartans easily won the national championship. Magic Johnson had now claimed the Michigan High School Class A Championship and the NCAA National Title within three years. But he hadn't seen the last of Larry Bird.

Magic was the number one pick in the draft of 1979. He left Michigan State after his sophomore year as the school's all-time assists leader. The Los Angeles Lakers' owner Jack Kent Cooke signed Magic to a 5-year deal worth $500,000 a year. It was the highest salary for a rookie ever. However, Larry Bird signed with the Celtics later that year for $600,000 a year.

Earvin started working his magic immediately in the NBA. Teaming up with Kareem Abdul Jabbar, he brought "showtime" to Los Angeles fans. He quarterbacked the Lakers all the way to the NBA Finals in 1980. However, in game six, Jabbar went down with a sprained ankle. Johnson went to then head coach Paul Westphal and persuaded the coach to let him play center for Jabbar. Keep in mind that Magic had played point guard for most of the season. After laughing hysterically, Westphal later agreed, and Magic lit up the Philadelphia 76'ers for 42 points and 15 rebounds. He was named the NBA Finals MVP, and the legend of Magic Johnson was born. He had now won an unprecedented three titles in four years, dating back to his senior year in high school.

Even though Magic had worked wonders in his rookie season, Larry Bird was named the Rookie of the Year. Magic and Larry met three times in the NBA finals. And even as recently as 2000, they met again when Larry Bird coached the Indiana Pacers to the NBA Finals against the Lakers, a team partially owned by Magic Johnson.

Magic and the "showtime" Lakers won 5 NBA Championships: 1980, 1982, 1985 and back-to-back titles in 1987 and 1988. He was voted the Finals Most Valuable Player in 1980 and 1987. He was selected as the league Most Valuable Player in 1987, 1989 and 1990. Johnson was a 12-time NBA All Star and was named the All Star Game MVP in 1990 and 1992. In addition to all of these honors, he won an Olympic gold medal for the United States in 1992 when he played for the Dream Team in Barcelona.

Early in the 1991-1992 season, Magic Johnson stunned the world when he announced his retirement from basketball. He had tested positive for HIV. But his peers wanted him to start in the 1992 All Star Game anyway, and he took home the MVP honors with a performance that basketball fans will never forget. After that he made a brief comeback and took over as the coach of the Lakers for a short time. In 1996, he made a final return and looked very strong leading the Lakers into the playoffs once again. At the end of that year, he retired for good.

Magic Johnson walked into green room "V" at QVC around 8 P.M. on Friday, June 2, 2000. As soon as I shook his hand, I felt as if I had known him for years. He looked great and his smile lit up the room. He appeared to be trimmer and even more toned than he had been during his playing days. I asked him how he stayed in such great shape, and he said that he was working out almost every day at Billy Blank's Tae-Bo studio in L.A.

As soon as I told him that I was from Michigan, we formed an instant bond. We even have a couple of mutual friends from there. I told him I had played high school basketball against Edgar Wilson out of Dowagiac, Michigan. I knew that Edgar had gone on to play at Michigan State before Magic arrived. It turns out that Magic and Edgar were great friends, and Magic still keeps in touch with Edgar and his wife to this day. I also knew David Adkins (better known as Sinbad the comedian/actor) in high school, from the days when we had played on a team that went to Canada together after our sophomore year in high school. Magic and Sinbad are friends as well.

Even though he has risen to the top of the world of professional sports, Magic has never strayed far from his Michigan roots. I told him about the article my friend had sent me in college, and he said he remembered that Benton Harbor game vividly. He recalled that during warm-ups, a couple of the Benton Harbor players walked up to him and asked who Earvin Johnson was.

"I am," was his response.

"Yeah, we're going to tear you up," they announced.

" We'll see," was his response.

"I then proceeded to score 36 points. But I was kind of nervous going into that game, because Benton Harbor was considered to be a powerhouse, and my school usually wasn't very good," he told me.

It's funny because every time I see Magic on television, he is always dressed to the nines. So, I wore my most expensive suit to work that night—and wouldn't you know, Magic showed up in a light blue knit shirt and dark slacks. It was a very nice shirt and slacks, mind you, and due to Magic's six-feet-nine frame, his outfit probably cost as much as my suit. But it worked out fine, and he was in great spirits.

Magic was my guest for a one-hour edition of Basketball Collectibles that aired from 9 P.M. to 10 P.M. eastern time. Unfortunately, we were up against the NBA Western Conference Finals between the Lakers and Indiana Pacers. This show had been booked months in advance, and nobody had any idea what the playoff situation would be like at the time.

I had a feeling Magic would be a good guest because he has always seemed very comfortable in front of a television camera. But he turned out to be even better than I hoped for. He was *great* and actually understood the QVC approach to electronic retailing very well. He shared some fascinating stories and interesting memories of his career. He also had excellent comments about the other players who were featured in the memorabilia that we offered on the show.

At the start of the hour, I mentioned the article I received in college and he shared his recollections of that high school game. We then moved into his college career, as our first item was a Magic Johnson & Michael Jordan Mint Rookie Combo card. His face lit up with pride as he recalled playing with his Michigan State teammates. He was quick to praise guys like Greg Kelser, Jay Vincent and others as well as their coach, Jud Heathcote.

"This is the first time I have seen this card. Look at how skinny we both were. We both had hair. Michael's got his tongue out and I've got my patented look," he said as he described the card.

I was very impressed with the way Magic helped me to romance each piece of merchandise. You can tell he is a skilled businessman. Not only is he a part owner of the Los Angeles Lakers basketball team, he also owns a huge theater complex in Los Angeles and is involved in several other businesses. Some of the athletes who are featured guests on our sports shows at QVC don't understand our format. They have been known to tell long stories that don't hold viewer attention, or even venture into inappropriate territory for on-air discussion. Magic, however, understood the system well. He spoke in what we call "soundbites"—crisp 15- to 20-second statements. He had something to add to the description of each and every product.

Most people wouldn't say that "humility" is an attribute that describes many of today's professional athletes, but it definitely applies to Magic. I sensed it the moment I met him. He seemed genuinely pleased to be at QVC—as if it were an honor for him to be there rather than a privilege for me. He talked about Michael Jordan with a feeling of gratitude that he was able to call him a friend. He offered great insight into Michael the basketball player and the man.

I asked him about Jordan's complete game, and he pointed out that he was defensively minded first because when he stopped his man on defense, his offense was even better. But then he really got into the heart of why Michael was so outstanding as a player.

"...he was a winner. He was a guy who said, 'I want to step on this court and win, and I'll do whatever it takes to win.' And that's what made him one of the greatest basketball players and one of the greatest athletes ever."

When I inquired as to what it was like to play against Jordan, Magic responded by saying, "I knew he was going to bring his A-plus game, and you couldn't just bring your A game. That wasn't good enough ... and then you also had to compete against him. A lot of people were afraid to compete against him because he was so awesome. I just said *Look, I'm going to try my best*. I'm not going to try to get into a scoring battle with Michael, because he's always going to win that one. All I'm going to do are the things that I do best to help my team win. And one thing I just love about

Michael is that he carries that over into his everyday life. Whether we are playing cards or checkers or anything else we are both going to do everything we can to win."

Another winner for whom Magic has a great deal of respect is his long-time rival, Larry Bird. Their competitive fires ignited a new level of excitement in the NBA. In fact, it was so intense between them that Magic told me for the first five or six years, they never spoke to each other off of the court. They later became lifelong friends.

"I cared about winning . . . and making the players on my team better. That's what Larry Bird did and that's what Michael did," Magic explained. Because of that attitude, they were three of the greatest players in history. Magic and Larry brought the game to a new level in the 1980s. Because they were both so team-oriented, they were two of the best passers ever to play the game. In fact, one of Magic's best tricks was his ability to make the ball instantly disappear from his hands and magically appear in the hands of a teammate underneath the basket.

On April 15, 1991, Magic broke Oscar Robertson's all-time assist record of 9,887. When I asked him what that felt like, he responded, "It was a great feeling. I knew I would only have it [the record] a little while especially with a guy like John Stockton right behind me, but it was a great feeling. It's a feeling that you are a team player who passed the ball and took pride in making good passes. And I want to tell all of the young fans out there to take pride in learning the fundamentals of the game because that's what it's all about, and then you can become a great player from that."

The NBA had never seen a player like Earvin "Magic" Johnson. He was a 6' 9" point guard who could play forward and center as well. In fact, he kind of created a new position that I call "rover." As I mentioned earlier, he filled in at center for Kareem in his rookie year during the NBA Finals.

He told me that he had always had a good time roving around and playing all positions, even in high school and college. But his first love was passing. He learned to make great passes as a young boy in Lansing, Michigan.

"When I was little, I was dominating the action. We would score like 30 points as a team, and I would personally have scored like 29 of the points. The other kids would go home crying and upset because they didn't score, so I said, *I've got to start passing the ball so they can be happy too.*"

"Do you remember one pass that was the ultimate of your career?" I asked.

"I think the pass was in Las Vegas to Kareem when he broke the all-time NBA scoring record. I went inside to him and he scored on a hook shot against the Utah Jazz."

That statement shows the kind of unselfish player that Magic Johnson was. He was thrilled that he had helped Kareem reach the scoring pinnacle. This unselfish attitude is something that we don't see enough of in today's athletes. However, there are definitely some great players in the NBA, and we discussed some of today's superstars.

When we presented cards of Kobe Bryant and Shaquille O'Neal, Magic beamed with pride. As I mention later in the chapter on Shaq, he really came into his own during the 1999-2000 season. Magic agreed.

"Shaq really took it to another level this year. Under Coach Phil Jackson's direction he really took off at both the offensive end and the defensive end. He's really blossomed as the most dominant player in the game today," he stated.

He feels Kobe Bryant is one of the most exciting players in the NBA. When he jumped into the NBA directly out of Lower Merion High School in the Philadelphia area, a lot of people said that he wasn't ready.

"And he proved us all wrong," Magic added. "The thing about him is he is so mature for his age. This year he made the first team on the All Defensive Team. He excelled on both ends of the court. He didn't make bad decisions like he did years before because I think Phil helped him to understand that he doesn't have to take a shot with three guys on him. He can just take his time and let the game come to him, and he blossomed under that system. I'll tell you, give him one or two more years and he will be the guy everybody is looking to say, *Wow, that guy has taken over.*"

Magic believes that Kobe has an uncanny ability to see the game several minutes ahead of time and that is what makes him a great player. He also feels that Kobe is a superstar draw for the fans.

"He sends a buzz in the arena. When he comes to play, the arena is jumping whether he's at home or away." When Magic said that, I reminded him that he had had the same kind of effect on the crowd when he was playing. He simply smiled.

Allen Iverson is another one of today's superstar players that Magic really likes. He admires the way that Iverson goes inside and takes the punishment although he only weighs about 150 pounds. He also said that he hopes Iverson can stay in Philadelphia because the 76'ers are a team of the future. With the other teams in the east aging, Magic believes that the Sixers are just one or two players away from being a championship-contending team. "I hope they can work it out because you can't win the championship without superstars, and Allen Iverson is a superstar," he commented.

While Iverson is still looking for his first championship as of the writing of this book, Bryant and O'Neal have just won their first title. However, they all have a long way to go to match the accomplishments of Earvin "Magic" Johnson. When I asked Magic what set his Laker teams of the eighties apart from the competition, he explained that they set their sights on winning it all every year in training camp.

"We went to the finals 9 times out of 12 years. It was really just a beautiful and great run. I played with some of the greatest players in Kareem, James Worthy, Michael Cooper, Kurt Rambis, Jamaal Wilkes, Norm Nixon and others. I just was very thankful and then when you look at Pat Riley who coached us, it was fantastic. I just want to thank all of the fans out there, because they were very important in my career, and I just tried to do the right thing and put on a show for them. But also, I just tried to win."

And win he did. He garnered a total of five championships during his career, a statistic that pushed his friend and foe Michael Jordan even higher. "We both wanted to have as many championships as the other guy. When I retired, I had five and the only reason he [Jordan] kept playing was to get six!" Magic explained as he exploded in laughter.

The 1992 All Star Game is forever etched in Magic's mind and the minds of basketball fans everywhere. He shared his memories with me. "I was out of basketball and was given the opportunity to come back and play in the All Star game by my peers, the players, as well as Commissioner David Stern. I want to thank all of them for that opportunity, and I especially want to thank Tim Hardaway, who said that it was all right for me to start in his place. When the game started, my emotions just took over and I was really ready. I just wanted to show people that I could still play at a high level with the best in the world. I was able to accomplish that on that particular afternoon, and it was a way for me to say, 'You know what? It's OK to retire.' So, it was just great."

The great athletes who achieve legendary status learn to adapt their game as their physical skills lessen late in their careers. Magic and Michael did this very well. When I asked Magic about it, he explained how he handled it.

"I said, *OK, I'm getting older. I can't do the things I used to do, so let me learn how to post up now*. So then I added the hook shot, and I went to the drop step. I improved my free throw shooting. I started to really improve my outside shooting. I learned to shoot from the three-point line. Like Michael, people don't understand that what made us the players we were is that we added something to our game every year. Michael could only drive when he first came into the league. Then they said, *OK, we're going to try to shut off the drive.* Then he said, *Oh, I'll work on my 20-footer.* Then he became a jump shooter. Then he worked on his three-point shooting. Now everybody said, *We can't do nothing with this guy.* Then he said, *Oh, one more thing. I'm going to go down and shoot the fall-away on the baseline!*" Magic once again burst out into laughter.

Near the end of the show, I made the statement that Magic and Michael were two of the greatest players of all time. In typical Magic Johnson style he very quickly passed the attention to Michael.

"He's number one by far. No comparison. Everybody did it different, but when you look at Wilt Chamberlain, Bill Russell, myself, Oscar Robertson, Jerry West, Larry Bird and on and on and on, you realize that this guy was definitely the best because he was a winner too. He was a winner, and he could do it like nobody else. And he was exciting! I had my run, and I was proud of my career. And like Larry, we were able to help make the NBA what it is today ... but I'm trying to gobble up everything with Michael Jordan on it. Not only am I a friend, but I am a big fan. One day when my son gets old enough—my youngest son is seven—I want him to understand who was the greatest player. So, that's the highest respect I can pay Michael Jordan. This card, the card with him and me, his jerseys, even his baseball jersey, I'm trying to collect everything." He added, "Michael is Michael. There is never going to be another Michael, so I hope you had your tapes out when he was playing, and you'd better get all the jerseys, basketballs and cards that you can. These are super cards because he was superman."

I get the impression that Magic is a great friend to have. It seems like he still keeps in touch not only with his buddies from the NBA, but also his friends from his early days in Michigan. Even those people whom he battled on the court are now friends. In fact, I asked him what it was like to finally play on the same team with long-time rival Larry Bird when they represented the United States on the Dream Team in 1992 at the Summer Olympic Games. He responded, "That was at the end of both of our careers, so it was special for us to team up together and represent our country and do it in a way that nobody else has, as far as the Olympics were concerned, because we beat teams by 60 and 70 points. We really represented our country very well."

One of my last questions for Magic: out of all of his accomplishments, which one stands out as the best?

"The Championship at Michigan State University and then beating the Celtics for the first time, because the Lakers were 0-9 against the Celtics before that in the NBA Finals. And then the Olympics. Without a doubt the Olympics are number one. Playing with Michael, representing your country, playing with Larry Bird, Charles Barkley, Scottie Pippen, Patrick Ewing and putting on that USA jersey every night was special, and I'll never forget that."

He then told me that the most important thing that a person gets out of sports is friendships. He said that he cherishes his friendship with Larry Bird, Michael Jordan, Isaiah Thomas, Dr. J, Kareem and many others.

Magic Johnson fans called in during our show that night to talk with him on the air. You could hear love in their voices. Patricia from Michigan said, "Magic, we have been fans of yours for 20 years. We love you! You are Mr. Basketball." She then asked him how his wife and kids were and he said,

"Cookie is doing great. The kids are growing. I have two boys and a girl. I work out every day, and we are all doing fantastic. It continues to get better as I go along." Near the end of the show he added, "The things that I've been able to achieve in my career, the All-Star Games, the five championships, the collegiate championship, the MVP awards, it's just been a blessing. It's just been great."

Magic Johnson won an Olympic gold medal playing on the Dream Team and ultimately, he went further than even his childhood dreams could ever take him. At the end of the show, he very humbly said, "I never thought, as a kid growing up in Lansing, Michigan, that I would one day be sitting on QVC offering my autographed basketball. I dreamed but I never dreamed that big."

And I never dreamed back in 1975, at Evangel College, that I would one day be interviewing and writing about the kid I read about in the article from my hometown newspaper. When I think about it, it really does seem *Magical*.

Chapter 4

Joe Willie Namath

"Take it off. Take it all off!" the sultry blonde with the European accent purred. A swing band was playing the "stripper" song as a razor shaved the face of Joe Namath. It was a television commercial for Noxzema Medicated Comfort Shave. I vividly remember watching this commercial as a teenager. The message of this spot was that if you want the smoothest, closest shave possible, use Noxzema. After all, it works on Mr. Smooth himself, Joe Namath.

He was smooth on and off the football field in those days. "Joe Willie" or "Broadway Joe," as he was known, was one of the best passing quarterbacks in football history. He became a national celebrity after leading the New York Jets to a stunning 16-7 upset over the Baltimore Colts in Super Bowl III in 1969. He had "guaranteed" that the Jets would upset the heavily favored Colts—and he made good on his promise.

Joe was born in Beavers Falls, Pennsylvania, on May 31, 1943. In high school, he excelled at football, basketball and baseball. He attended the University of Alabama, where he starred in football under legendary head coach Paul "Bear" Bryant. After his team lost in the 1965 Orange Bowl, Joe signed a contract to play professional football for the New York Jets. In just his second season, he led the American Football League in pass completions and threw for a record 4,007 yards. Joe quarterbacked the Jets through the 1976 season, then played one year for the Los Angeles Rams before retiring. He set the season record for most games with 300 yards or more passing and was elected to the National Pro Football Hall of Fame in 1985.

It seemed to me that Joe Namath was the Muhammad Ali of professional football. He seemed brash and even arrogant at times. He definitely had the image of a fast-moving, jet-setting playboy. He was given the nickname "Broadway Joe" because of his ownership of a New York City nightclub. He could always be seen with beautiful women and one year attended the Academy Awards with actress Raquel Welch.

One of the things I remember about Joe was his penchant for wearing eye-catching clothes. If you are old enough to remember the style of the late sixties, you'll recall there were some pretty loud patterns and unusual color combinations in the fashion world. Broadway Joe definitely had a flair for the fashion of his time. I remember seeing a picture of Joe wearing a full-length overcoat with fur trim around the collar and sleeves.

Everything I have read about Joe from this time period leads me to believe that his life moved at an incredibly hectic pace. He seemed to handle it all the same way he handled passing under pressure in the American Football League: smoothly and worry-free. I once read that Joe did not like the feeling of worry, so he never allowed himself to get caught up in the intense pressure that comes with being a celebrity and a pro quarterback.

"Broadway Joe" did not go along with the status quo. Even his passing style was unique. He didn't step forward as he passed, nor did he follow through straight ahead the way other quarterbacks did. Joe stepped out to the side a little and turned around to his left. He was one of the first quarterbacks who sometimes ran away from the line of scrimmage instead of moving forward. His throwing motion was extremely fluid, which is why I called him "Mr. Smooth." He made all of his movements look effortless, which is amazing considering the fact that he wore large braces on both of his knees.

I hadn't heard much about Joe Namath after his playing career was over, until the fall of 1993. Joe was coming to QVC for a special show marking the 25th anniversary of the Jets' tremendous victory in Super Bowl III. To this day, that was the Jets' only appearance in the Big Dance. I was really anxious to meet him and relive some of the great moments of his career.

The chiseled dimple in the chin and the sparkle in the eyes were still there when Joe walked into the QVC green room about an hour before the show. His hair was starting to gray, and his movements were slower, but overall he looked great. As we chatted, I was struck by his kindness and humility. I kept asking myself, "Is this really Broadway Joe?" He kept mentioning how blessed he was to have a wonderful wife and kids. His demeanor had definitely mellowed over the years.

The time just flew by during our two-hour show. Joe is one of the legends who truly enjoys talking about his sport. He recalled Super Bowl III with a look of excitement in his eyes. I asked him if he had been nervous before the game, and he admitted that he had been, mainly because he had "guaranteed" victory. He told me he was really confident that his team could beat the Colts, so he tried not to even entertain the possibility of losing. Joe stressed the importance of a quarterback keeping his mind in shape for the game. From hour after hour of preparation with head coach, Weeb Ewbank, his confidence remained high. Obviously, the Jets executed their game plan to perfection when the big game finally rolled around.

Joe told me that his unique throwing motion was easy and natural—as any quarterback's moves should be. "If I have good form, if I look good throwing, then I know I'm doing it right. Anytime I start to look or feel awkward, I know I'm doing something wrong," he said.

At one point during the show, our conversation turned to the subject of Dennis Byrd, the Jets' defensive end who suffered a paralyzing neck injury in 1990. Joe told me that Dennis had had a tremendous impact on his life and that something spiritual had taken place when he visited Dennis in the hospital. I thought this was really interesting, and I would love to have the time someday to talk with him more about it, because I imagine the experience must have been intense.

I have read Dennis Byrd's autobiography, entitled *Rise Up and Walk.* It's a fascinating story about how Dennis's life was dramatically changed in an instant when he inadvertently collided with his own teammate. One moment he was sprinting around the football field, hitting linemen and sacking the opposing team's quarterback. The next moment, he was lying paralyzed on the ground unable to move even his little finger. Dennis has always had a strong faith in the Lord Jesus Christ, which he believes pulled him through this tragedy. While the doctors and nurses gave him very little hope of ever walking again, he proved them wrong. The book really makes you evaluate your priorities in life.

As soon as the show was over, Joe showed me what was important in his life. We hurried back to the green room so he could show me pictures of his children. As I was admiring them, he asked, "Hey, do you have any pictures of your kids?"

Of course, I said, "I sure do."

We took turns looking at pictures of our daughters and bragging about their accomplishments. Joe definitely seemed extremely happy and content with life. I got the impression that he followed today's football teams, but the sport is no longer the most important thing in his life. Joe is another guy who doesn't spend much time looking back.

I really wanted to add Joe Namath to my autograph collection, but I didn't have anything with me for him to sign. He asked the people from the Scoreboard Company if they had anything, and before they could answer he saw a full-size 25th Anniversary Jets helmet sitting in a box. He grabbed it before anyone could protest and wrote on it with a blue Sharpie pen: "Hey Dan, I enjoyed our visit! Good Luck Pal! Joe Namath X12." I couldn't believe he was giving me this helmet. It remains one of my favorite pieces of sports memorabilia. I'll always treasure it, and my friends also give it rave reviews whenever I pull it out of my collection.

I ran into Joe again in the spring of 1996. I was in Los Angeles for a cable television show and was having dinner at Spago's with several QVC executives. When we walked in, Joe was the first person I saw. I said hello and reminded him who I was. He was very polite and said he remembered me. He was surrounded by a lot of important-looking people, so I figured he was doing some public relations work. We probably only talked for two minutes, but it was nice to see him.

In January of 1999, I was thrilled when I learned that Joe was going to appear with me on our pre-Super Bowl show from the *NFL Experience* in Miami. We had a good crowd for the show that day, and when Joe walked onto the stage, they went wild. As soon as they started clapping and cheering, Joe's eyes lit up and a big smile came over his face. It had been exactly 30 years since he made his bold guarantee of victory in Super Bowl III, and it had happened in Miami. He told me he remembered it like it was yesterday. We talked a lot about that victory and how it really served to unite the AFL and the NFL. He was at his absolute best that day as he recalled several of the key plays in that game. He looked tanned, relaxed and totally at peace.

I remember reading an article about Joe a few years ago that talked about the drastic change in his lifestyle since his playing days. The writer was as surprised as I was to learn that Joe was enjoying a fairly quiet life with his family in Florida. The image of Joe Namath as a brash, if not cocky, free-wheeling bachelor seems to be locked in the collective mind of football fans everywhere. It is sometimes hard to imagine him any other way.

In one of the pictures that accompanied this particular article, Joe was working out on a piece of exercise equipment known as a skier/strider. He said this particular exercise was the main way that he stayed in shape. Because of his battle-scarred knees he really can't do any high-impact exercises. Besides, he really likes the motion, which is almost as smooth as the operator himself.

Chapter 5

Pete Rose

A coach in a popular movie about the women's baseball league said that baseball players don't cry. Well, the script for that movie was wrong. On the evening of September 11, 1985, I, along with millions of other baseball fans, watched the toughest player ever to put on a uniform cry like a baby. After Pete Rose drilled Eric Show's 2-1 fastball into left centerfield for career hit number 4,192, his emotions got the best of him. How could he not cry after finally replacing Ty Cobb as baseball's All-Time Hit King? On that September evening, at the age of 44, baseball immortality was finally his.

Pete Rose played the game the way it was meant to be played. "Between the foul lines," nobody did it better. He wasn't blessed with the speed of Lou Brock, the power of Willie Mays or the rifle arm of Roberto Clemente. But nobody did more with his God-given baseball talents than Pete. He played all out, full tilt on every play of every game. He stretched singles into doubles and doubles into triples. His nickname was appropriate, "Charlie Hustle."

Ty Cobb's all-time hit record propelled Pete in the final years of his career. At the age of 36, Pete said he felt like he was going on 21. His amazing accomplishment came along just in time for the game of baseball. Free agency had opened the door for players to command unbelievable sums of money to play a game. The public was being deluged with different reports of yet higher salaries every night in the news. Americans were ready to look for a new favorite pastime.

So, on that September evening in 1985, Pete Rose proved that there *is* crying in baseball. If Pete Rose cried, then it was all right for any ballplayer to be overcome with emotion for America's favorite game. However, just a few short years later, Pete made us all cry when an investigation into his gambling produced strong evidence that he had bet on baseball. In 1989, then baseball commissioner A. Bartlett Giamatti declared that Pete Rose would be banned from baseball for life! A man who loved the game of baseball and excelled at it would no longer be allowed to be associated with it in any way. He was one of the game's greatest players. He played in more games, had more at-bats and stroked more base hits than any player in the history of the game, and he was being banned. In 1990, the board of directors of baseball's Hall of Fame voted to exclude banned players from the writers' ballots. This prevented Rose from almost certain election into the Hall. There would never be a plaque for baseball's All-Time Hit King in Cooperstown, New York.

I was a host for the Cable Value Network (CVN) in 1990, when Pete was scheduled to be a guest on one of our baseball collectibles shows with my friend, Alan Skantz. It just so happened that the official announcement of Pete's lifetime ban came on the same day that he was to appear. I'll never forget walking out of CVN's headquarters that day. Several microphones were shoved in my face as soon as I reached daylight. Reporters asked me what I thought about the fact that Pete would be appearing on CVN the very day he was banned from the game. What could I say? We were all devastated. My response was a simple, "No comment." Our studio was crawling with members of the media from around the country that day—they had to sneak Pete in through the back doors of our warehouse for his appearance.

The next day, a picture of Pete and Alan on the set of CVN appeared in newspapers and magazines around the country. The news services simply took the image off the television screen during the show. Interestingly enough, every autographed piece of Pete Rose memorabilia that was presented that evening completely sold out of CVN's inventory.

Life's ironies are what make it an adventure. The next time I saw Pete in person was September 11, 1997, which marked 12 years to the day since he broke Ty Cobb's record to become baseball's All-Time Hit King. Here is where the story becomes interesting. When I walked into QVC's green room to greet "Charlie Hustle," I knew immediately that he was in great spirits. At first I thought it was because his son, Pete Rose II (most people call him Pete Rose, Jr. or Petey) had finally made it to the big leagues after nine long years in the minors. In fact, less than two weeks earlier, Petey had stroked his first major league base hit. His accomplishment came in Cincinnati, wearing a Cincinnati Reds uniform with Pete Sr.'s number 14 on it. I'm sure that Pete's good spirits were at least partially due to his son's feat. Pete then told me that he had received a call that morning from his lawyer telling him that the interim Commissioner of Baseball, Bud Selig, had contacted him to set up a meeting regarding Pete's future. His spirits were definitely buoyed by the possibility of his lifetime ban from baseball being lifted.

Pete Rose was in such a good mood on this particular night that when I walked into the green room the first thing he said was, "Dan, sit down, I've got a great joke for you." After he told me the joke, we laughed, and I congratulated him on his son's recent accomplishments. He beamed with pride as he told me that Petey had hung in there through nine long years in the minor leagues. I then asked him if it would be all right to discuss the movement that was afloat among many of his ex-teammates to get him reinstated. He said whatever I wanted to discuss on the show would be fine with him. Pete then told me about the call from his lawyer that morning, and the fact that a meeting between his people and Major League Baseball appeared to be on the horizon.

Pete and I appeared on QVC at exactly 7:00 P.M. eastern time that September evening. Pete was in rare form. He was lively, engaging and playful. I began by asking him about the origins of his nickname "Charlie Hustle." He told me that Mickey Mantle and Whitey Ford were watching him from the bench during the exhibition season of his rookie campaign with the Reds. He received a base on balls and sprinted to first base in his customary fashion. Whitey tapped Mickey on the shoulder and said, "Hey, check out Charlie Hustle." The nickname stuck.

As a young boy, Pete watched the Reds on television with his dad, Harry. One day the legendary Enos Slaughter received a base on balls and sprinted to first base. Harry told his attentive, young son that Enos played the game the way it was meant to be played. He suggested that Pete play the same way. He was eight years old at the time and began to play with that same kind of intensity and hustle. He never changed his style.

I mentioned the fact that it was exactly 12 years to the day since he had broken Ty Cobb's record. I asked him to describe what was going through his mind after he got the base hit. As I mentioned at the beginning of this chapter, the world watched one of the toughest competitors in the history of sports break down and cry like a baby that night. Pete explained that people were seeing "three generations of Pete Rose." His son, Petey, who was the batboy, ran out and hugged Pete. As they hugged, Pete looked up in the sky and pictured his deceased father, Harry, looking down from heaven. Sitting next to Harry he saw Ty Cobb. "As I looked up, my dad told Ty to get in the back row. Knowing my dad and knowing the way Ty Cobb was, they probably had a donnybrook right in heaven that night," Pete explained.

At this point, we were about 10 minutes into the show and my producer told me that we had a caller ready to go on the air. I welcomed Carol to the show and introduced her to Pete. "Where are you calling from, Carol?" he asked. There was a brief pause and then she said, "Las Vegas." Pete and I looked at each other and he said, "Why Las Vegas? Of all the towns you have to be from Las Vegas!" How ironic it was to have our first call for Pete Rose come from the gambling capital of the world. We all enjoyed a good laugh. Carol went on to explain that her husband was originally from Cincinnati and used to watch Pete play regularly. She was ordering Pete's autographed baseball for her husband. It was postmarked "September 11, 1997" with the cancellation from the Cincinnati Post Office.

I find it fascinating that so many great athletes were influenced by their fathers in their pursuit of athletic excellence. I think of Barry Bonds, the son of baseball great Bobby Bonds; Ken Griffey, Jr., who is the son of Pete's former teammate Ken Griffey; Brett Boone, the son of former Cincinnati Red Bob Boone; and of course, Pete Rose II, son of Pete Rose.

Pete told me that when he was a member of the "Big Red Machine," their toughest game of the year was the Father/Son game. "Imagine how much fun it was for us to watch these kids at six, seven and eight years old. They already had their stance down. Our pitchers couldn't sneak up too close to pitch the ball because they'd smack 'em right back up the middle. You had to be on your toes against these kids!" he chuckled.

Pete was deeply influenced by his father and an uncle who was a scout for the Cincinnati Reds. His uncle suggested that he build up his arms by taking one hundred swings from both sides of the plate before going to bed each night. He practiced this habit religiously and it helped him to develop into the game's most prolific switch-hitter of all time. I remember Mickey Mantle telling me about how his dad trained him to be a switch-hitter from an early age. Pete was schooled in the same way. In fact, his father told all of his coaches that he would never take him away on vacation during baseball season on the condition that he always be allowed to switch-hit.

When I interview the true legends of the game, I always enjoy asking them what their proudest accomplishment is, apart from the well-known records they hold. Some athletes have to think about that question for a few moments but Pete didn't hesitate for a second. He answered, "The fact that I played in 1,972 winning games. I have to believe because of the amount of games we play as baseball players, that makes me the biggest winner in the history of sports. To put it in perspective, the 1,972 wins are 600 more than the total number of games that Joe DiMaggio played in."

I wasn't aware of that statistic before the show. While on the surface, this might seem like a boastful statement, it does in fact demonstrate that Pete Rose really was a dedicated team player. He went on to talk about what a great manager Sparky Anderson was. Anderson guided the Reds to 70 victories in their first hundred games of the 1970 season. Rose praised his teammates and talked about how fortunate he had been to play with some of the game's greatest.

Mike Schmidt was the "best player I ever played with," Pete said. "Johnny Bench was the best catcher that you or I will ever see play the game, and Joe Morgan was the greatest second baseman ever to play the game." He definitely credits his teammates with a lot of his success on the baseball field. You can see it in his eyes when he talks about them.

He loves the camaraderie that comes with being a part of a sports team. Pete Rose is the kind of teammate every player wants to have.

Hard work and determination were Pete's constant companions throughout his career. About halfway into our two-hour show, I asked him if he had any rituals that he used before a game. He responded that the only ritual he practiced was that he always used the same bat in batting practice that he used in the game. "All batting practice is, it's a confidence builder. So, I tried to take my confidence into a game," he explained. I asked him if he ever switched bats after a bad batting practice. He responded, "No, I just tried to get back into the cage and take more batting practice."

Pete doesn't understand why baseball players today change their stance. This was a cardinal rule for Pete Rose, the game's most prolific hitter. "I never changed my stance," he said emphatically. It used to anger him to see guys who hit .300 with 30 homeruns in a year in the big leagues suddenly decide to change their stance because they were in a slump. "Why would a guy want to change his stance after making it to the big leagues?" he asked. I didn't have the answer. But I enjoyed watching Pete's eyes light up as he discussed the finer points of his favorite subject: hitting. It reminded me of the fire in Ted Williams's eyes when he expounded on the same subject. The great hitters in baseball consider it a fine art. When they talk about it, they suddenly become energized.

Pete told me he had a great batting practice the night that he broke Cobb's record. He was "seeing the ball real well." But the thing that really stands out in his mind is the press conference he held the night before. While he was chasing Ty Cobb for the all-time record for career base hits, he held a press conference before and after every game. He had gone 0-for-4 the previous night when one of the reporters raised his hand and asked him when he was going

52

to get the hit. This guy was hoping it would be soon because he had to send his clothes out to the cleaners several times, and he was running out of clothes. "Well, he made me feel bad. So, I went home and said these guys are starting to get on my case because I didn't get a base hit. I'd better do it soon!" Pete recalled. The very next night he carved his name into baseball's record books with a sharply hit line drive into left centerfield.

I had a lot of fun teasing Pete about that hit. At one point, I said he "slapped" it into left center. He protested, so I said, "O.K. you sprayed it."

Pete said, "Come on, Wheels *[he called me by my nickname throughout the two-hour show]*. I drilled it. It was a shot." He was right. I've looked at the tape of that game and it looked like that baseball was fired from a howitzer.

While Pete enjoys singing the praises of his team-mates, he is also quick to compliment some of today's super-stars. His pick for the best player in the game today? Ken Griffey, Jr. He remembers watching Junior play in the club-house in Cincinnati with his son Petey when they were small children.

"The reason he'll be in the 500 Homerun Club one day is because he loves the game. He'll probably play until he's at least 38 years old. These guys today make so much money that the owners can't afford to pay them for 20 years. Look Wheels, if you come up today and you're 20 years old, and you play 20 seasons and average 35 homeruns a season, you're still 55 short of Hank Aaron's homerun record. If you play 20 years and average 200 hits a year, you're still 256 shy of my hit record. It's not that they can't beat the records, Wheels. The players won't be around long enough to beat the records. They don't need to. You know as well as I that we Americans are trying to find ways to retire as early as we can because life is fun. It's tough going to the ballpark. It's tough traveling all the time, and there's a lot of tough things about this game," Pete said.

While I found Pete's comments interesting, I also know there are hundreds of millions of Americans who would love to have the "tough" life of a professional athlete. When you are being paid millions of dollars to play a game you love, I somehow think you can force yourself to go to the ballpark. The majority of Americans stay at jobs they don't necessarily like at all because of these little obligations called "bills."

I can't blame Pete for thinking this way. Most of the professional athletes I have interviewed are equally out of touch with the lifestyle of average Americans. I think it is very difficult for wealthy, superstar athletes to understand the challenges that face the majority of Americans. Not only are their salaries disproportionately high, but they also become accustomed to everybody else picking up the tab. When they travel anywhere, they expect "first class" treatment all the way around. They rarely have to pay for anything. John Q. Public always offers to buy them a drink or a meal. Restaurant owners often pick up their tabs, because they want athletes in their restaurants as a draw for the public. Isn't it ironic that the people who need handouts the least often get them the most?

While a lot of great athletes watch their competitive fire burn out with time, Pete Rose seemed to fan the fire until the day he retired. I doubt if there has ever been a man who worked harder at the game of baseball. He stroked over 1,000 hits after the age of 38 in order to beat Cobb. (By the way, this is one statistic that Pete told me he wasn't aware of until I mentioned it during the show. I love surprising guys like Pete with at least one thing that they don't know about themselves.) At the age of 40, in 1981, Rose led the National League in hits. Interestingly, 1981 was a strike-shortened season. He tied Stan Musial's National League record for career hits the night before the strike went into effect. He then had to wait

56 days before he could break the record. I asked him how he handled the time off. "I don't think I ever worked so hard in my life. I took batting practice two times a day, every day, for the entire 56 days," he said. "I didn't just convince myself that the strike would last all year. I really worked hard and I think it showed. That's why I was able to lead the league in hits. A lot of guys took off and needed the first two to three weeks to get back in shape when we resumed playing ball again."

Pete was always driven to outwork and outhustle his competition. While it may have been O.K. for other players to give 100 percent, Pete had to give 110 percent. He didn't have the speed of Lou Brock or the power of Willie Mays, so he made up for it up with sheer hard work. He told me, "The way I always looked at it, Wheels, is God gave me other things that he didn't give some people. He gave me work ethic, desire, enthusiasm and he did give me good eye/hand coordination. So, those are God-given talents also, not just speed, power and a strong arm. Like you said, Roberto Clemente had the greatest arm of anyone I ever played with or against. I had an adequate arm, but I had to charge the ball harder to get to the ball quicker to throw people out. You have to make adjustments."

Most people aren't aware that Pete Rose began his baseball career as a catcher. It wasn't until his sophomore year in high school that his coaches determined he was too small to catch. They took him out from behind the plate and put him down on the other end of the throw at second base. When he signed his first professional contract after graduating from high school, he had only played second base for a couple years. Stories about Pete staying after practice and begging people to work with him at second base are legendary. He was never satisfied putting in the same number of hours as the other players. After being stuck behind the plate all those years, he felt like he had a lot of ground to make up at second base, so he often worked on turning the double-play long after everyone else had gone home. Even after winning the National League Rookie of the Year award in 1963, Pete went to Venezuela to play winter ball because he wanted the extra practice at second base.

The truly great athletes, the ones who go after the career records, are guys like Pete Rose, Nolan Ryan and Hank Aaron. They all pushed their bodies hard after the age of 35. Pete shared his philosophy by saying, "It seems like the older you get, if you're smart, you realize you have to work harder. And by that time, you learn how to work hard. I did something that most players do today but they didn't do it in the sixties or seventies. I stayed in shape all year round. Johnny Bench and I had a basketball team, and we'd go around playing high school coaches and teachers. We gave the proceeds to the high school. So, we tried to stay in shape all year round."

Interestingly enough, the same night that Pete was on the show, I also interviewed Roberto Clemente, Jr. Nineteen ninety-seven marked the 25th anniversary since his father, Pittsburgh Pirate superstar Roberto Clemente, died in a plane as he was transporting supplies to earthquake victims in Puerto Rico. Roberto, Jr., is a very polite, well-spoken young man. He was doing Spanish radio broadcasts for the New York Yankees at the time. He played professional baseball for a few years but developed some pretty serious back problems. Most fans my age remember that his father suffered from back and neck problems as well. Roberto, Sr. always gave his neck a trademark twist as he stepped into the batter's box.

Roberto Clemente, Jr. was just six years old when his father died. He told me that the thing about his father that makes him the proudest is simply "the man that he was." While he is proud of his father's baseball accomplishments, he admired the way he lived his life even more. Twenty-five years after his death, people still showed him respect by keeping his legacy alive through season-long tributes. This is what made his son proud. Roberto Clemente was voted into the Hall of Fame in 1973, less than one year after he passed away. He collected his 3,000th hit in his final game, on the last day of the season in 1972. Roberto, Jr., told me that his father somehow knew he was going to die young. He said that his father told his mother if he didn't get his 3,000th hit in the 1972 season, he never would.

When Pete Rose returned to the set after Roberto Clemente, Jr., he had a somber look on his face. He said, "As I was listening to you and Roberto, Jr. talking, I wondered if he really knew how great a ballplayer his father really was." Pete went on to say that Clemente had the greatest arm he had ever seen. They had become friends while playing together in several All-Star Games for the National League. They talked quite a bit in the tunnel of Forbes Field. In fact, in 1969, Pete and Roberto battled for the National League batting title right down to the last game of the season. Pete edged Clemente out by cracking a base hit in his final trip to the plate. But there is no doubt in my mind that Pete Rose carries a great deal of respect in his heart for the late, great Roberto Clemente.

The battle with Clemente for the 1969 batting crown was not the only close race Pete had for the title. In 1972, he and Matty Alou had a blazing battle of the bats, right down to the last game of the season. In the second to the last game that year, Pete faced Gaylord Perry in Cincinnati while Alou was playing in Chicago. Matty went four-for-four against the Cubs' pitchers that day and Pete went five-for-five off Gaylord Perry. "And four of those hits came off spit balls," Pete recalled. "Did Gaylord cheat? I *know* so." The next day Alou was oh-for-four, and Pete went one-for-three to win the crown. When there was a title on the line, Pete Rose was as fierce a competitor as there ever was.

Retiring is not easy for great warriors. Whether your name is Douglas MacArthur or Pete Rose, you miss the excitement of the battle when you no longer wear the uniform. As we began the presentation of his autographed Rawlings bat, he picked it up and said, "This really brings back memories, holding this bat in my hands. I want to knock the dirt out of my shoe and step up to the plate." I asked him if he could still hit and he said, "Sure. I do a Bucky Dent baseball school in Florida every year. It's a week of hitting, and I get in the cage and take my cuts." He told me he enjoyed practicing with his 12-year-old son Tyler's Little League team. He had to be extra careful because he could really "smoke" it with the aluminum bats. The kids needed to back up a bit when he stepped up to the plate. By the way, he is adamantly against players ever using aluminum bats in the Major Leagues because he feels "somebody would get killed."

Pete spoke with a lot of pride about all of his kids. His son Tyler was not only an avid Little Leaguer, but he also loved to collect sports memorabilia. He beamed with pride as he told me about his youngest daughter who had a fine acting career going. She had already appeared on the TV shows "Ellen," "Touched by an Angel," "The Pretender" and "Step by Step." Pete bragged that she was "a hot little star at just eight years old."

Toward the end of the show, Pete picked up a trading card from the Pete Rose card set we were presenting. A smile slowly came to his face. The card featured a shot of Pete and Petey in their younger days. "He's now 6' 2" and weighs 230 pounds. He's gonna play in Philadelphia tomorrow night. This picture on this card is when he was the batboy for the Phillies. That was the night I broke Stan Musial's National League record for career hits," he said. There was an air of melancholy about him as he reminisced. Perhaps he thought about missed hugs with a boy who always idolized him. In fact, Petey's entire baseball career has been an expression of love for his father. When he takes the field he writes "4256" in the infield dirt as a tribute to his dad's all-time record for base hits. He wears the same number 14 that his dad wore. He hung on in the minor leagues for nine long years just to get the chance one day to play for the Cincinnati Reds in the major leagues.

It finally happened in late August of 1997, and Pete Rose, Sr. was there. As he reflected back on the game, he added, "I wish every father could go through what I went through a couple of weeks ago. You talk about a goose bumpy day. Maybe because it was in our hometown of Cincinnati, where the ballpark is on Pete Rose Way, but to see that kid run out there and take that third base position with number 14 on his back; it was more goose bumpy than the night I broke the record. It really was . . . he hung in there. He didn't quit though man, he has been just relentless."

I believe Pete Rose has mellowed a great deal over the years. Like all of us, he has his regrets. Of course, his biggest disappointment is not being elected to Baseball's Hall of Fame in Cooperstown, New York. On the evening of September 11, 1997, he was definitely energized by the possibility of a meeting with Bud Selig, the Acting Commissioner of Baseball at the time. But as of the writing of this book, baseball's All-Time Hit King, the man who came to bat more than any other player in history and perhaps its fiercest competitor, remains banned from the game he loves.

Toward the end of our two-hour show he said, "I'd love to go and tell them how I'm doing and what's going on in my life. There are a lot of positive things happening. I've got a successful radio show and a couple successful restaurants. My son is in the big leagues, and my little daughter is in the entertainment field. Tyler, my 12-year-old, is on the Beverly Hills Little League All-Star team that recently played in

Venezuela for eight days. So, I think there is a lot of positive in my life right now."

I worked with Pete again in the spring of 1998 and on September 11, 1998. The latter was the 13-year anniversary of his record-breaking hit. The spring show took place in front of a live audience. I took an informal poll, and every person in that audience believed Pete belonged in Baseball's Hall of Fame. During that show, Hank Aaron called in and helped us present a couple of items. Hank was livelier and more energized than ever. It is obvious that he thinks the world of Pete. One of the items we presented was an autographed lithograph entitled, "The Kings of Baseball." It featured the portraits and signatures of Nolan Ryan, Rickey Henderson, Hank Aaron and Pete Rose. As I listened to Hank and Pete talk about the difference between the players of their era and the players today, I was struck by their passion for the game. It was truly some of the best baseball analysis I have ever heard. I was honored to be talking baseball with the All-Time Home-run and RBI King and the All-Time Hit King.

September 11, 1998 fell right in the middle of the greatest homerun race in the history of baseball. Mark McGwire had broken Roger Maris's single-season homerun record just three nights earlier on September 8th. Sammy Sosa had 58 round-trippers and was about to explode for 4 more over the next 3 days. Americans everywhere had been stricken with baseball fever. Pete and I had a lot to talk about that night. He was really excited about the accomplishments of these two great ballplayers.

After the show, Pete, his agent, Ken Goldin, and I went out for dinner. We discussed the homerun race at length. Pete told me that McGwire and Sosa had brought baseball back to its glory. However, he wondered why Ken Griffey, Jr., Sammy Sosa and Mark McGwire all hit over 50 homeruns in the same season. Since this never happened before, and other guys like Greg Vaughn and Albert Belle were also closing in on 50, Pete told me that he thought they might be winding the balls tighter. Of course, he believes, along with many baseball experts, that expansion has weakened the pitching. All of that being said, he still agreed that Mark McGwire and Sammy Sosa had done wonderful things for the game of baseball. Their Ruthian clouts came along at a time in American history when we all needed something to cheer about. Pete Rose was probably as happy as any baseball fan could be about what was happening.

Pete Rose is one of my favorite people to interview. He is always upbeat, engaging and insightful. His knowledge of the game of baseball is incomparable. I always look forward to working with him because I never know what is going to happen, but I always know that it will be fun. The last time I worked with Pete was a prime example of this. I walked into the green room to say hello and Pete was standing at the counter eating a plate of food. He was wearing shoes, socks, a shirt, tie and underwear. What a funny sight it was to see Pete Rose standing there fully clothed except for his pants! When I walked in, he nonchalantly said, "Hey Wheels, how's it going?" I'm thinking he didn't want to wrinkle his pants before show time, but I could be wrong ... you never know what is going on in the active mind of Pete Rose.

I remember near the end of the first show that I ever hosted with Pete, we presented an autographed Mike Schmidt baseball card. Pete sang Schmidt's praises as a great defensive player, a tremendous base runner and "a guy who learned to win games with his leadership and his arm." I mentioned the fact that Schmidt had been inducted into the Hall of Fame with the late, great Richie Ashburn. Ashburn had passed away just a week or two earlier. Pete gave a beautiful tribute to Richie by saying, "He was a Hall of Fame player, Hall of Fame announcer and an icon in the Delaware Valley. . . . I never saw him without his hat or without his pipe, and I never saw him mad at anybody. He was just a prince of a guy. Philadelphia fans and baseball fans are really going to miss him. People realize what kind of a guy he was. Why do we always wait for someone to die before we realize how really valuable and how important they really are?"

When the show was over that night, Pete and I walked back to the green room where we talked for a few more minutes before saying our good-byes. As I slowly walked up the spiral staircase at the back of QVC's old studios, I thought about Pete's words regarding Richie Ashburn. Princess Diana had just passed away a week before Ashburn, and we often heard reporters say that she had no idea how deeply she was loved. Pete was right. We have to let people know how much we appreciate them while they are alive. I think this applies to Pete.

I wonder if Pete Rose will ever see his plaque hang in Cooperstown, New York. If we were to take a close look at the players whose names are there, I'm sure we would discover more sinners than saints. If we were to scrutinize each player's deeds, I'm sure we would find some offenses that are as bad or worse than Pete's gambling. I'm not saying that what he did was right. It was wrong. He made some serious mistakes. But so did many others. The sad fact is that the most prolific hitter of all time may never see his name and likeness on a Hall of Fame plaque. I wish he could find some peace and forgiveness. Let's not wait until he is gone to honor his baseball accomplishments. Nobody played the game better "between the lines."

There is crying in baseball, and I'd like to see Pete Rose cry one more time . . . in Cooperstown.

Chapter 6

George Foreman

The bluish-white flicker from our old black-and-white television set cut through the darkness like Ali's left jab. The concentration on my dad's face was intense as we watched the Saturday night boxing match on TV. Boxing and baseball are the only two things I ever remember watching on television with my dad. I was probably eight or nine years old. This was long before Pay-Per-View, HBO and ShowTime. It was when you could actually watch the biggest boxing matches of the year for the cost of the electricity it took to run your television set. The fight cards contained legendary names like Emil Griffith, Dick Tiger, Floyd Patterson, Sonny Liston and a young upstart from Louisville, Kentucky, named Cassius Clay—or if you're too young to remember that, I'm sure you know him better as Muhammad Ali.

When I heard that Clay had actually knocked out the powerful Sonny Liston in the first round, I was shocked. I knew this guy was going to be something special. During the years that followed, there was only one fighter who seemed to consistently give Ali trouble in the ring, Smokin' Joe Frazier. The Ali-Frazier battles were legendary. I'll never forget the night Frazier stunned the boxing world by taking the heavyweight title and the belt from Ali in a slugfest to the finish. Joe Frazier was like a superhuman warrior on that night.

Not long after that fight, Frazier agreed to defend his title against the 1968 Olympic gold medalist in the heavyweight division. The guy who waved the tiny American flag around the ring, after punching his way to Olympic gold in 1968, was big George Foreman. He was a fierce fighter who carried thunder in his right hand. His opponents rarely lasted past the early rounds. Most boxing experts, however, thought Frazier had superior boxing skills. On January 22, 1973, Foreman entered the ring to find out where he stood against Smokin' Joe. George came out swinging, and Frazier didn't know what hit him. Big George bounced Joe around the ring like a basketball before the referee finally had mercy on him and stopped the fight in the second round. George Foreman had stunned the boxing world by winning the heavyweight title on a technical knockout (TKO). Foreman appeared to be invincible.

Later that year, Big George put away Jose "King" Roman in less than one round in his first title defense. On October 30, 1974, 25-year-old George Foreman entered a boxing ring in Zaire, Africa, to defend his title against the fading ex-champ Muhammad Ali. Even Ali was afraid of Foreman's overpowering right hand. However, the crafty Ali had a plan—his famous "rope-a-dope" strategy. Basically, he leaned against the ropes and let big George whale away for seven rounds. Foreman eventually punched himself out in the African heat. In the middle of the seventh round, he missed on a hook, and Ali caught him off balance with a right to the head. Foreman went tumbling to the canvas and failed to stand before the end of the ten-count. Muhammad Ali had won the World Heavyweight Boxing Title for an unprecedented third time.

Foreman staged a major comeback after that fight. On January 24, 1976, he knocked out highly regarded Ron Lyle in the fifth round. In June of that year, he knocked out Joe Frazier for the second time in the fifth round. He sent

Scott LeDoux sprawling to the canvas in round three of their fight in August of 1976. John "Dino" Denis lasted only four rounds against the vengeful blows of Foreman in October. Pedro Agosta was stopped cold in the fourth round of his battle with Foreman in January of 1977. A $13 million rematch with Muhammad Ali was in the works.

On March 13, 1977, Foreman entered a ring in San Juan, Puerto Rico, for a tune-up against Jimmy Young, who had deceptive moves but little power behind his punches. Big George wanted to prove he could go the distance with any opponent, but he miscalculated the Puerto Rican heat and somehow lost the decision after going all 12 rounds.

Foreman says he experienced a "spiritual rebirth" in the locker room following that fight. He then walked away from the world of professional boxing at the age of 28 to enter a full-time preaching ministry. At this point in time, I lost track of George Foreman. He wasn't in the ring anymore, so like most boxing fans, I hardly gave him a thought.

Eight years later, in 1985, I was working as a producer for WCFC-TV, a Christian television station in Chicago, Illinois. It is now called the *Total Living Network*. I read an article one day in *Sports Illustrated* about George Foreman and Muhammad Ali. The article talked about how George had developed a genuine love and concern for Muhammad Ali. George was now the pastor of a tiny church located just outside of Houston, Texas, called the Church of the Lord Jesus Christ. The article said that Foreman and Ali had been honored at a recent dinner. As Ali got up to accept his award, George noticed Ali's shirt was un-tucked, so he stopped him and tucked it in just before he went to the podium. Parkinson's disease was beginning to take its toll on Ali. Foreman felt partially responsible for Ali's decline because of the vicious blows he had unleashed to Ali's head during their 1974 Rumble in the Jungle.

At this point in my career, I had produced six television documentaries. The *Sports Illustrated* article fascinated me, so I thought it would be interesting to produce a documentary on the life of George Foreman. After several phone calls, I found myself on the phone with the man himself. I told him I was intrigued by the article and wanted to come down to Texas with a television crew to document his story. He was very cautious and wanted to know what my angle would be. I told him I just wanted to tell his story in an honest and meaningful way. It took a few more phone calls and some pretty persuasive talking before he agreed to let me and my crew come down for three days of shooting.

The day finally arrived for us to fly to Houston. I boarded a plane at O'Hare airport with Dean Anderson and Wade Bobbitt, my excellent production team. They were both extremely capable in all aspects of television production, including camera, audio and lighting. The three of us had spent many days, weeks and months together on the road working on other documentaries, as well as a weekly half-hour magazine show called *A Closer Look*. We had a great working relationship and remain good friends to this day. In fact, both Dean and Wade work on the *Oprah* show produced by Harpo Productions in Chicago. Dean is Oprah's floor director. She often talks to him during the show, affectionately referring to him as "Dean-o." Wade is a senior engineer for the show.

We flew to Houston and checked into our hotel that first night. Early the next morning we were on the road in a rental car heading for Marshall, Texas, which is located about four hours north of Houston. George owned a ranch there and invited us to spend our first day videotaping him on the ranch. My plan was to travel back down to Houston to tape on Saturday and Sunday. As we pulled into the long driveway that led up to the ranch house, we saw a giant of a man emerge from the front door. George Foreman looked bigger than John Wayne ever did on the silver screen. He was wearing blue jeans, a denim shirt, cowboy boots and a big, white cowboy hat. I think the boots and the hat made him appear even bigger than he actually was. He stood over six feet four inches tall and, at the time, weighed well over three hundred pounds.

George was cordial and invited us in to sit down and talk about our schedule for the day. My goal was to shoot enough footage for a one-hour documentary. I knew this was ambitious, because when you are working on a television documentary your shooting ratio is usually anywhere from 10-to-1 to 20-to-1. This means, for a one-hour documentary, you usually shoot anywhere from 15 to 20 hours' worth of footage, a process that usually takes several weeks. Viewers have grown accustomed to television moving fast, you never want to keep them looking at any one shot for more than three seconds. In addition to all of the interviews, it is necessary to shoot hours of "cover footage" (it covers longer sections of narration or dialogue). In the back of my mind, I knew I would probably get enough for a strong half-hour documentary in our allotted three days of shooting with George.

During that first day, we taped George riding a tractor, feeding his longhorn steers, riding a horse, fishing, rowing a boat (using a two-by-six board for an oar), reading his Bible, jogging down a long, dirt road and feeding his geese by the pond. It was an action-packed day, and George was extremely cooperative. In the middle of the afternoon, he asked us if we wanted to see the gym where he used to train for all of his major fights. "How far away is it?" I asked.

He pointed across the way to a big, red barn and said, "It's right there."

"Let's go!" I responded.

George unlocked the door, and we stepped back into boxing history. Everything was exactly the way it had been eight years earlier, when he walked away from the sport. A large boxing ring still stood in the middle of the barn. There were wads of used athletic tape lying around it. The pungent odor of muscle ointment permeated the air, thanks to an open jar of Atomic Balm that sat in one corner of the ring. Leaned up against the base of the ring on the floor was a large oil painting of George wearing the heavyweight belt.

George told me he had only been inside this gym a couple of times since 1977. He climbed through the ropes and started shadow boxing in the ring. We couldn't have scripted anything better. There was an air of melancholy about him as he looked around and talked about all of the memories this gym held. After he talked a while, he invited me into the ring. I couldn't resist throwing a few playful punches at the champ, fully aware that if he ever hit me, I would probably never wake up.

George Foreman is a powerful man. His forearms are the size of my thighs. His fist is easily twice the size of mine. At the time, I thought that if he really wanted to, he could probably still fight professionally. I knew he still had the power. However, I questioned if he had the endurance. At the end of the day, when I asked him to jog about 100 yards down a dirt road for a concluding shot, he warned me that we needed to get it in one take because he didn't have the stamina to do it again—300 pounds was quite a load to carry even on his powerful frame.

We stopped taping around 5:30 P.M. that first night because we still had a four-hour drive back to Houston ahead of us. George would also be driving back to the Houston area to meet us the next day at his church. I told him that I would like to start shooting around noon the next day. He gave me his phone number and directions from our hotel to his church so we could meet. As he gave me the directions, I feverishly attempted to copy them down. Since George has a bit of a Texan drawl, I was having trouble understanding him. When he said to turn left at the "horse-pidal," I had no idea what he was talking about. I finished writing down the directions and then asked, "What exactly is this horse pidal? Is it a statue of a horse or a fountain or what?"

George laughed good-naturedly and said, "Come on, you know what a horse-pidal is!"

Wade and Dean were trying to get my attention by whispering, "Hospital. *Hospital.*"

I still didn't get it until George said, "You know they take care of sick people there!" I was very embarrassed and extremely thankful that George had a good sense of humor. When we got in the car, Dean and Wade said they had visions of my being hammered by a George Foreman right hand!

The next morning, Wade, Dean and I enjoyed a leisurely breakfast. After watching some of the tapes from the previous day, I was feeling pretty good about the way things were going. Around 11:30 A.M., I called George's house but nobody answered. I figured he had just run out for a few minutes, so I waited 15 minutes before I dialed his number again. After letting the phone ring for quite some time, I decided to call his brother Roy. He answered but had no idea where George was. Roy suggested I call his mother's house, which I did but to no avail. At 2:00 P.M., I was worried that George either didn't make it back from Marshall, or that he was bailing out on the project.

I finally tracked him down around 2:30 P.M. He sounded very different from the day before. His manner was distant, almost cold. He said he was tired and really didn't feel like doing any taping that day. I explained that we were working on a very tight schedule. I told him that I really needed to get something accomplished, even if we only taped for a couple of hours. He reluctantly agreed to meet us at the church at 3:30 P.M.

When we arrived at the church, George was already working out in the yard. His youngest son, George III, his daughter and his wife were all helping. A pick-up truck was parked in the church driveway with five or six lawnmowers in the back. When I asked George why he had so many lawnmowers, he said they kept breaking down so he kept buying new ones! Since I could tell he wasn't in the best of moods, I decided to roll up my sleeves and help him while the crew videotaped us. I actually interviewed him while we were swinging scythes and chopping down weeds along the outskirts of the church property.

This was definitely not the congenial George Foreman that we had worked with the previous day. I felt like he was upset with me for wanting to shoot more footage. After an hour or so, he became more accommodating. I decided, however, that I shouldn't push him, so I had the crew wrap things up after just two hours. I told him we had enough for the day and that we would see him tomorrow. He said that was a smart decision and assured me that we would be able to videotape his church service the next morning and interview members of his congregation afterward.

After we left the church, Dean, Wade and I drove to the tough Houston neighborhood where George Foreman grew up. As we began shooting cover footage, we quickly realized we were not in a top vacation spot of the world. Several of the neighborhoods we taped in looked "war torn" from gang activity. It was easy to understand how George had become street-tough at an early age. After we finished, we decided to drive into downtown Houston and enjoy a nice dinner. We found a great outdoor cafe, ate a wonderful meal and walked around the downtown area. We appreciated it much more after seeing the way people lived in Houston's rougher sections.

The Church of the Lord Jesus Christ in Humble, Texas, is a far cry from Madison Square Garden. But on this particular Sunday morning, the former Heavyweight Boxing Champ of the World came out swinging. He was no longer jabbing for the jaw; instead, he hammered for the heart. Big George is a passionate preacher, and when his very large hand strikes the pulpit, people pay attention. His sermon focused on being "fishers of men," as Jesus admonished His disciples to be in Matthew 4:19. He talked about how it took the Lord 28 years to land him. "That was a big one he threw in the boat that day. I came out flappin' and hollerin', but He pulled me in. Now, you've got to give the Lord a clap offering for that one," Pastor Foreman exhorted as the congregation broke into applause.

The sanctuary wasn't exactly jam-packed full of people. I would guess the attendance on this Sunday numbered between 30 and 40 people. The vast majority of the worshippers were members of George's extended family. But that did not dampen his enthusiasm or his determination to preach the Gospel. His nephew, James Steptoe, played electric guitar for the worship service and his wife, Joan, kept beat with a tambourine. I'll never forget the sight and sound of Pastor George Foreman leading the congregation in *Wade in the Water*. As Nat King Cole sang, it was truly "unforgettable." I must say that I thoroughly enjoyed attending the Church of the Lord Jesus Christ that morning in Humble, Texas.

As the service was letting out, George walked up to me and said that he had lined up several people for us to interview. I was happy to see that George was back to his congenial self. After what I had gone through the day before, I was extremely grateful.

James Steptoe told us about the transformation he had seen in George since he left boxing for the ministry. "He was about the meanest guy I ever knew before the Lord got a hold of him. He wasn't the type of person you wanted to be around at all. He was just mean. But now, he's like a brother

71

to me. Really, he's like a father to me," he explained. Another young man from his congregation said George had told him things that he never knew before about God. It seemed like George had a way of making the Scriptures easy for him to understand.

As I was finishing up my last interview, George walked up, slapped me on the back and said, "Dan, why don't you and the boys come on over to my house for dinner? I'll barbecue up some chicken and ribs and you guys can video-tape me and interview my mom and my brothers." Again, I couldn't believe my ears. There was no way I would pass up this opportunity. I definitely needed the footage for the doc-umentary, but I also had a hunch that Big George knew how to prepare some pretty tasty ribs.

We followed George to his house, which was located in a nice, middle-class suburban neighborhood. As we pulled into the driveway, we were surprised to discover that George lived in a fairly modest home. The lawn was well groomed, but it wasn't the type of mansion that you would expect the former Heavyweight Boxing Champion of the World to be living in. It was a 5-bedroom house that had, at the most, 3,000 square feet of living space. The house and the yard were well cared for, but there was no gated entrance, no guards, not even a long, winding driveway. It looked like a typical house that you could find in any suburb in America.

George went straight to the barbecue and fired it up. He had a lot of people to cook for that day. His brothers, Roy and Sonny, and their families were there along with his mother, Nancy. In addition, he had three hungry television guys. Everyone was extremely friendly and made us feel right at home. I'll never forget watching George cooking away at the barbecue. He had the biggest grin on his face and appeared to be as relaxed and happy as we had seen him. You could tell he was doing one of his favorite things. In fact, today, whenever I see George on QVC with the George Foreman Health Grill, I remember this scene. George is definitely more than just a "celebrity spokesperson" for this product. As soon as I tasted the delicious ribs and chicken legs, I knew George Foreman was an expert on the topic of grilling. The meat literally fell off of those ribs, and we ate until we could eat no more.

George Foreman was never really hurt in the ring during his first boxing career. In fact, few fighters ever made solid contact to his head or face. When I asked him about the Ali fight, he told me he was very tired in the seventh round when Ali caught him off balance, but he said that Ali's punch didn't hurt him at all. George explained that a fighter is trained to look to his corner when he is knocked down. He is supposed to wait for his manager to signal for him to get up. When his manager signaled for him to get up that night, he jumped to his feet but the referee had counted him out and the fight was over.

To this day, George believes something funny went on that night in Zaire. His brother Roy confirmed that when we interviewed him for the documentary. We set up his interview that Sunday afternoon after cleaning up the dishes.

Roy discussed the Ali/Foreman fight in depth. It was known as the infamous Rumble in the Jungle in Zaire in 1974. He recalled the night of the fight and explained that when George entered the ring, he knew something was wrong. Whereas George usually bounced around the ring and tested the ropes, on this night he seemed like he was trying to conserve every ounce of energy he had. He barely loosened up at all. Roy suspected someone might have slipped something into George's drinking water to cause this unusual lethargy, yet he said that regardless of the outcome of that one fight, George was ultimately on course to run into the higher power of the Lord. And when he did, it dramatically changed his life for the better.

Roy talked about George's boxing career and how it affected his personal life. He recalled how George was always generous with his wealth, but sometimes Roy thought he confused money with love. While Roy was often the recipient of gifts of money and cars and clothes, he said there were times when he wanted to give it all back to just have George. "The George Foreman you see here today is nowhere near the George Foreman that used to be. What you see now is the real thing. He is genuinely loving and caring. But he used to be mean and unhappy," Roy explained.

George's mom, Nancy Foreman, gave our next interview. George has the deepest admiration and love for his mom. She often worked two jobs to keep food on the table for her seven children. With George's voracious appetite among them, this was no small task. George's father was absent much more than he was present around the Foreman house. In his autobiography, *By George*, George talks about his dad: "Mom couldn't count on him for anything. Unless she found him early on a Friday night, he drank away most of his railroad worker's salary." Nancy worked seven days a week to keep her children fed. Her main job was working as a short-order cook. George told me that although they were poor growing up, they never really knew they were because his mom wouldn't let them talk about what they didn't have. They never measured what they had against what other people had.

Nancy is extremely proud of all of her children. When I asked her if she thought George was a good preacher, she responded, "I think George is a good man, period." She explained, however, that he was "more than a handful" growing up. He apparently got into a lot of fights on the streets of Houston and had several "scrapes with the law" as a teenager.

Our last interview of the day was with George himself. He talked about everything. His quick wit had us all in stitches several times. His description of his first fight in the

Job Corps was as humorous as any comedy routine I've ever heard. He had invited all of his friends to come and watch him "whoop this little skinny kid. He was so skinny you could see his ribs. I thought, boy am I ever going to beat him up. Look at how skinny he is! Well, I never could find him. I'd swing and he'd just move out of the way and hit me on the nose. I lost that fight, and I was never so embarrassed in all of my life," George recalled. Obviously, he was a quick learner because he captured the Olympic Gold medal in Mexico City just six months later.

From that point on, he became accustomed to knocking out his opponents in the early rounds. After pummeling Joe Frazier to capture Boxing's Heavyweight Championship, he felt invincible. But on October 30, 1974, he faced the former world champion, Muhammad Ali, in Zaire, Africa.

I asked George if he was worried going into the Ali fight. He responded, "Not at all. In fact, Ali was the one opponent I faced when I was completely overconfident." He described the night of the fight in the same way Roy had. He told me that the water that his trainer, Dick Sadler, gave him to drink just before the fight tasted like medicine. He remembered when he climbed into the ring to face Ali, he still had the aftertaste in his mouth.

George told me he hit Ali with some vicious shots that night, but every time he connected, the crowd booed. Ali, of course, just absorbed the blows and gave George an occasional little jab as he worked his "rope-a-dope" strategy. In the eighth round, he was feeling extremely tired, and Ali caught him with a one-two combination that sent him to the mat. He said he wasn't hurt at all but was actually excited that Ali was now willing to mix it up with him.

"In those days," George said, "you were trained not to look at the referee, but at your corner for your trainer. When he gave you the signal you were to stand up. As soon as my trainer signaled, I jumped to my feet, but the referee had counted the fight over." George feels that he ran into a power much greater than himself.

But it wasn't until the night of his fight with Jimmy Young in Puerto Rico three years later that George finally experienced that power to its fullest extent. George described to me in detail the supernatural events that took place in the locker room following that fight.

"I kept telling myself that everything was all right. I thought, well, I'm still George Foreman, I can come back and fight again and die. For some reason, the word 'die' had crept into my vocabulary. I had never really thought about death or dying much before, but it was as if another voice was speaking to me. I thought, well, I can box and do good things. I can give money to charities and help a lot of people. Then the voice said, 'I don't want your money, I want you.' My trainers and managers were holding onto me, they thought I was out of my mind. But I kept having this conversation with myself. I kept thinking, I'm George Foreman, I've got everything money can buy, I can go home and retire and die. I said, I don't want to die. The voice said, 'If you believe in God why are you afraid to die?' " George explained.

He then described how he had the feeling of being transported to different places, and in each place he became a different person, speaking a different language and feeling that person's feelings. He also saw blood coming from his forehead where a crown of thorns was placed. Finally, he told his managers and trainers they could let go of him because they had just witnessed a miracle. He shouted, "Jesus Christ is coming alive in me." After this incident, George walked away from the boxing ring and into a full-time preaching ministry.

Our interview lasted about two hours that afternoon. We covered many different subjects, and George was animated and well-spoken. As we began breaking down our equipment, Dean noticed a piano in the corner of the living room. He asked George if he played and George said, "No, do you?" Dean said that he did and then jumped on the piano and started playing. George then brought out an electric guitar and asked if anyone played guitar. I grabbed the guitar and started jamming with Dean and we all began singing Christian choruses. George seemed to really enjoy this, and we stayed there singing for about another hour and a half.

As we were saying our good-byes, George asked what time our flight was the next day. I told him it was in the afternoon. He then asked if we would be interested in coming by the George Foreman Youth and Community Center the next morning to do some more taping. I found it ironic that just the day before, I had had to track George down and beg him to let us tape. Now he was offering us every possible opportunity he could think of. When I asked George why his attitude had changed, he told me that he was testing me the day before. "I wanted to see how badly you wanted this story. I figured that if you put up with me the way you did, you would probably do a good job of telling my story in an honest and fair manner," he explained. I was very glad he had reached that conclusion.

The next morning, we met George and Roy at the Youth Center. George explained that in 1983, Roy was volunteering his time to work with kids who wanted to learn how to box. George visited Roy one day and met a kid who later wound up in jail. George was upset that he hadn't reached out to help the kid and decided that he had to find a way to help other teenagers in that same situation. He started looking for a place to build a youth center where he could steer kids into some worthwhile activities to keep them off the streets. Before long he found and purchased an abandoned warehouse. He outfitted it with boxing rings and all kinds of physical fitness equipment, including punching bags and weights. This was the beginning of the George Foreman Youth and Community Center. We videotaped some young boxers as they worked out, as well as some NBA hopefuls who were playing basketball on the outdoor court.

It was obvious that George had a real heart for these kids. He wanted them all to have a chance to make something out of themselves the way that he did. His goal was to take as many as possible off of the streets and to get them interested in a productive activity. Since many of their fathers were absent from their lives, George wanted to be a positive role model for them. George told me he was looking for new ways to fund the center. Apparently, the government had promised him a substantial monetary grant that had fallen through.

The documentary I produced on George was entitled, *Winner by Decision: George Foreman.* I really enjoyed putting it together. After I returned to Chicago, I spent three consecutive weeks in an editing suite putting together both a one-hour and a half-hour version of the documentary. It aired on TV-38 in Chicago and several other Christian television stations around the country.

I sent a copy of the finished documentary to George and he called me after he watched it to tell me it was the best thing that had ever been done on him. He thought we told his story in an honest and accurate manner.

I stayed in touch with George's brother, Roy, for quite some time after that. Less than a year after the documentary aired, Roy told me that George had decided to return to boxing as a way to raise funds for the George Foreman Youth and Community Center. I was excited and honestly believed that George could recapture the Heavyweight Title of the World. Of course, all of my friends told me I was crazy and that George was too old and too overweight to box again. I wanted to produce another documentary on George's comeback. I tried to raise the money to do it, but nobody else seemed to believe that George had a prayer. In retrospect, I should have just taken out a loan from a bank. The idea of borrowing large sums of money, however, has always made me nervous, so I didn't do it. I guess I didn't really have enough faith in George at the time either.

As we all know now, George's comeback story is one of the most exciting in all of sports history. His first fight on the comeback trail was against Steve Zouski, in March of 1987, in Sacramento, California. George won by technical knockout in the fourth round. He was on his way. The boxing world did not make it easy for "Big George." At times he had to set up his fights on his own. He punched his way back in small clubs and venues across America. These little halls would fill to overflowing with fans who were curious about the former Heavyweight Champ of the World. They usually brought in extra seating and still had to turn many people away. After beating several tough professionals, George began fighting ranked opponents.

Finally, on November 5, 1994, at the MGM Grand Garden in Las Vegas, George stepped into the ring to face the World Boxing Association's Heavyweight Champion, Michael Moorer. Moorer had defeated Evander Holyfield in April of that year for the heavyweight belt. George sapped Moorer's strength throughout the fight by jabbing hard to his body. In the tenth round, he caught Moorer square on the chin with a quick upper cut that sent Moorer straight to the mat for the ten-count. George Foreman had stunned the world by regaining the Heavyweight Championship of the World at the age of 45! He is the oldest man in history to win the title and the only man to regain the title 21 years after winning it the first time.

George retired from boxing, again, at the age of 48. This time it is for good, I think (never say never?). After losing a very controversial fight to a young boxer, George graciously congratulated his opponent and announced that he had fought his last fight.

I ran into George in 1998 at QVC. He told me the documentary I had produced on him, back in 1986, was still the best and most complete video production ever done on his life. I told him that I was very proud of his comeback, and then I reminded him about the time I made him jog a hundred yards down a dirt road. We laughed as we remembered how out of breath he was. If he had told me on that day that he was going to be the Heavyweight Champion of the World eight years later, I probably would have had serious doubts. But George Foreman is an extraordinary person and an extraordinary athlete.

Most boxing experts call Muhammad Ali "the greatest of all time." In fact, if you asked George, he would probably agree that Ali was the greatest boxer in history. While Ali's accomplishments are considerable, I personally think George's are even more impressive. I know how tough it is for me to get in shape every spring and fall to play soccer in a men's "over-35" league. It's murder. I am 45 at the writing of this book. My back and legs get stiffer with every season. Whereas I used to get loosened up for an athletic contest in about a half-hour, it now takes me an hour and a half to fully stretch and prepare. I just can't imagine how George trained the way he did, in his mid-forties, and knocked out the Heavyweight Champion of the World who was young enough to be his son!

There is no doubt that Big George Foreman is a true legend in the sport of boxing. But even more importantly, he is a legendary human being. He is still swinging for the hearts of men and women and boys and girls. His message is as straightforward as his awesome jab:

If you want to be a true champion for all time, follow the Lord Jesus Christ. He'll never let you stay down for the count.

Today, when George runs into Muhammad Ali, he no longer wants to knock him out. Instead, he wants to lift him up to the Lord so that he can wear a crown that will never tarnish. George's prayer is that Ali will realize that "the greatest of all time" walked the earth 2,000 years ago and never threw a punch.

Chapter 7

Nadia Comaneci

Nothing in the world of sports captivates me like the Summer Olympic Games. As a kid, I remember being glued to my television set for those two glorious weeks. To me it was the greatest exhibition of athletic skill on the face of the planet. The Olympic Games had it all! Running, jumping, lifting, boxing, swimming, diving, basketball and all of the other sports that bring out a young boy's developing sense of machismo. But in 1972, I was totally taken by surprise to discover that my favorite sport to watch was, dare I say it, gymnastics! Not only that, but my favorite athlete to watch didn't fit my preconceived notions of what an athlete should look like. Instead of possessing a massive body rippling with muscles, this athlete was tiny, almost diminutive. While most of my sports heroes looked mean and tough, this one looked like an angel in pigtails. My entire world view was shaken to its very foundations!

Sixteen-year-old Olga Korbut was originally an alternate for the Soviet Union's Women's Gymnastics team in 1972. She ended up competing and grabbed international attention with her lively routines and sparkling personality. She captured three gold medals and one silver. Her performance ignited a new enthusiasm for gymnastics and set the stage for an even younger and brighter star who was preparing to burst onto the scene at the 1976 Olympic Games in Montreal, Canada.

Nadia Comaneci, a 14-year-old gymnast from Romania, participated in her first major contest at the 1975 Champions All Tournament. She earned a silver medal and three golds. In 1976, at the Montreal Summer Olympic Games, she single-handedly lifted the sport of gymnastics to a new level. She earned the first perfect score of 10 ever awarded in the history of the Summer Olympic Games, and she did it at the tender age of 14. Nadia went on to earn seven scores of 10 and took gold medals in the uneven bars, balance beam and all-around competitions. At the 1980 Olympic Games in Moscow, Comaneci again garnered gold medals in the balance beam and floor exercise events. I'll never forget her flawless performances and electric smile. If Nadia was performing, I was in front of the television. The fans, judges and even other gymnasts, were in awe of her athletic ability, poise and grace.

Comaneci's fame spread beyond the world of gymnastics. In fact, she soon became known simply as Nadia. Her image was everywhere. "Nadia's Theme" was instantly recognizable as her signature song. She was an international star and one of only nine people in the history of the Modern Olympic Games, dating back to 1896, to receive the coveted Olympic Wreath.

Back home in Romania, Nadia's life was far from the perfect 10 she was scoring in competition. A Communist ruler named Ceaucescu controlled her country. Nadia actually dated his son for a time. But once her gymnastics career was over, apparently so was her usefulness. The country, which once lauded her as a hero, locked her out of the gym. She became depressed and suicidal. Things got so bad that in 1989, Nadia defected to the United States with the help of an American businessman. Her departure was so secretive that she left without her Olympic medals and the coveted Olympic Wreath. Her brother eventually smuggled them out of the country for her.

Nadia seemed to disappear from public view after that time—although there were several rumors flying about her and even about her relationship with the businessman who helped her escape Romania. But I have learned to discard rumors. They can destroy a person's reputation even when they are false. Many times I have heard disparaging remarks about a certain guest scheduled to appear with me on QVC. More often than not, my experience with the person was the opposite of what I had heard. If you have ever heard rumors about yourself that were not true, you know how badly they hurt. We all need to spend more time focusing on the good in other people and less time spreading something around through gossip.

I had heard very little about Nadia Comaneci, other than that one rumor, until I learned that she was coming to QVC in November of 1993. She was to appear with her fiancé at the time, Bart Conner, to represent a fitness product called the Step Circuit Trainer. Bart is a former U.S. World and Olympic Gymnastics Champion. In fact, he is the only male American gymnast to win gold at every level of national and international competition.

It's always a little weird meeting someone who was famous as a teenager and then disappeared from the spotlight. You wonder what they are going to look like. I remembered Nadia as an elfin 14-year-old dressed in her Romanian gymnastics uniform. When I walked into QVC's green room on that November evening, I recognized her immediately. There was no mistaking those dark, penetrating eyes and that electric smile. It was the same smile that had captured the hearts of people around the world in 1976. During the first few minutes, she was polite, but I could tell she was extremely shy.

Bart Conner, who is now Nadia's husband, did most of the talking. He is one of the nicest people I have ever met and was extremely accommodating. As we talked about the show, Nadia slowly began to open up. Her Romanian accent was strong, but I was impressed with her command of the English language. Although she had grown into a beautiful woman, she still possessed the childlike wonder that made her so refreshing as a gymnast. She was a pure delight to be around.

About 20 minutes into the meeting, a public relations lady who accompanied Nadia and Bart told me that Nadia had brought along something very special. Nadia reached into her gym bag and brought out what appeared to be a large jewelry box. As Nadia handed it to me, she said, almost apologetically, "I don't know if you are interested in these or not." When I opened the box, I couldn't believe my eyes. I was staring at Olympic history! All of Nadia's Olympic medals and the coveted Olympic Wreath were lying on top of each other inside this box.

Sadly, the medals were tarnished and in serious need of polishing. The Olympic Wreath, which has been given to only nine people in all of history, was broken in two. I picked up the two halves and said, "Nadia, don't you think you should have these soldered together?" She laughed and said that she would probably get around to fixing it someday. As I looked back into the box, I discovered that mixed in with these symbols of her tremendous accomplishments were pieces of old, stale candy. Can you imagine carrying around the ultimate symbol of athletic excellence in a box with old candy? I was flabbergasted. After regaining my composure, I thanked her for bringing them and told her I definitely wanted to show her medals at the beginning of our presentation on QVC.

I have a few boxes of sports trophies in the basement of my house. They used to be important to me, but they just collect dust now. For some reason, I haven't been able to part with them. But my trophies are from Little League, high school and college sports. If I had ever won an Olympic medal of any kind, I think I would have it hanging in a special display case. Here were Nadia's nine Olympic medals and the award that only nine people in history have won. I couldn't believe that they were tarnishing away in a jewelry box. I asked Bart why she didn't have them locked up in a nice case. He told me that they were no longer that important to her because of all of the bad memories associated with that time in her life. He did say that he was hoping that, after they got married, he would be able to display them either in their home or at the gym they were going to run in Oklahoma.

Isn't it funny how most of us think that winning an Olympic gold medal would have to be one of the greatest things that could ever happen to a person? Nadia has nine Olympic medals, several of them are gold, and she just leaves them put away inside a box—not because of any disrespect for her sport, but because of the sad memories those times bring back to her. The truth is Nadia is much happier now than she was back in 1976, when she was winning all of those medals.

Our presentation on QVC went extremely well that night. Nadia and Bart were professional and fun. One of the items in the circuit training package we offered is called a slide. This is basically a piece of flexible plastic that is about seven feet wide by three feet in length. The surface is slippery, so that when you put cloth booties over your shoes, you can quickly slide back and forth from side-to-side. Your thighs and buttocks get a terrific workout. In fact, several professional baseball teams have used this piece of equipment to help their players increase their lateral movement on the base paths and in the field. Nadia, Bart and I had the best time presenting this product. We began doing the "moonwalk" like

Michael Jackson. I remember looking at Nadia and seeing that wonderful twinkle in her eyes. She was giggling with that same joy that she had exuded so many summers before when the world was her stage for those unforgettable Olympic performances. It was another one of those magical moments. My job with QVC has offered me many great opportunities like this one. Many people would pay to have the chance to talk to Nadia Comaneci. She is definitely a legend in Olympic history. But that night on QVC, she was like a little girl who was showing Americans that fitness can be a lot of fun.

I usually try to get an autograph from the legends I interview, but on this particular night, I was so busy that I simply did not have a chance. I had to stay on the air for another two hours after Nadia and Bart's appearance. The next day at QVC, I ran into our fitness buyer at the time, Karen Fonner. She said, "Hey, I've got something for you in my office." I followed her to her office and she presented me with two five-by-seven color photos of Nadia and Bart. They had both signed them to me. Nadia wrote, "To Dan, Best Wishes, Love Nadia." I was thrilled.

Over the years, I have turned into a pretty serious collector of sports memorabilia. Whenever I have friends over to my house who are really into sports, I pull out some of my favorite pieces. Nadia's picture is one that I always bring out because people are still fascinated with her. My friends are always amazed when I tell them the story of her tarnished medals and broken Olympic Wreath. It just goes to show you that there is a lot more to life and happiness than winning Olympic gold.

Nadia seems to be very happy with her life now. She has married a wonderful guy. Bart Conner is a true gentleman and is as nice as the day is long. They seem to balance each other very well even when they're not on the beam. (Sorry, I couldn't resist a gymnastics pun.)

When I think about Nadia, I think of how she came as close to achieving perfection at her sport as any athlete ever has. I remember how her performances stood out, not only because of her incredible athletic ability, but also because of the grace and childlike joy that she seemed to weave into every movement. The world had no idea that away from the gym, she experienced very little joy at all. Her tarnished medals and broken wreath are somewhat symbolic of her life at that time. I'm happy for her because she seems to have rediscovered her joy. When you see her smile and you hear her laughter, you realize that neither time nor circumstance have tarnished them. And, regardless of what may happen to her Olympic medals, she'll always have those wonderful qualities hanging around her neck.

Chapter 8

Cal Ripken, Jr.

My kids often tease me when they catch me with tears running down my face at a sad movie. I am an emotional sap. The first time I watched Gary Cooper deliver Lou Gehrig's farewell speech in *The Lou Gehrig Story,* I cried like a baby. Nobody could figure out why the mighty "Iron Horse" of baseball was falling apart before their eyes during the season of 1939. When the Mayo Clinic finally discovered he had an illness that attacks the central nervous system, they announced he would no longer be able to play the game he loved. Yet on July 4, 1939, Gehrig stood before his fans and teammates and declared himself "the luckiest man on the face of the earth." I wish I could have seen him play.

Gary Cooper did a masterful job portraying Lou Gehrig. But I wonder who will one day play the part of baseball's "new Iron Horse," Cal Ripken, Jr. He has been compared to Lou Gehrig thousands of times. Like Gehrig, he's a wonderful family man. Like Gehrig, he always shows up for work and he always gives 110 percent. Although I never met Lou Gehrig, I know he would approve of Cal Ripken, Jr. as his heir —Cal happens to be one of the nicest people I have ever met.

He may not be as dramatic as Gary Cooper, but on the night of September 6, 1995, there was as much high drama in Oriole Park at Camden Yards as there had ever been on any Broadway stage. The reluctant star of the show was Cal Ripken, Jr. The night before, he not only tied Lou Gehrig's record for consecutive games played at 2,130, but he hit a homerun in the Orioles 8-0 rout of the California Angels. Cal didn't need a team of scriptwriters for his record-breaking performance, either. He took matters into his own hands and homered once again. When the game had reached the mandatory four and a half innings to become official, complete bedlam broke loose.

The game came to a screeching halt, and the standing ovations began. They went on and on and on. Cal's teammates finally pushed him out of the dugout. He told me he didn't know what to do so he went over to his family. He embraced his wife, Kelly, and hugged his kids. He took off his jersey to reveal a shirt that his children had given him which said, "2,131 hugs and kisses for daddy." He then found himself jogging around the entire stadium shaking hands with the fans and slapping high-fives. The ovation continued for 22 minutes. One of the most amazing—and nicest—things about this for the fans watching at home was that Chris Berman, one of the game's announcers, was completely silent for the entire 22-minute celebration! The network just let America enjoy Cal's amazing accomplishment. The fans were celebrating greatness, the kind that can only be achieved through hard work and consistency.

September 6, 1995 may go down in history as the day Cal Ripken, Jr. saved the game of baseball. The players' strike had ruined the fall of '94 and the spring of '95 for baseball fans everywhere. Once the '95 season finally got underway, there was a real effort on the part of the owners and players to try to bring the fans back out to the parks. By midseason, they were losing the battle to bring them back. But as Cal began his march toward baseball immortality, the excitement reverberated through office buildings, schools, recreation parks, television studios and homes across America. Cal's streak injected new life and hope into a national pastime which barely had a pulse.

As Cal took the field on the night of September 6, 1995, I took my seat at the *QVC Sports* desk. One of the many great things about *QVC Sports* is that when a major professional sports event takes place, we interrupt our regular programming and present the official merchandise, the instant that it happens. We call it a "QVC Sports Flash." For example, every year for the past five years, we have broadcast live from the stadium where the Super Bowl is played. As soon as the game ends, QVC offers official locker room hats and t-shirts, the same ones that the winning players are wearing on the field.

On this particular night, as soon as Cal took the field for game number 2,131, we offered Cal Ripken, Jr. autographed memorabilia. Cal had agreed to sign 1,000 baseballs for us that he dated "9/6/95." Our phone lines were jammed and within 10 minutes, all 1,000 autographed baseballs had been ordered at $249.00 each. Poor Cal was signing baseballs every spare second he could find during this historic time. When our Cal Ripken, Jr. presentation ended 1 hour and 20 minutes later, sales for his merchandise totaled $1.7 million.

Baseball's humble hero began his incredible Streak on May 30, 1982. For the next 16 1/2 years, he played all out. He dove, leaped and slid with the best in the game. He excelled on the field, winning the Rookie of the Year award, two American League Most Valuable Player awards and two Gold Glove awards. He has hit more homeruns than any shortstop in the history of the game. He played in 16 consecutive All-Star games, and he did it all his way: with grace, humility and style.

I'll never forget hurrying home after the QVC Sports Flash on the night Cal broke Lou Gehrig's record, to watch the rest of the game and to hear Cal's speech. I was impressed with his honesty and forthright style. Cal told me later that he worked very hard on that speech and that the words were his own. The same vigor and determination you see in Cal on the ball field go into everything he does, even speech writing—and you could tell it that night. One line in particular struck a note with me. It went something like this, "All I ever tried to do was play baseball the best that I could every day." Well, Cal did that every day for over 16 years straight!

His dedication and endurance reminded me of a notable scene in the movie *Dad*. Jack Lemmon, lying in a hospital bed, recalls the 1947 World Series to his son, portrayed by Ted Danson. He describes a game-saving catch by a little-known reserve outfielder for the Brooklyn Dodgers named Al Gionfriddo. In the sixth game of the Subway Series between the Dodgers and the New York Yankees, with the game on the line in the late innings, the great Joe DiMaggio hit a smash into deep left field that looked like it was a sure homerun. At the last possible moment, Gionfriddo leaped as high as he could and robbed Joltin' Joe of a homerun. DiMaggio, who rarely showed emotion on the field, was so upset he kicked the infield dirt near second base. As Lemmon finishes the story in the movie, he looks up at Danson and asks, "Do you know what that means to me? In America anything is possible if you show up for work!"

Cal Ripken, Jr. not only showed up for work every day for more than 16 years, but he consistently excelled at his profession. He holds many Major League records, including the longest streak for consecutive innings by a shortstop without committing an error. He has hit more homeruns than any other shortstop in history. He has won league MVP and All Star MVP awards, and I could go on and on and on. But I've found that the single most impressive thing about Cal Ripken, Jr., is his kindness. (Many women think his piercing blue eyes are a close second.) Cal has always been polite to everyone he comes in contact with at QVC. I can always tell something about a person's character by the way he or she treats the people who work behind the scenes. Cal is friendly not only to the producers, buyers and executives, but he is also friendly to the product coordinators, janitors, phone operators and, in short, everyone he comes in contact with. Cal is a great guy.

At a time when the game of baseball was in serious danger of extinction, Cal Ripken, Jr. was a much-needed hero. But Cal is much more than a hero. He is the guy that I would recommend as a role model for America's youth. In fact, he's my number one pick. Cal does not take a penny of his personal proceeds from the sale of his autographed memorabilia. It all goes directly to the Kelly and Cal Ripken Jr. Foundation to teach people to read and to help the underprivileged in the Baltimore area. The foundation isn't just a charity of choice for Cal. He and Kelly are personally involved in the work. Cal sees it as a way to give back to the community. Kelly Ripken spends a great deal of time working with the foundation, in addition to running the Ripken household and making sure that Cal and their children are where they need to be every day. In Cal's words, "She's an amazing woman." While Cal enjoys talking baseball, if you really want to see those blue eyes light up, ask him about his family.

Like Mickey Mantle and Pete Rose, Cal Ripken, Jr. learned to love the game of baseball from his father. Cal Ripken, Sr. was involved with professional baseball most of his life. He played, coached and managed in the Baltimore Orioles organization for 35 years. When Cal, Jr. was a young boy he loved to ride to the ballpark with his dad. He fondly recalls the talks they had riding back and forth between their home and the park. It was during those rides that Cal's love for base-ball began to grow. He learned the fundamentals of the game the Orioles' way. So, when Cal was drafted by the Orioles out of high school, he was more than ready.

Cal is one of several professional athletes I have met who demonstrates the important influence a father has on his young children. He knows how precious the time is that a parent spends with his children, and he works hard to pro-tect that important time. I don't know how he does it, because the game of baseball demands a lot of his time. But no matter how demanding his schedule may be, he always makes his family a top priority. Cal is not only an All-Star infielder; he's an All-Star dad. Let me say here that I think the most important role model in a child's life should *not* be a professional athlete. It should be a parent. This is why I find Cal Ripken, Jr. so refreshing. For all of his accomplishments in professional baseball, he finds his proudest achievement in the three simple letters "D-A-D."

Cal Ripken, Sr. was a guest on a QVC Baseball Col-lectibles show on September 6, 1997. This was the two-year anniversary of Cal's record-breaking night. Cal's mom, Vi, came along to the show. Vi and Cal Ripken, Sr. were two of the world's most down-to-earth people. They really took Cal Jr.'s success in stride. They obviously beamed with pride when they talked about him, but they had the same expression of pride when discussing any one of their four children.

Before the show, I took Vi and Cal Sr. on a tour of our backstage sets and props area. Vi wanted to buy some of our older pieces of furniture. She found an old Victorian style couch that she absolutely adored. She told me that one of her favorite hobbies is attending garage sales. During the show, Cal Sr. and I discussed baseball, family life, gardening and the Ripken Family Museum.

Cal Ripken, Sr. passed away at the start of the 1999 baseball season. It was a tremendous loss for Cal. He lost his father, his mentor and his best friend. Baseball lost a man who deeply loved the game.

When people ask me who my favorite athletes are to interview, Cal Ripken, Jr., is always at the top of my list. On the four or five different occasions I have worked with Cal, he has always been polite and he has always given an engaging interview. You can tell he thoroughly enjoys talking about all aspects of the game of baseball. Cal can eloquently describe the strengths of other players and he easily moves from the topic of hitting to fielding to base running and even coaching strategy.

Lou Gehrig is a fascinating topic for discussion with Cal. He readily accepts the fact that history will forever tie their names together because of their consecutive-games-played streaks. In fact, Cal has taken the time to learn as much about Gehrig's career and life as possible. When Cal appeared on QVC on February 11, 1997, he told me that he was looking forward to learning even more about Lou Gehrig when his playing days are over, and he has more time for hobbies and leisure.

On the night of September 20, 1998, Cal Ripken, Jr. did something extraordinary. He rested. After taking batting practice, he walked into the office of Orioles' manager, Ray Miller, and said, "I think the time is right." And just like that, the famous Streak was over. After playing in 2,632 consecutive games, Baseball's Iron Man decided to end The Streak on his own terms. It was Baltimore's final home game of the 1998 season. He wanted it to end where it all began 16 1/2 years earlier. Ironically enough, he ended it against Lou Gehrig's team, the New York Yankees.

When most major sports milestones are achieved, everybody knows about it. But Cal wanted to end The Streak

with little fanfare. Most of the people in the stands that night
had no idea they were witnessing history until the first out of
the game was made. At that point, the New York Yankees
walked up to the top step of their dugout and began applaud-
ing. The crowd then realized what was happening, and they
gave Cal a thunderous ovation. Cal emerged from the dugout
and acknowledged the fans with a look of relief on his face.
He wouldn't have to endure another winter full of questions
about when The Streak would end. He would no longer have
to listen to the critics who thought The Streak was interfer-
ing with the Orioles' success. He could finally free himself
from the unique pressure that comes with playing in every
game for 16 1/2 years.

I was surprised, at first, that Cal ended The Streak
during the most incredible homerun race of all time. Mark
McGwire and Sammy Sosa had been dominating the head-
lines for weeks as they chased and passed Roger Maris on the
single-season homerun list. But the more I thought about it,
the more perfect it seemed. Cal didn't want to attract a lot of
attention to himself. His personal numbers had slipped a bit,
and he felt it was time to give the younger players a chance.
The day he decided to end it was a day when Americans
needed some good news. We had been deluged with tran-
scripts and videotapes of our President's indiscretions. Wall
Street was on the down side of a roller-coaster ride. Cal Ripken, Jr. reminded us all that integrity and dependability do
matter. In fact, during his postgame press conference he said
that what he took pride in the most was not the number
2,632 but the fact that his coaches, teammates and the fans
could count on him to give his best effort every day.

It's a shame that so many people today seem to dis-
like their jobs. Cal feels blessed to love his job so much. He
showed up for work every day for 16 1/2 years and not only
showed up but *excelled* at his craft. Whenever you mention

the enormity of his accomplishments, he quickly points out two things: first of all, he was blessed with a body that heals quickly; secondly, he had a little luck along the way. For example, he says Kelly had perfect timing with regard to the birth of his children. Neither one was born on a game day. He will also tell you that whenever he experienced an injury, he had the necessary time to recover.

In several instances, that recovery time was extremely short by mere mortal standards. He told me about a time when he was sure The Streak was over. He had severely sprained his ankle sliding into second base during a night game. When he awoke the next morning, it was swollen to twice its normal size. As he stepped out of bed, he realized he was unable to place any weight on it. It looked as though his name would not be in the starting lineup that night, but he decided to get to the park early and begin therapy. The Orioles' trainers must perform their jobs very well because by game time Cal was ready to play. Don't ever underestimate the power of hard work, prayer and athletic tape!

I remember watching the Chicago White Sox on television with my dad in the early 1960s. His favorite player was Luis Aparicio, who was the diminutive shortstop for the Sox. My dad used to say he was "faster than greased lightning!" He was the prototypical shortstop of that era. He was of small stature but was extremely quick moving to the ball. Most of the shortstops at that time were built close to the ground. Their defensive skills seemed to be of much greater importance than their offensive prowess. They usually hit around .250 for average and rarely hit the long ball. In fact, the only tall shortstop that I remember was Don Kessinger of the Chicago Cubs.

Cal Ripken, Jr. has led the way for a new breed of major league shortstops. When you meet Cal in person, you realize that he is built like a tank. He stands 6' 4" and weighs about 220 pounds. At the age of 40, he is in prime physical condition. One of the ways he stays in such tremendous shape is by playing basketball. He has a full court in his home gymnasium, and he often invites college players to his house for some pretty intense pick-up games. Alex Rodriguez, the All-Star shortstop for the Seattle Mariners, told me that playing Cal one-on-one is like going to war. Cal definitely likes to take the younger guys to the school of hard knocks hoops.

One of my favorite pieces of baseball memorabilia is a photo of Cal Ripken, Jr. and Nolan Ryan. The photo was taken at the last All-Star game that Nolan appeared in. It is autographed by both of these legends of the game. This is special because these guys have been called "America's Last True Heroes" by more than one sportswriter. They are definitely cut from the same cloth when it comes to work ethic. Nolan pitched for a record 27 seasons in the major leagues, which is just one of over 50 records which he held at the time of his retirement. Nolan told me that whenever he finished pitching a game, he would immediately begin training for his next start. I guess you could say that Nolan is the Cal Ripken of pitching and Cal is the Nolan Ryan of infielding. I'll write more about Nolan Ryan later, but in my opinion they are the two great legends of modern baseball. That photo of them in uniform at Oriole Park at Camden Yards in Baltimore features the autographs of two great ballplayers and two great men.

I could probably write an entire book just about Cal Ripken, Jr. But I'll close this chapter by describing an incident involving Cal that is a very special memory for me.

QVC Sports, working closely with Goldin Sports Marketing out of Cherry Hill, New Jersey, often travels to the spring training home of Baseball's World Champions from the previous season. In March of 1996, we were in West Palm Beach, Florida, which at the time was the spring home of the 1995 World Champion Atlanta Braves.

The day before our scheduled live remote broadcast, I went over to the field to videotape what we call "roll-ins" for the show. "Roll-ins" are pre-taped pieces that are rolled into the live show. We shot footage of various players whose memorabilia we were going to feature in the show. We also shot what we call "bumper footage," which includes cover shots of the stadium and action shots to bump in and out of the spot breaks. I like to do some fun pieces too, so I put on an Atlanta Braves uniform and pretended to be trying out for the team. After all, you never know when they are going to need a 40-something rookie to add some flair to the lineup. The only problem was that after I attempted to slide into second, I remembered that it takes an entire afternoon just to get the mud out of your pants and undershorts.

The Braves were hosting the Baltimore Orioles that day for a spring exhibition game. When the Orioles came onto the field, I was standing in the area designated for members of the media. Reporters and technical crews were required to stay in this area during the pre-game activities. Media coordinators brought certain players and coaches over to this area for interviews.

I was going through a very sad time personally at this point. My dad, Dr. Joseph D. Wheeler, was dying of cancer and battling Alzheimer's disease in South Haven, Michigan. The night before he had taken a real turn for the worse. I spoke to him from a pay phone at a restaurant, and he wasn't sure who I was. I'll never forget that night. I had arrived in town before the rest of the crew, so I was dining alone. The only thing worse than eating alone in a restaurant is eating alone with the knowledge that someone you love is dying in another part of the country.

It never fails to lift my spirits just to be out at the ballpark, but I still had a lot on my mind. When I spotted Cal, I didn't pass up the chance to say hello, and he recognized me and invited me to come over and chat while he played catch with a teammate. I looked around and figured if I was with Cal, nobody would say anything. I was right. He asked me how certain products were doing on QVC. He takes a personal interest because the proceeds go to the Cal and Kelly Ripken Foundation. We had a nice conversation for about 10 minutes. I wished him well and returned to the media area.

As I was walking back, a reporter from a major sports publication who had been standing with me in the media area earlier asked, "Who are you and how do you know Cal so well?" I explained to him that I was a host on QVC and that while most members of the media only spend a few minutes with the athletes doing 30-second "sound bites," I have the unique opportunity to spend several hours interviewing them on the show. I also have the chance to spend time with them before and after the show.

It made me feel good that Cal remembered me and took a personal interest that day. His kindness really helped to lift my spirits at that difficult time. He had no idea what was going on with me that weekend or how bad I was feeling about my dad. But his simple act of kindness went a long way toward brightening my day. When I think about it, I realize he was just being Cal. It reminds me of a saying that an old radio deejay friend of mine used to close his shows with. He would always end by saying, "Remember friends, it's nice to be important, but it's more important to be nice." Cal is just a nice guy, and at a sad time in my life, he helped me feel a little bit better.

Of course, QVC was extremely supportive of me during this time, too. Jack Comstock, QVC's Vice President of TV Sales, and Mary Harlyvetch, TV Sales Scheduling Specialist, had been terrific about reworking the schedules of 22 hosts in order to give me a few days off so that I could fly to Michigan to be with Dad during his illness. My dad passed away on

May 27, 1996. I was flying home from a remote broadcast site, and I had the distinct feeling that he had gone on to his heavenly home.

When I think back to that time, it's a bright spot in a bleak memory that Cal Ripken, Jr. gave me a few minutes of his time when I was feeling low.

By the way, the exhibition game that day between the Orioles and the Braves was rained out in the third inning. As the crew and I made our way down the bleachers, we noticed one ballplayer standing underneath an umbrella signing autographs. All of the other players were either in the showers or driving away from the park. Do I even need to tell you who it was? Baseball's "Iron Man," of course. Whether they ever make a movie about Cal Ripken, Jr. or not, I think he deserves an Academy Award for kindness and a Lifetime Achievement Award for saving the game of baseball.

Chapter 9

The Super Bowl

Super Bowl XXIX
Parties, Payton & Young in Miami

"I'll give you 2,000 dollars cash for your ticket right now!" the man said as I walked toward the stadium.

I didn't even think about it. "Sorry pal, this is my first trip to the Big Dance and there is no way I'm stopping now!" I responded with a big smile on my face. It was Sunday, January 29, 1995, and I was about to enter Joe Robbie Stadium in Miami. This was the first Super Bowl I had ever attended, and I was as excited as any 10-year-old kid. Super Bowl XXIX was the culmination of a very special season for the NFL. Professional football was celebrating its 75th anniversary, and there had been festivities and ceremonies all season long. The NFL players wore a special patch on their uniforms commemorating the milestone.

The NFC Champion San Francisco 49'ers were taking on the AFC Champs, the San Diego Chargers. As Craig Adler, QVC's sports producer, and I walked into the stadium, I kept staring down at my ticket. I couldn't believe I was finally going to be at the biggest sporting event of the year "live and in person." But even before this stellar event, my week had already been made—I had been to another Super Bowl extravaganza, the NFL Properties party. How did I get this prestigious invitation?

QVC's Monday Night *NFL Team Shop* was in its

second year and was quickly becoming one of our most popular shows. I had hosted a three-hour special from the *NFL Experience* the day before. The *NFL Experience* is similar to *Major League Baseball's Fanfest.* It's really a theme park for football fans of all ages. My special guests included Brett Favre, Marshall Faulk and other NFL stars. This was QVC's first show from the actual site of the Super Bowl. Jill Bauer was the roving reporter at the *Experience* and had been in Miami for several days taping reports that were rolled in during the live show.

Our broadcast was a huge success and afterward Jill, Craig Adler and I had the honor of attending a party that was being thrown by NFL Properties. I thought I had attended some pretty fancy parties in my life up until this night—but I had no idea just what kind of a party could be thrown with a budget of over a million dollars!

While approximately 70,000 people are able to attend the Super Bowl itself (depending on the size of the stadium in which it is being played), only a couple thousand people are invited to the NFL Properties party. Most of the people who get invited are directly affiliated with the NFL or the sale of NFL merchandise. Ken Goldin, who was the president of the Scoreboard Company in Cherry Hill, New Jersey, at the time, gave us our invitations. The Scoreboard Company had been the primary provider of sports memorabilia to QVC over the years before the formation of Goldin Sports Marketing.

The party was thrown at a Port of Entry for Miami, so we drove toward the Pacific Ocean in anticipation of the party of a lifetime. We felt a little funny pulling up in our Chevy Malibu rental car, since most of the vehicles around us were stretch limousines. Upon arriving at the door, we were greeted by the Miami Dolphin cheerleaders. As I entered the party, I recognized the gentleman in front of me as none other than the NFL's all-time leading rusher, the late, great Walter Payton. I had interviewed Walter in the early eighties while working for TV-38 in Chicago. I said hello, but I'm sure he had no idea who I was. As usual, Walter was cordial. He always seemed to live up to his nickname, "Sweetness." At this point, I knew we were in for a Hall of Fame evening.

The party actually took place in seven different rooms—and each room was huge! The first offered a choice of every kind of seafood imaginable: rowboats filled with ice displaying shrimp, lobster, scallops, crab legs and practically everything edible from the ocean. Another room was dedicated to various cuts of beef and poultry. Every type of main course had its own designated area. Dessert even had a special room. Of course, there were beverages of every kind, and everything was free courtesy of the NFL Properties. It was now 9:30 P.M., and we hadn't eaten since noon. After filling our plates to overflowing, we found our way to the biggest room of all. This was actually an outdoor patio. Half of the patio had tables and chairs. The other half was a dance floor with a massive stage. *The Commitments* were playing on the stage. The movie by the same title had come out just a year or two earlier.

If you have ever watched me on QVC, you are probably aware that I love to dance. After dinner, I talked Jill into hitting the dance floor. We got quite a workout dancin' to the oldies. At one point, I accidentally bumped into a rather large, solid individual. When I looked up, I realized I'd just collided with John Elway, the quarterback for the Denver Broncos. It was definitely a night to remember. We left the party at a respectable hour because Jill had to fly back to Philadelphia the next day, but Craig and I stayed for the game on Sunday.

We were fortunate enough to get invited to the NFL's infamous *Super Bowl Tail Gate Party*. It was thrown in the parking lot of Joe Robbie Stadium from 1:30 P.M. to 5:00

P.M. This is the single most difficult ticket of all to come by. A mere 2,000 people are invited. Craig and I made it a point to be there at 1:30 P.M. sharp. Once again, the Miami Dolphin cheerleaders greeted us. As we walked in, we noticed that the food and beverages were being served at tables running down the middle and along the perimeter of the largest tent/building structure we had ever seen.

The food was exquisite. As we were finishing dessert (I probably gained five pounds that week), a voice came over the loudspeaker system announcing that the music entertainment was about to begin on the main stage. I can't remember the name of the opening band, but they belted out some great Jamaican tunes. They were followed by the main act, none other than the Allman Brothers. Craig and I looked at each other and bolted for the stage area. We stood about ten feet away from the band as they played for two hours straight. By five o'clock, we were pretty tired, but realized it was time to head for the stadium. We had no idea how exhausting Super Bowl weekend could be!

Of course, ticketless fans were offering big money for our tickets, but there was no way we were going to make it this far and not go in. Our seats were in the second row of the San Diego Chargers' end zone. In fact, we sat next to the San Diego Chicken. He seemed like a pretty nice guy, but this was before he punched Barney the Dinosaur.

The Super Bowl is not just another football game. This is the game that the players work toward from the first day of training camp. It is much more than a game, it is truly an entertainment extravaganza. Major entertainment happens on the field from the moment they open the gates. It never stops, even while the players are warming up. The scoreboards flash all kinds of interesting football information, the cheerleaders dance, and the music blares. By the time the game begins, the crowd is so fired up that they are almost in a frenzy. I have no idea how the players can concentrate on the game at all.

On this particular night, however, Steve Young and the San Francisco 49'ers had absolutely no problem concentrating on their game plan. Young went right to work. On the third play from scrimmage, he "threaded the needle," hitting Jerry Rice in stride on a deep post pattern. Rice sprinted directly toward us into the end zone for the touchdown. I can still see that play clearly in my mind's eye. It was at that moment that Craig and I realized we were sitting in two of the best seats in the house. That was the first of six touchdown passes that Steve Young rifled on his way to breaking the record for most touchdown passes thrown in a Super Bowl. He had finally exorcised the ghost of Joe Montana that had haunted him during his entire career in San Francisco. Interestingly enough, it was Montana's Super Bowl record that he broke. I was happy for Steve. He had been my guest on a couple of football collectibles shows on QVC and was always polite and cooperative. Jerry Rice and Ricky Watters tied the Super Bowl record for most touchdowns scored, with three apiece, as the 49'ers rolled to a Super Bowl XXIX victory by the score of 49-26. This game was filled with several outstanding performances, including San Diego rookie Andre Coleman's record-tying 98-yard kickoff return.

I made it back to the hotel around 11:30 that night. The problem was, I had a flight out of Fort Lauderdale the next morning leaving at 6:00 A.M. I packed my bags and slept for two hours. I wanted to be on the road by 3:00 A.M. since I wasn't quite certain of the route to the airport. The reason I had to catch such an early plane was that I was scheduled to host a Super Bowl Wrap Up Show from QVC at 7:00 that evening. My first Super Bowl was behind me and I must say it was one of the most exhilarating and exhausting experiences of my life.

Super Bowl XXX
Chaos, Howie & Diana in the Desert

Before I knew it, Super Bowl XXX was here. The 1995 season saw substantial growth for QVC's *NFL Monday Night Team Shop*. Fans across America were discovering that QVC was a great place to shop for officially licensed NFL merchandise. Most stores carry only the merchandise of the local team. If you're a New England Patriots fan living in San Francisco, it is very difficult to find your team's merchandise. QVC, on the other hand, has always tried to offer all 31 teams in every item. It's really a convenient service to football fans. QVC had become the official electronic retailer of the NFL and this year we were invited to produce a show from the *NFL Experience* in Tempe, Arizona, as well as a show from the press box at the stadium immediately following the Super Bowl game.

Our show from the *NFL Experience* was another hit. My guests were Howie Long, Steve Young and Rashaan Salaam. These shows always present our production team with some interesting challenges. Each player is scheduled to appear for a specific time period. We try to schedule the products that are most appropriate for that player during his time. For example, if I have a piece of memorabilia featuring Jerry Rice, I want to have his quarterback, Steve Young, on to give insights into Rice. If I have something featuring an Oakland Raider, it makes sense to have Howie Long, a former Raider, to talk about that player, etc. The challenge is that the players usually have many different appearances scheduled during Super Bowl weekend, so they don't always arrive on time. Everybody involved with the QVC production has to be extremely flexible. Steve Young was running way behind schedule on this particular day, so we really had to juggle things around.

Because of the location of our stage, the players had to walk through a large crowd of people to get up to the set. This is no easy feat when you're an NFL superstar and you are walking through a crowd of diehard football fans. I remember watching Howie Long literally fight his way through the crowd. This was an instance where his substantial size and strength helped tremendously, as fans were trying to hang on to his arms and shoulders.

My co-host for this show was Dave King. Dave was fairly new to QVC at the time. He played college football for Penn State and is a huge sports fan himself. We went out to dinner that night with some of Dave's friends. We were both extremely tired after dinner and still had over an hour drive to our hotel. While the stadium was in Tempe, our hotel was located 60 miles south of the city. It was an older resort where the San Francisco Giants baseball team used to stay during spring training in the fifties and sixties. It was far from an ideal situation and really required a lot of extra time and effort just to get back and forth to our broadcast sites. When you are dealing with the Super Bowl, you have to make reservations a year in advance to have decent accommodations within a half-hour of the stadium. Dave and I and the rest of the crew, however, were still thrilled to be at the Big Dance, although we felt like we were staying in another state.

Super Bowl XXX pitted the AFC Champion Pittsburgh Steelers against the NFC Champion Dallas Cowboys. This was the Cowboys' third trip to the Super Bowl in four years. They won Super Bowls XXVII and XXVIII by defeating Jim Kelly and the Buffalo Bills by scores of 52-17 and 30-13 respectively. The Cowboys once again had their offensive triumvirate of Troy Aikman, Michael Irvin and Emmitt Smith to go along with a pretty solid defense. They were coming off a regular season record of 12-4 with playoff victories over Philadelphia and Green Bay. The Steelers, on the other hand, had a defense that was reminiscent of the "Steel Curtain" of the seventies. They featured hard-hitting Greg Lloyd and Kevin Greene at the outside linebacker positions and the talented Levon Kirkland on the inside. On offense, quarterback Neil O'Donnell had a brilliant season with his favorite targets being Erric Pegram and Yancey Thigpen. The Steelers playoff road went through Buffalo and Indianapolis.

The game was scheduled to begin at 4:00 P.M. Arizona time, so we arrived at the stadium at high noon to make sure we didn't miss any of the festivities. Our press passes allowed us access to the international TV booth, which sat high atop the stadium. The crew at Sun Devil Stadium in Tempe had built a special viewing area for all of the members of the international press and people like us who were working after the game. The view was incredible! We were looking almost straight down onto the field and could see every play developing. We literally had a bird's-eye view.

Joe Montana and the Super Bowl MVPs from the previous 29 Super Bowls were present for the coin toss. Recording artist and movie star, Vanessa Williams, sang the National Anthem. One of the most impressive things about the National Anthem is that as soon as the singer hits the final note, a squadron of jets roars over the top of the stadium. The year before, Craig and I were taken by surprise, but this year I was watching for them. Since we were on the overlook at the very top of the stadium, I had a great view in all directions. I'll never forget watching the magnificent sunset over the Arizona desert. It was one of the most beautiful sights I have ever seen. Suddenly, toward the end of the song, I spotted the jets on the horizon and in a matter of seconds they zoomed over the stadium on the last note of the song! I am always amazed at how they time that out to the precise second.

The halftime show this year was nothing short of spectacular. Diana Ross, one of the world's most famous entertainers, performed with a singing and dancing ensemble. The 1,000-member World Choir along with thousands of Phoenix-area children represented Phoenix's diverse population. The extravaganza culminated with Diana Ross airlifted off the field by helicopter. She was whisked up and away right past our viewing area as she exited the stadium.

Another truly amazing aspect of the Super Bowl is the lightning-fast set-up and teardown of the halftime show stage. This involves a massive coordination effort. Several hundred people help roll out stages, lights and instruments. Numerous others handle all of the production elements of the show. It's quite impressive to watch them completely transform a football field into one of the world's largest stages in a matter of three to four minutes! When it's over, they tear it down in even less time. Radio City Productions produced this halftime event. The television director was the legendary Steve Binder, who directed Elvis Presley's famous Comeback Special in 1968.

The majority of Super Bowls over the years have been one-sided. The 49'ers dominated the game from the opening drive the previous year. But this one was close until the latter stages of the game. In fact, if Neil O'Donnell had not thrown a critical interception late in the game, the Steelers might have pulled this one out. But the gun-slinging Cowboys prevailed 27-17. I must say, I was surprised to see all of the black and gold worn to the game. We expected Sun Devil Stadium to be filled with a majority of Cowboys fans since Dallas is much closer to Tempe than to Pittsburgh. But those Steeler fans are loyal and they were there in full force supporting their team.

After the game, things got crazy. This was our first live remote from the stadium after a Super Bowl game. We were actually sharing a TV booth with the British Broadcasting Corporation (BBC). They were broadcasting from the booth during the game and then, within a few minutes after the game ended, they signed off and we went on. Those few minutes were among the wildest I have ever seen. Our crew waited for the BBC crew to clear everyone out of the booth. My friend, Drew Pearson, formerly of the Dallas Cowboys, came out of the booth along with Marv Levy, the coach of the Buffalo Bills at the time. They had been doing the commentary on the game for the BBC. Our production staff went to work immediately setting up banners and rearranging the booth for our show. To save time, we used the same cameras and microphones that were already in the booth. One of the BBC's technicians stayed with us for our show in case there were any technical problems.

I was standing outside the booth reviewing all of the statistics from the game, waiting for my cue. I had every statistic imaginable. The press information available at the Super Bowl is tremendous. There is a central media room that distributes complete game statistics at the end of each quarter. They also give you any Super Bowl records that have been tied or broken, along with other background information. Runners bring this information to every TV and radio booth in the stadium. This is no small task since there are media there from all over the world.

As soon as the booth was ready, they called me in, sat me down, put the headset on me and cued me. I love the excitement and rush of live TV. Dave King was down on the field grabbing players and coaches for interviews while I presented Super Bowl Champion Dallas Cowboy merchandise. Since QVC was the official electronic retailer of the NFL, we were the first to offer the public the official locker room championship merchandise. Starter manufactured the t-shirts that the players wore on the field immediately following the game and Logo Athletic manufactured the championship hats. Sports fans across the country have learned to tune into QVC as soon as any major sports event ends, because we usually "break-in" to our regular programming with a special presentation of *QVC Sports*. We offer the official championship gear. Every year for four consecutive years, we completely sold out of the championship hats during our live broadcast from the Super Bowl. I believe we had 27,000 hats this first year and they were sold out in about 20 minutes. Dallas had been the most popular team all year long in our *NFL Team Shop*, so we knew the show would do extremely well if they won. In an hour and a half, sales for Dallas Cowboy merchandise topped $1.8 million.

The majority of football fans watch the Super Bowl on television every year, but only a tiny fraction of the population ever has the opportunity to attend the Big Dance in person. I was feeling extremely fortunate that I had now been to two of them. Then before I knew it, I was heading to New Orleans, Louisiana, for Super Bowl XXXI.

Super Bowl XXXI
The Pack & Bourbon Street

The Green Bay Packers had finally made it back to the Big Game for the first time in 30 years. They were facing the AFC Champion New England Patriots. We were scheduled, once again, to produce a three-hour show from the *NFL Experience* on Saturday, January 25 and then a two-hour show immediately following the game from the Louisiana Superdome on the 26th. I'll never forget this weekend because it started for me very early in the morning on Friday, January 24.

Two of QVC's biggest days each year fall on August 17 and January 24. These are our popular Gold Rush Days.

The dates mark the anniversaries of the Klondike and California Gold Rushes, respectively. Our gold buyers bring in brand new gold pieces at exceptional prices, which are good for these 24-hour events only. I have hosted a slot on every major gold event except one, since I began with QVC on September 3, 1991. Gold Days are always exciting, and I love being a part of them. The hard part about this one was that I was scheduled to host the 6:00 A.M. to 9:00 A.M. portion of Gold Day on Friday the 24th. Most QVC hosts arrive at work about three hours before their scheduled time on the air in order to properly prepare. So, I woke up at 2:00 A.M. to be into work by 3:00 A.M. My slot went extremely well and around 10:30 in the morning, I drove to the airport to catch an early afternoon flight to New Orleans. I'll never forget how tired I was when I finally checked into my hotel that evening.

When I arrived at the front desk, however, there was a message from Greg Bertoni, QVC's Director of Merchandise for the Sports and Fitness areas. When I called him, he enthusiastically encouraged me to get dressed for dinner with some people from NFL Properties. Well, as tired as I was, I knew it was important for me to attend this dinner. NFL Properties was the main reason we were able to offer officially licensed NFL merchandise on QVC. I took a brisk shower and somehow managed to make it through dinner without my head hitting the plate.

When I returned to my hotel room that night, I turned on the news as I often do when I'm getting ready for bed. I was horrified as I watched a report about a woman who was practicing for the Super Bowl Halftime Show that evening. She was tragically killed practicing a bungee cord dive. Somebody made a mistake measuring the length of her cord. She apparently hit the concrete floor of the Superdome with full force. Her husband was there practicing

113

and actually witnessed this terrible tragedy. That put a damper on all of the weekend's events. The producers of the halftime show very wisely canceled the bungee diving portion of the program.

The next day I arrived by cab at the New Orleans Convention Center, which was the site for the 1997 *NFL Experience*. The QVC Local bus was parked at least a quarter of a mile behind the convention center. Since the producer, Rob Anderson, had my press credentials, I was instructed to report to the bus when I arrived. The problem was, my cab driver could not figure out how we could get close to the bus, since there was an eight-foot concrete wall separating the road from the area where the Local was parked. I told him to just let me off there and I scaled the wall. I'm lucky I didn't rip my khaki pants climbing over that thing.

My guests on the show that day were Jason Sehorn, Kordell Stewart and the legendary Green Bay Packer, the late Ray Nitschke. It was a special treat to have Ray Nitschke on the show because the Green Bay Packers had not been World Champions since Ray's playing days back in Super Bowl II. Green Bay had been waiting 30 years for the Lombardi Trophy to come back to Titletown. I'll never forget Ray talking about how proud he was of the Packer team.

When I asked Ray about Vince Lombardi, his eyes filled with tears as he fondly recalled the man after whom the Super Bowl trophy is named. He loved Vince Lombardi as a coach and as a person. Ray Nitschke was another one of the true legends who was such a pleasure to interview. He played the game of football because he loved it. His fingers were bent, and his nose was crooked from having been broken so many times. In fact, Ray played on several occasions with broken bones. When I asked him why he did that, he said he just didn't want to miss a game because of a little broken bone. Times have changed, haven't they?

Our *NFL Experience* show was once again very popular with America. After the show, Dave and I were pleased to learn that we would be attending the NFL Properties party. It was thrown at a huge building that was situated directly on the mighty Mississippi River, not far from the convention center. I remember rushing back to my hotel room to grab a quick shower and change of clothes after the show.

When I came back down, I ran into Drew Pearson in the lobby. Drew is the former All-Pro wide receiver of the Dallas Cowboys. He is probably best remembered for his Hail Mary catch that defeated the Minnesota Vikings in a playoff game in 1974. Drew now runs the Drew Pearson Company, which primarily manufactures unique sports hats. He has been a frequent guest on the *NFL Team Shop* and his hats are always extremely popular with our viewers. Drew has been a successful professional football player and is now a highly successful entrepreneur. But what makes Drew such a special guy is his kindness. Every time I run into him, he gives me a big hug and tells me he's glad to see me. He is a terrific guy and is always a pleasure to be around.

We had talked for about 10 minutes when I noticed that he seemed to be in some discomfort. He told me he had played in the Old Timers game at the *NFL Experience* earlier that evening and his quarterback was Randall Cunningham. Randall was temporarily retired from the NFL at the time. Drew told me he was throwing rockets in the game. "Unfortunately, Randall drilled one right here. I caught it, but it felt like it got stuck in one of my ribs!" Drew moaned. He told me he thought Randall could still play quarterback in the NFL. He was right, of course, because the very next season the Minnesota Vikings brought Randall out of retirement. In fact, at the end of the 1998 season, he was named the NFL Player of the Year. I wished Drew well and told him I was heading to

115

the NFL Properties party. He said he would see me there if he were able to walk.

This party was even bigger and better than the one I attended two years earlier in Miami. This time the New Orleans Saints' cheerleaders greeted us. Once again, the party took place in a very large facility with many large rooms. This year each room was decorated like the stage of a Broadway play reflecting life in the Big Easy. The first room featured backdrops that made it look like a Mississippi River steamboat. Naturally, this was the seafood room. This time, however, the seafood was prepared in typical New Orleans Cajun fashion. Umm! Umm! It was delicious. The next room we walked into looked like Bourbon Street. Another room was designed to resemble a famous New Orleans restaurant. Basically every room was done up in similar fashion, each having its own version of New Orleans flavor.

After dinner, Dave and I wandered into the entertainment area just in time to hear the announcer introduce New Orleans' own Neville Brothers. We fought our way through the crowd and ended up standing about 15 feet in front of Aaron Neville. They put on some kind of a show that night. They sang every one of their hits and more. It was another magical moment where I thought to myself, "I have a great job!" I must say, NFL Properties certainly knows how to throw a party! We stayed and sang along with the Neville Brothers until the wee hours.

When I threw open the curtains in my hotel room late the next morning, I saw the Goodyear blimp outside my window (my room was on the 33rd floor of the hotel). Whenever I see the blimp, I realize that I am where the sports fans of the world want to be. I showered, ate lunch and then met Dave down in front of the hotel. We arrived at the stadium around two in the afternoon for the 6:00 P.M. game.

Dave and I had developed a pre-Super Bowl ritual by now. We usually checked in with our producer at the Local and then wandered around the stadium to take in the sights and sounds of the big game. We walked out onto the outskirts of the playing field area and had our pictures taken with both the Green Bay Packer cheerleaders and the New England Patriot cheerleaders. These seemed like neat shots for our scrapbooks. Dave and I got separated at some point, and I ended up watching the start of the game from the press box. Unlike Sun Devil Stadium the year before, there was no overlook area for members of the international press at the Superdome. So, we were on our own trying to find seats. Luther Vandross, who happens to be one of my favorite singers, sang the National Anthem, and then the Big Show began.

Brett Favre brought the Packers down for a quick score and the Packers were in control of the game through the first half. The momentum began to shift, however, in the third quarter. The Patriots scored a touchdown and tied the game at 21 all. Desmond Howard then electrified the crowd by taking the ensuing kickoff 98 yards for a touchdown, and the Super Bowl record for longest kickoff return. That put the Packers back in the driver's seat. Howard was named the Most Valuable Player (MVP) of Super Bowl XXXI. He also set the record for the most punt return yards in a Super Bowl, with 90. All together, Howard returned 4 kickoffs for a total of 154 yards, and 6 punts for yet another Super Bowl record of 244 return yards. He became the first special teams player in history to be named the Super Bowl MVP.

I lost my seat in the press box area about halfway through the second quarter. When I went back to the bus, I ran into Ken Goldin of the Scoreboard Company and he informed me that the seat next to him was empty. What a stroke of luck. The seat was right at the start of the second section up from the field on about the 40-yard line. It was one of the best in the house. I had a tremendous view of all of that exciting second half action.

As I mentioned earlier, going on the air live after a Super Bowl is organized chaos. A couple of minutes before the end of the game, I began making my way up the steps so that I could be waiting outside of the press box that we, once again, shared with the BBC. Apparently, most of the fans in the stadium decided to leave at the same time, because when I got into the hallway, it was wall-to-wall people. I was trying to go up a winding ramp that was filled with thousands of people who were coming down! I began to worry that I would never make it up to the press box in time. Suddenly, a woman in the crowd recognized me and shouted for everyone to let me through. People began clearing an outside aisle and I made it up to our broadcast booth just as the BBC crew was coming out. I wish I knew who that lady was, because I owe her a big "thank you!"

Our postgame show almost melted QVC's phone lines, even though our phone centers were geared up with extra operators. This time we had ordered 30,000 of the locker room hats by Logo Athletic and all 30,000 were ordered within the first half-hour of the show. In addition, over 20,000 locker room t-shirts and several thousand sweatshirts by Starter were ordered. The Pack was back and Green Bay fans were going wild. I remember looking over my shoulder onto the field at the start of the show, and it was covered with a sea of confetti. An hour after the game had ended, Packer fans were still celebrating, and our phone lines were still jammed. The sales for the post game show totaled over $2.1 million in about 2 hours! Keep in mind that most of the items ordered were in the $25 to $30 range. This means that QVC took over 85,000 orders in that 2-hour period.

Dave and I joined some of the production crew down on Bourbon Street at about 1:30 A.M. The streets were absolutely jam-packed with people wearing green and gold jerseys. I remember thinking that even though it was the wee hours of the morning, it felt like it was noon. Around 2:30 A.M., I decided to "Pack it in." I had seen enough drunken people to last a lifetime. My flight was around noon the next day and, once again, I collapsed into my seat on the airplane happy to have survived my third consecutive Super Bowl.

Super Bowl XXXII
Elway & Party Animals

Heading into the 1997 season, the pigskin prognosticators were predicting a return to The Dance by the Green Bay Packers. Some were saying they had a chance to become only the second team in the history of the NFL to go through the regular season undefeated. Many were proclaiming the Packers as the new dynasty. However, injuries took their toll on the Pack early in the season. After a couple of losses, Coach Mike Holmgren wisely gave his team the bye week off to recuperate.

Normally, I wouldn't have cared about a coach giving his team a rest, but we were scheduled to do a remote with Brett Favre during the bye week. The location had been set for the Brett Favre Steak House in Milwaukee, Wisconsin. I was looking forward to spending some time with my mom and my sister's family in New Berlin, which is located just outside of Milwaukee. However, when Holmgren announced that he was giving his team the week off, Brett decided he wanted to go home to Mississippi. As I said earlier, when you are dealing with professional athletes, you have to be flexible.

Brett's agent contacted our people and it was decided that the show would now originate in Mississippi. On Friday, October 17, 1997, I hosted a two-hour football collectibles show with Brett Favre from the Old Waverly Golf Club in West Pointe, Mississippi. (For more on that, see the chapter on Brett.)

That week off really proved to be a wise move by Holmgren. The Packers' key players had a chance to recuperate from their injuries and Green Bay went on a roll the rest of the season. They ended up with a 13-3 record in the regular season and easily handled both the Tampa Bay Buccaneers and the San Francisco 49'ers in the playoffs. They had indeed made it back to the Big Dance, but their opponent for Super Bowl XXXII was a very determined Denver Broncos team. The Broncos seemed intent on putting an end to the AFC's 13-year Super Bowl drought.

The Broncs had a much more difficult playoff road than the Packers did. With a 12-4 season record, they came into the playoffs as the wild card team. After beating Jacksonville 42-17 to avenge the previous year's surprising playoff loss, they went into Kansas City and stopped the Chiefs 14-10. They then invaded Three Rivers Stadium and escaped with a 24-21 victory over a versatile and tough Pittsburgh Steelers team. The stage was set for a showdown between two of the best quarterbacks ever to play the game: 3-time NFL MVP, Brett Favre would face 37-year-old legend, John Elway.

The modern-day OK Corral was QualComm Stadium in sunny San Diego, California. I never mind visiting warm climates in late January. My Super Bowl stops have included Miami, Tempe, New Orleans and now San Diego. They were all tough assignments, but I guess if you have to go to the Super Bowl in late January, it might as well be in a warm location.

I decided to fly into Los Angeles and spend my two days off that week visiting an actor friend of mine named Rod Sell. Rod has appeared in movies like *Groundhog Day* starring Bill Murray and *Home Alone II* (he was the police chief looking for Macaulay Culkin). I stayed in the beautiful Summit Hotel in Bel Air. My friend, Roselyn Cosantino, was the director of Business Development at the Summit. She is also an avid QVC viewer. When I arrived she said, "I hope you don't mind having dinner with Bo Jackson. He's already in the dining room waiting for you." Roselyn treated Bo and me to a wonderful dinner that evening. He is a really nice guy and we had a great time talking about all kinds of sports. The next night I got together with Rod, and we had a lot of laughs reminiscing about the years that we worked together at WCFC-TV in Chicago.

The time and day of the week for this three-hour football collectibles show were far from ideal. The show began at 5:00 P.M. eastern time, which was 2 P.M. Pacific time. There just aren't many football fans at home during a weekday afternoon. All things considered, the show went pretty well.

My guests for the show were Desmond Howard, Franco Harris and Marcus Allen. Desmond had done a show with me the previous year about a week after the Super Bowl. He was now a member of the Oakland Raiders, and I'm sure he was a little sad over the fact that his former team was back playing in the Super Bowl and he was going to be watching from the stands. He seemed to be in pretty good spirits, however, as did Marcus Allen. Unfortunately, Franco Harris never showed up.

The next day, Ken Goldin and Barry Didinsky of Goldin Sports Marketing were able to obtain tickets for Dave and me to attend Leigh Steinberg and Jeffrey Moorad's party at the San Diego Zoo. Leigh Steinberg is the biggest sports agent in the business. I read a newspaper article that said the movie *Jerry McGuire* was loosely based on his life. When we arrived at the party, we joined several hundred people who were being directed down a long runway. It kind of felt like the Academy Awards, without all the outrageous attire. Warren Moon, Kordell Stewart, Drew Bledsoe, Desmond Howard, Ricky Watters and Emmitt Smith were all in attendance, along with Leigh's newest recruit, Ryan Leaf. Leaf was the quarterback who led Washington State in a valiant effort against the number-one ranked Michigan Wolverines in the '98 Rose Bowl. Desmond Howard, a former Heisman Trophy winner from the University of Michigan, and I walked by Leaf and yelled, "M go blue!" Growing up in Michigan, I became a diehard Wolverine fan and was thrilled over the Wolverines' National Championship. We ran into Emmitt Smith of the Dallas Cowboys, and his girlfriend, Patti, whose uncle, Malcolm Mitchell, is the General Manager of QVC's phone center in Chesapeake, Virginia. Dave and I had a nice talk with her and Emmitt. They are both very pleasant, down-to-earth people. During the party, workers from the zoo brought various animals into the party. One lady was carrying around a chinchilla. This animal is so soft that the trainer had me close my eyes as she ran the chinchilla's fur through my fingers. I honestly couldn't tell I was touching anything. They are very cuddly, loveable animals. They also brought in exotic birds, but I think they went too far when they brought in a camel. The camel kept "breaking wind," and this was not a pleasant thing to experience.

Super Bowls are exhausting—not so much because of the game, but because of all of the parties and events surrounding the game. I can hear you thinking, "I can't believe that Dan Wheeler is complaining about having to attend the Super Bowl and all of the parties!" Hey, I'm not complaining, I'm just saying that it takes a lot of energy to keep up with all of the revelry. I am very grateful for the opportunity to be a part of it. I was just preparing you for the fact that later that evening, we had to get ready to attend the famous NFL Properties party.

This time we caught a special bus at the Catamaran Hotel and rode for about a half-hour to the party. Our bus had a police escort all the way. I kept thinking, "I hope the criminals in this city don't know where all of the police are."

We were surprised to discover that the San Diego Charger cheerleaders did not greet us at the door. Space people greeted us instead. The theme of this party was futuristic, so the greeters actually wore alien space suits. Who knows? The space aliens may have actually been the Charger cheerleaders after all. The first room featured hors d'oeuvres. The second room was bigger than a football field. There were two music stages set up at both ends of the room. The lead singer for the Stray Cats was backed up by a big band on one stage, and the other one featured a good old-fashioned rock 'n' roll band. When one group stopped playing, the other one kicked in immediately.

The food tables were located around the perimeter of the room. I ate sliced roast beef, crab cakes, chicken and lots of vegetables. After dinner, Dave and I roamed around and chatted with all kinds of people. I discovered that by your fourth Super Bowl you start to know some of the people. Drew Pearson was there and we talked for about 15 minutes. He was his usual affable self. I asked him if he had played in the Old Timers' Game at the *Experience* and he said that he had. He told me he was glad that Randall Cunningham went back into the NFL, so he didn't have to catch any more of his bullets to the ribs. Dave and I talked to Jack Fitzgibbons

123

and Roger Atwater from NFL Properties for at least a half-hour. We then decided it was time to hit the dance floor before the band quit playing. We jumped on the floor and before we knew it, we were in a Conga line that snaked its way everywhere, including up on to the stage. Once again a great time was had by all!

Since we were on the West Coast, the game started at 3:00 P.M. the next day. Dave and I didn't arrive at Qual-Comm until around 12:30 P.M. because the traffic was horrendous. Our hotel was only about 10 minutes away from the stadium on a normal day, but on Super Sunday it took us over an hour to get there. In the bumper-to-bumper traffic, people were waving flags, holding up signs and even hanging out of their windows shouting for their team.

We checked in with our producer, Bobby Collom, at the Local, which was parked in the television compound. Every year there are more television and satellite trucks at this one game than I have previously seen in my lifetime. When you are in the compound, you are in the middle of a virtual sea of satellite dishes and trucks. You can almost feel the television signals blasting through the air.

After checking in, we were off again on our pre-game ritual. We walked into the stadium at the second section up from the Packers' end zone. There are usually still a lot of empty seats this early, so we sat down and enjoyed all of the pre-game entertainment. I have described the on-field entertainment of previous Super Bowls in glowing terms. But this year, it was beyond anything you could imagine. The pre-game show included performances by the Fifth Dimension, Mike Love and Bruce Johnston of the Beach Boys, Lee Greenwood, Glen Campbell, John Stamos, Dean Torrance and David Marx. The late Phil Hartman narrated the show. The National Anthem was performed by San Diego area resident and recording star, Jewel.

I returned to the bus near the end of their performances to pick up a ticket that was left for me by Ross Auerbach, the president of the Northwest Company. Northwest makes a lot of the NFL throws that we offer on QVC during the *NFL Team Shop*. He happened to have an extra ticket, so I was fortunate once again to have a prime seat. This one was located on the 35-yard line in the second section up from the field. In fact, when I looked down the row that I was sitting in, I saw the legendary Jim Brown about 10 seats away. I was actually closer to the 50-yard line than Jim Brown.

The Green Bay Packers wasted no time scoring once the game began. Brett Favre marched his team the length of the field and dropped a beautiful pass into the hands of Antonio Freeman in the corner of the end zone for a touchdown. At this point, I thought, "Here we go. The Packers are going to blow the Broncos out." But John Elway and the Broncos had other plans. They came roaring back and struck pay dirt on their first possession, with Terrell Davis blasting up the middle from a few yards out. We were in for one of the best games in Super Bowl history.

The halftime show was as engaging as the game itself. It featured a salute to Motown, which was celebrating its 40th anniversary. The all-star lineup included Martha Reeves, Smokey Robinson, the Temptations, the Four Tops, Queen Latifah and Boyz II Men.

Denver and Green Bay slugged it out in the second half. The Broncos went up 31-24, and the Packers' hopes of a repeat title were dashed when Brett Favre's final pass to Mark Chmura was batted away by the Bronco's Steve Atwater with just a few ticks remaining on the clock. John Elway and the Broncos had done it! They ended the NFC's 13-year Super Bowl reign. Terrell Davis was named the game's MVP in front of his hometown fans. In fact, he became the first NFL player in history to be named the Super Bowl MVP in his hometown. John Elway played like a 25-year old superstar. What an awesome game it was!

Denver Bronco fans and John Elway fans across America were calling in to QVC during our postgame show. This year we had 35,000 of the Logo Athletic locker room hats. By the end of our show, we had none. QVC's phone lines were jammed, once again, for the entire hour and 20 minutes after the game. At midnight eastern time, I threw it back to QVC's studios in West Chester for an hour of jewelry. We then came back to QualComm Stadium for another hour of Denver Broncos championship merchandise from 1:00 A.M. to 2:00 A.M. eastern time.

Just minutes before we were to come back on from the stadium, one of the other television crews accidentally unplugged our main power line as they were tearing down. One of our crew members traced the line into the depths of QualComm Stadium and got us up and running again in just a few minutes. QVC's production team is second to none.

After three unsuccessful trips to the Super Bowl, the Denver Broncos had won the Lombardi Trophy. John Elway finally won the big game, assuring his place among football's all-time greatest quarterbacks. Finally, a quarterback from that famous draft of 1983 had guided his team all the way to the pinnacle of professional football. Our sales for the postgame shows totaled $2.2 million.

It was another long night at the football stadium. Dave and I left around 11:30 P.M. San Diego time. We had to give Brendan McQuillan, QVC's buyer of licensed sports merchandise at the time, a ride back to his hotel, which was about 15 minutes in the opposite direction from ours. After we dropped him off, we made a few stops to pick up souvenirs for our kids. I always try to bring my daughters, Kirstyn and Kelsey, special souvenirs from my travels. Dave does the same for his two sons.

I walked into my hotel room around 1:00 A.M. Unfortunately, I had an 8:00 A.M. flight out of Los Angeles International Airport, or LAX, as it is known. This airport is 2-1/2 hours from San Diego. This time I packed my bags, slept for only one hour and hit the road. As always, I collapsed into my seat on the airplane, having now survived four Super Bowls in a row.

My flight arrived in Philadelphia at 4 P.M. I wanted to get back home to have an evening with my family because I was scheduled to be on the air for three hours the next night. Two of those hours were for a Super Bowl Wrap Up show with Rod Smith, wide receiver for the Denver Broncos. It is difficult working evenings when you have school-age children. Basically, as they are coming home from school, I have to leave for work. I don't get to see them much during the week, so when I have an evening off, I try to protect that time.

The show with Rod Smith went smoothly. We were able to get a rush order of 5,000 more of the locker room hats from Logo Athletic and all 5,000 were ordered. A total of 40,000 of the Denver Broncos Championship Locker Room Hats were ordered from QVC following Super Bowl XXXII.

The following Sunday, I hosted one more Super Bowl Wrap Up show. My guest was Franco Harris. He showed up this time and did a great job. Franco was a very nice man and was quite helpful during the show. He gladly assisted me in holding up the championship throw rug, and he commented favorably about all of the merchandise we presented. John Elway called in near the end of the show. I asked him if he was going to retire, and he said it would be very difficult to do it with his team playing so well. I guess he knew he had one more great year left in him.

Super Bowl XXXIII
Namath Returns, Broncos Repeat in Miami

Super Bowl XXXIII had us flying to Miami. Dave had been down taping most of the week at the *NFL Experience*. I was able to fly down a day early, so Dave and I scheduled an afternoon visit to South Beach. The weather was perfect. Skies were sunny and the temperature was around 75 degrees. We walked on the beach for about a mile before finding some comfortable beach chairs for rent. We settled down and had a couple of sandwiches on the South Beach sand. Dave had a camcorder that we were going to be presenting the following week on QVC, so we videotaped a special Super Bowl preview capturing some of the South Beach excitement. We also showed that we were working very hard as we did our Super Bowl preparation on the beach.

About an hour later, we walked up to the street that runs along South Beach. It is lined with all kinds of upscale shops and eateries. As we were walking off the beach, Dave recognized two members of the singing group, Boyz II Men, as they walked by us. When we arrived at the street, it was jam-packed with all kinds of crazy football fans. One guy had a huge boa constrictor around his neck. You see all kinds of things at the Super Bowl.

The *NFL Experience* Show this year was one of our best ever. My special guests were Broadway Joe Namath and Doug Flutie. Joe brought the house down when he walked out. He still draws a big crowd wherever he goes. He is a legend because of his bold guarantee of victory in Super Bowl III. He lived up to it by leading his New York Jets to the win over the Baltimore Colts, 16-7. That game, by the way, took place in Miami exactly 30 years earlier. My other guest, Doug Flutie, was coming off his best season ever in the NFL. He had put up some impressive numbers as the starting quarterback for the Buffalo Bills.

This year was the first time that QVC had its own broadcast booth at the Super Bowl. Pro Player Stadium was big enough to house all of the media properly. It was such a luxury for us to sit in our own booth and enjoy the game. We were at the top of the stadium and once again had an aerial view of the field. As soon as the game ended, we were ready to go with our show because everything was set and lit before the game started.

The Atlanta Falcons, under head coach Dan Reeves, had captured the NFC title and made their first appearance ever in a Super Bowl. John Elway had led his Denver Broncos back to the Big Dance for the second year in a row. This game featured a great match-up at the running back position with the Broncos' Terrell Davis and the Falcons' Jamal Anderson. Davis had been named the league MVP that season.

The Broncos controlled this one and cruised to a 34-19 victory to repeat as Super Bowl Champions. John Elway, in the final game of his career, was named the Super Bowl MVP. I remember we were wondering going into this game if the Broncos' merchandise would be nearly as popular as the previous year if they won. Well, the answer was resounding. Our postgame show total soared to a record $2.5 million. We offered several unique John Elway autographed items and they all sold out quickly.

I had now attended five great Super Bowls in a row, but my streak was about to come to an end.

Super Bowl XXXIV
Vermeil & Warner Arrive in Atlanta

Super Bowl XXXIV in Atlanta was very disappointing for me. Because the Georgia Dome is a comparatively small stadium, the NFL was not able to offer us our own booth. Our QVC Local personnel did not want to go through all of the hassle of sharing a booth. Instead, I would fly to Atlanta for the *NFL Experience* Show on Saturday and fly back to Philadelphia right after the show to anchor the post-game broadcast from our studios in West Chester, Pennsylvania. Dave King would stay in Atlanta and report from the field after the game.

The previous years had spoiled me. It just didn't seem like the Super Bowl to me, since I wasn't going to be able to attend the game. By now, this had become the highlight of the year for Dave and me.

I decided to fly to Atlanta a day early to visit my good friend, Brian Roland, whom you'll read more about later in the chapter on the Atlanta Centennial Olympic Games. Brian had just purchased a home in the Atlanta area, so I thought it would be great to see his new place.

The Georgia World Congress Center was the site for the 2000 *NFL Experience*. It was an ideal location. QVC had an eye-catching stage area which featured large, cheesecloth backgrounds. Our lighting guys did a wonderful job of lighting these up with our *QVC Sports* logos and splashes of color. Our guests for this show included Brad Johnson, quarterback for the Washington Redskins; Terrell Owens, wide receiver for the San Francisco 49'ers; Roger Craig, the former great 49'er running back and former Rams' standout Deacon Jones.

I had worked with Deacon Jones and Roger Craig before. Deacon is always a lot of fun to have on, and Roger Craig is a very pleasant, humble guy. Brad Johnson and Terrell Owens were making their first appearances on QVC.

Brad Johnson really impressed me. After experiencing a few tough breaks in Minnesota, he had been traded to the Redskins following the 1998 season. He really put it all together in 1999 with Washington. He took the Skins to within one point of the NFC Championship game. I have to say that he was one of the nicest young men I have ever met. He came up onto the set while we were in a pre-taped spot. The first thing he said to me was, "It's really an honor for me to be on the *QVC Team Shop*. I watch your show a lot and you have some great players on. I can't believe I finally made it on as one of your guests." His genuine character and humility were refreshing.

Terrell Owens did a nice job, very smooth, and nearly as sincere-sounding as Brad. Deacon Jones was his usual outgoing self and Roger Craig, as before, did a wonderful job during his presentation. He was working for a software company and gave them a nice plug on national television.

The show went well from a technical standpoint until the power went out in the building! I was in the middle of a presentation of an Upper Deck card set. All of a sudden, our set went completely dark. When you are on live television, you can never panic in these situations. I just kept talking and acted like everything was fine. My guest took my cue and kept the presentation going nicely.

Luckily, the cameras were not on us, or the viewing audience would have seen we were in total darkness—we had just gone into a piece of videotape about the cards, and the audience could only hear our voices. By the time the tape ran out and the cameras came back to us, our lighting guys had our lights back up. Our power came from our own generator, so when the house lights went down, we were able to keep the show going. Our viewers never even knew anything was wrong.

In the middle of the show, my producer told me that my flight back to Philadelphia had been canceled. The ice storm finally came, and a lot of people were stranded at Atlanta's Hartsfield Airport. After the show, Brian and I had to scramble to find a hotel room for the night. Fortunately for us, one of the drivers of the QVC Local decided to hit the road that night. He still had a hotel room booked in the same hotel that we had stayed in the night before, so he gave it to us. I had housekeeping bring up a roll-away bed.

That evening we decided to go for a steak at Ruth's Chris Steak House in Atlanta. We didn't have a reservation, so we knew we were in for a rather lengthy wait. As we were walking into the waiting area, we recognized the very large man in front of us as Jackie Slater, the former Rams' great lineman. He shook hands with a gentleman whom we quickly recognized as Eric Dickerson, the Hall of Fame running back. These guys had played together for the Rams, and they were in town to watch their former franchise, the St. Louis Rams, take on the Tennessee Titans in Super Bowl XXXIV. About 15 minutes later, we saw Cecil Fielder. Cecil was a guest on one of my World Series Wrap Up shows when he played for the World Champion New York Yankees. Brian also knew Cecil from a project he had worked on with him at Crawford Communications. We had a nice chat with Cecil, and he introduced us to his son.

We were finally seated about 11:00 P.M. Even though the hour was late, steak never tasted better. If you are ever in Atlanta, I highly recommend this restaurant. The meal was definitely worth the wait.

I had to rise at six in the morning to catch an 8:30 A.M. flight back to Philadelphia. The Weather Channel was forecasting a major snow storm for the Philadelphia area later in the day. My plane left Atlanta about an hour late. We had to have the wings de-iced a couple of times on the runway. Thankfully, I made it back to Philly before the snow storm began.

Super Bowl XXXIV was the best Super Bowl game I ever remember watching, even if I wasn't there in person to catch all the live excitement. The St. Louis Rams were a great story for several reasons. Dick Vermeil had come out of retirement, after a 15-year absence from coaching, the previous year. In his first year with the Rams, his team finished with the worst record in their division. This year they had the best, with an outstanding 13-3 record.

The Rams' starting quarterback, Kurt Warner, had come out of the Arena Football League and NFL Europe. He was the backup quarterback to starter Trent Green, at the beginning of the season. When Green went down with a season-ending injury in the first game, a lot of people thought the Rams' season was over. Warner surprised everyone and played like a veteran All Pro quarterback, throwing for 41 touchdowns in the regular season. His passer rating was a meteoric 109.2. He ran the St. Louis offense like a finely tuned engine. At the end of the season, he was named the Most Valuable Player of the National Football League.

Running back Marshall Faulk had been traded to the Rams from the Indianapolis Colts. He never really reached his potential with Indianapolis but sure put it all together in his first season with St. Louis. The five-foot, ten-inch Faulk set the NFL mark for total yards from scrimmage. He rushed 253 times for 1,381 yards and caught 87 passes for 1,048 yards. He became only the second player in history to have over 1,000 yards rushing and over 1,000 yards receiving in the same season. Roger Craig, my guest on the *NFL Experience* Show this year, was the first to accomplish this rare feat. The Rams awarded Marshall their Team MVP award.

The Tennessee Titans had their share of great stories as well. After three consecutive mediocre seasons when they finished with 8-8 records, the Titans performed at an extremely high level all year long. They were the only team to beat Jacksonville during the regular season, and they did it again in the AFC Championship game. In college, quarterback Steve McNair had rewritten the record book at tiny Alcorn State, but most NFL teams didn't want to take a chance on him. He showed them—after a long apprenticeship, he took the Titans all the way to the Super Bowl on the strength of his arm and legs. McNair rushed for about 60 yards a game. And of course, the Titans had been a team of nomads for three years. When it was announced they would be moving to Tennessee, the fans in Houston basically abandoned them. Their first year in Tennessee they played to small crowds at the Liberty Bowl in Memphis. The second year they played to less-than-capacity crowds at Vanderbilt Stadium in Nashville. This year they finally settled into their permanent home, Adelphia Coliseum.

The Rams dominated in the first half, but had trouble punching it in once they reached the red zone. They drove the length of the field several times and came away with three points or less. In the second half, Tennessee came on strong and took the game down to the wire. With the final seconds ticking off the clock, Kevin Dyson courageously reached his outstretched arm with the football, only to end up one yard shy of the end zone. The Rams won Super Bowl XXXIV by the score of 23-16.

While these two teams had wonderful stories, we were concerned about our postgame show because we had never had two small-market teams in the Super Bowl. In previous years, we had teams like Denver, Green Bay, San Francisco and Dallas. These are all well-known, established teams with large national followings. St. Louis and Tennessee were unknowns for us as far as their popularity. Our phone lines lit up for St. Louis Rams Championship merchandise, however. Sales were not as strong as they had been in previous years, but our post game show still produced a respectable $1.7 million.

So, there you have all of my Super Bowl experiences. How do I sum it all up? I guess you could say I have danced at the Big Dance, and I have been fortunate enough to watch the Super Game from some of the best seats in the house. And you know what? If we are fortunate enough to produce another show from the stadium where the Super Bowl is played, and another guy comes up to me on my way into the game and offers me $3,000 for my ticket? I'll say, "No way. Keep your money, fella. I'm goin' inside to be a part of the biggest game and the greatest show on earth."

Chapter 10

Shaquille O'Neal

Standing only 4' 11" tall, my mom makes me feel like a giant. Fortunately, I attained my dad's height of 5' 8". But growing up, I was hoping I would reach a minimum height of 6' 4" so I could one day play point guard in the NBA. I tried everything I could think of to grow taller. I even asked my friend Tom Scheffler, who stood a towering 6' 9", how he got so tall. He told me he rubbed grease on his chest every morning. So, I went home and rubbed grease on my chest every day for a year. At the end of the year, I told Tom I had practiced this ritual every day for the past 365 days and had not grown a single inch. He asked me what kind of grease I had used. When I told him it was Crisco, he responded, "No wonder, that's shortening!" (O. K., it was a joke. I didn't really rub Crisco on my chest, but I would have tried it if I had thought it would help me grow.)

I pretty much knew early in my life that I wasn't going to be a giant. Whenever we were measured and weighed in grade school, I would get scorned for trying to stand up on my toes just to grab that extra half-inch. It was pretty tough being the shortest and lightest kid in my class for my entire grade school career. On one such measurement day, I came home at lunch time and stuffed myself with food.

I then loaded my pockets with BBs, hoping at least to lose my title as the lightest kid in class. It didn't work.

I have met some really large people in my life. But when I first met Shaquille O'Neal, I couldn't believe my eyes! Standing 7' 1" tall and weighing over 300 pounds, he is a modern-day Goliath. The fact that he is quick and agile and can dribble a basketball has made him extremely rich. Because of Shaquille, the 1992 NBA draft was one of the most anticipated ever.

He was such a dominating force in college that he became known simply as Shaq—no last name required. After his junior year at Louisiana State University (LSU), Shaq decided to enter the NBA. LSU was the college home of one of my boyhood heroes, "Pistol Pete" Maravich. I loved watching the Pistol perform magic with the basketball. His trademark long hair and floppy socks made him a phenomenon and helped put LSU on the map for a time. Shaq put it back into a place of prominence in the world of college hoops.

The Orlando Magic made Shaq their number-one pick and later paid him an unheard of $70 million, 10-year contract. In 1995, he signed an even heftier $120 million contract with the Los Angeles Lakers. He received the Rookie of the Year award following the 1992-93 season. He was also a big hit among sports collectors. His autographed cards, plaques and basketballs were extremely popular on QVC's basketball collectibles shows. During his rookie year, everything with his signature sold out quickly.

I was thrilled when I heard Shaq was coming to QVC on Saturday, September 24, 1994. Everybody at QVC Sports was sure he would be a big draw for many sports fans who had never watched QVC before. In fact, they even scheduled a show for Wednesday, September 21st, called "Shaq Preview," simply to promote the fact that he was coming to QVC on the weekend. Shaq was now on a par with our incredibly popular Super Bowl shows.

Maybe in the midst of the hoopla, we should have all remembered that a young athlete is just a young athlete. Shaq was only 23, and he had an intensive management and PR team in place to foster the image they had generated for him and protect him from making any false steps this early in his promising basketball and endorsement careers. In short, they wanted no surprises. And Shaq wanted the same thing any 23-year-old boy wants—to have fun, to talk about his current interests, and not to have to think too hard.

My first meeting with our sports buyers regarding Shaq's appearance was curious. They warned me that his agent and public relations person were very concerned about his appearance on QVC. His experience with live television was minimal. Most of his interviews had been videotaped and lasted less than five minutes. His handlers had been able to control the content of those interviews. The beauty of videotape is that it can be edited, so the prospect of Shaq talking "live and unedited" for three hours caused them great concern. They were also worried about the viewers who would be calling in and asking him questions.

Our buyers informed me that Shaq's people had requested my home phone number. I wasn't too thrilled about their having it, but I reluctantly agreed to give it to them. I received my first phone call at home from Shaq's public relations woman about a week and a half before the show. She wanted me to fax her a list of all the questions that I would be asking. She also wanted the questions written in the exact order in which I was going to ask them. I explained to her that since QVC is live, and things change constantly on live TV, I usually did not prepare a list of questions. I told her I do a thorough job of research so that I can conduct an interesting and informative interview, while going with the flow of the products and phone calls. I further explained to her that the product lineup often changes in the final hours prior to the show, so it would be impossible to plan an order to the questions that I could stick to.

My explanation did not make her very happy. After a rather lengthy discussion, I realized that Shaq's appearance would be in jeopardy if I did not appease her. I told her I would be glad to furnish her with a list of topics that I was hoping to address with Shaq and that if she had a problem with any of them, I would be glad to discuss it with her. This seemed to be satisfactory, so I faxed her the information the next day. It seemed like we were all set to go. I had no idea that we had only just begun.

The very next day, I received another call. The same woman told me, in no uncertain terms, that if I did not come up with a list of specific questions for Shaq by the next day, they were pulling out of the interview. This demand did not come at an opportune time for me. I've mentioned before that being a host on QVC is very much a full-time job. When I'm not on the air, I am often attending product seminars, participating in meetings with vendors and buyers, or traveling for the company. On this particular day, I had several meetings scheduled before my on-air shift that night. I looked at my watch and realized I had about a half-hour before I had to jump in the shower and get ready for work. I wrote down as many questions as I could think of in 30 minutes. I was scheduled to be on QVC until 11:00 P.M. that evening. I usually never leave work until a minimum of an hour after my show because there is always email and regular mail to catch up on. When I came into the host lounge that night after my shift, I went straight to work writing more questions for Shaq on the computer. I finished around 2:30 A.M. and left the list of questions, along with instructions for faxing them, with Elizabeth Buchan, who was the secretary for our department at the time.

The next day, I heard back from Shaq's PR person. She informed me that one-third of my questions had been rejected, so I would have to write more. A few days later, everyone seemed happy with the entire list of questions I had come up with. I made it a point, however, to let Shaq's people know that the questions would not necessarily be asked in the order in which they were listed, because the final order of products for the show would not be finalized until a few hours before air time. While they were not thrilled to hear it, they accepted the fact that there are certain aspects of live electronic retailing that cannot be precisely planned. I think this is what makes QVC such an exciting place to work. Everyone in the company has to be flexible. You simply have to go with the flow.

We finally made it to Saturday, the night of the big show with Shaquille O'Neal. While I knew Shaq's physical statistics as far as height, weight and even his shoe size, I was still taken aback the first time I saw him in person. He is absolutely mammoth. When I stood next to him, the top of my head barely came up to his chest. I now know what David must have felt like when he ran up to Goliath. I have never felt so small in my life. Shaq's forearms are the size of my thighs. His chest is twice the size of mine. When we compared the size of our hands, his were half again as big as mine. QVC's set and props people put out the tallest chairs they could find. My feet were dangling a couple of feet above the floor, while Shaq's were flat on it, and his legs were bent. My feet looked like a little boy's next to his since they were about half the size.

He seemed to be in a pretty good mood before the show. In fact, as I was taking him around the studio, the producer asked if he would mind spinning the prize wheel for a game that was being played on the air. Shaq said he would love to and proceeded to spin the wheel so hard we all thought it was going to come flying off the wall! I was fired up when I saw that he was in such a good mood. I started thinking we were going to have a terrific show.

When we opened the program, I decided it would be fun to have Shaq stand up next to me to give the viewers an idea of just how large he actually is. When I asked him to stand, however, he said he would rather not. Luckily, I was on my toes that night, so I immediately walked over by his chair and said, "Look, he's taller than I am even sitting down!" I should have known right then I was in for a very long night. I fired my first question toward him and got a one-word reply. Then I asked him how it felt to be named the NBA Rookie of the Year and I got another one-word answer, "Great!"

The three hours I spent with Shaq on QVC that night seemed like an eternity. He had two friends his age in the studio with him and he kept making faces at them throughout the show. We were presenting a Hakeem Olajuwon autographed basketball at one point in the show, and I asked Shaq how he played Hakeem defensively. He answered, "I get psyched!"

I tried to get him to elaborate by asking, "Do you try to force him outside or make him go to his left?"

He gave me the same answer but added one word: "I just get psyched."

When we talked about Shaquille's autographed basketball I held it up toward the camera to show his autograph, and he playfully slapped the ball out of my hands. I thought he was, at least, showing signs of life, so I told him he could hold the ball up. When he did, I slapped it back out of his hands. He seemed to get a kick out of this so we kept this running gag going throughout the show.

I still wasn't having much luck getting him to talk about the game of basketball in depth. However, I did discover that there were topics that he really did want to talk about. His favorite was rap music. He had just recorded his first rap album and was obviously very excited about it. Our buyers had given me a copy of his tape to listen to the previous week. I brought it home and played it for my daughter, Kirstyn, who was eight years old at the time. After she listened to it for a while, she popped the tape out of the player, handed it to me and said, "Dad, I think Shaq should stick to basketball!"

The second topic which really seemed to light him up was video games. He enjoyed talking about his new video game action hero called "Shaq Fu." Unfortunately, we were not offering his rap album or his video game that night on QVC, so these topics did not help the show much.

All in all, I would have to say that the much-anticipated show that night with Shaquille O'Neal was one of the most disappointing of my career. The fact that his PR team made me jump through so many hoops was frustrating. After interviewing him, I understood why his handlers were so worried. They had carefully shaped and molded his image and wanted to do their best to preserve that. Perhaps the most frustrating thing for me about the whole show was that I don't think Shaq himself ever read the list of questions that I was forced to prepare and submit. If he had read them, he certainly had not prepared any thought-provoking answers to them.

In Shaq's defense, as I mentioned, he was only 23 years old at the time. He was basically still a kid in an extremely large man's body. From my experience over the years interviewing scores of professional athletes, I have discovered that the older, more experienced athletes usually give the best interviews. The true sports legends are the best. I included Shaq in this book because, at this point in his career, he is considered one of the best players in the NBA. I think he may one day achieve that legendary status.

The 1999–2000 season was definitely his breakout year. He carried the Los Angeles Lakers on his very broad

shoulders and led them to the NBA championship. He garnered MVP awards for both the regular season and the NBA
Finals along the way. It will be interesting to see if he can sus-
tain that level of play and become a true legend. The fact that
he didn't seem very interested in discussing the sport that
made him rich and famous, however, concerns me. I have followed his career closely, and I believe that he finally played
up to his potential in the '99-'00 season. I would not put him
in the same class as Michael Jordan, Kareem Abdul Jabbar, Bill
Russell, Wilt Chamberlain, Jerry West, Magic Johnson, Oscar
Robertson or any of the others who are the "all-time elite" of
the NBA yet. Shaq spent quite a lot of time early in his career
doing commercials, movies, and albums. Maybe if he cuts
some of the "extras" out of his schedule and concentrates on
his game, he will one day deserve to be listed as one of the
best of all time.

Shaquille is older now and, hopefully, wiser. Maybe
we should consider having him as a guest on QVC once
again. If we do, I'd suggest we try a one-hour show, not three
hours. Sometimes the tallest guys are best when they appear
in the shortest segments.

Chapter 11

Willie Mays

In the late 1950s, baseball fans in New York City would argue for hours over the answer to one simple question. Who was baseball's greatest centerfielder? Was it Duke Snider, Mickey Mantle or Willie Mays? They all agreed on one thing. Baseball's greatest centerfielder was definitely playing for a New York team. All three of these outstanding centerfielders were playing in the Big Apple at the same time. Duke Snider was with the Brooklyn Dodgers, Mickey Mantle played for the New York Yankees and Willie Mays, "the Say Hey Kid," was roving the outfield for the New York Giants.

All three of these guys went on to achieve "legend" status. They have all been inducted into Baseball's Hall of Fame in Cooperstown, New York. Each left his permanent mark on the game of baseball. It is difficult to say who was the greatest. There was a period of time, in the fifties, when Duke Snider's bat was the most productive in either league. Of course, Mickey Mantle was "Mr. Clutch" for the most successful team in the history of sports. But if you look at a player's versatility and all-around ability, you would have to pick Willie Mays.

Mays was the National League Rookie of the Year in 1951. He won two National League Most Valuable Player awards in 1954 and 1956. His lifetime batting average was

.302. He belted 660 career homeruns and played in 24 All Star games. Defensively, he's in a league of his own, as the all-time leader in outfield putouts and total chances. In 1951, he caught a drive by Rocky Nelson in Pittsburgh's Forbes Field with his bare hand. He did the same thing to the great Roberto Clemente just a few years later in the same park.

In the 1954 World Series, Willie Mays made a play that has gone down in history as simply "The Catch." The Giants were playing Cleveland at the Polo Grounds. The score was tied 2-2 in the eighth inning when Indians' slugger Vic Wertz smashed a long fly ball to deep centerfield. Mays sprinted toward the ball with his back to the infield and made an incredible "over the shoulder" catch. In one motion, he whirled and released a perfect throw that prevented the man on second from scoring. That kept the score tied at 2-2. The Giants went on to win that first game and swept the series in four straight.

The first time I was scheduled to work with Willie Mays on QVC was on February 16, 1993. As I've mentioned before, I always like to get to the studio at least three hours before my show. On this particular evening, I think I was in the studio even earlier. I had been preparing for this show for a couple of weeks. I had done my homework on Willie. Since nothing on QVC is scripted, I like to have a good grasp of a player's background and statistics. I never know when I am going to need a quick fact or statistic to make the interview interesting.

About an hour before the show, I received a call from the Scoreboard Company informing me that Willie's plane had been delayed. Willie would not arrive until after the show began. This is never pleasant news. QVC usually promotes sports shows for several days prior to the show. We run spots showcasing some of the products and the special guest. I knew our audience was expecting to see Willie at

9:00 P.M. eastern time. At this point, I wasn't too worried, because I was told that he would be arriving within the first 15 minutes of the show. However, at 8:45 P.M., I received another call informing me that Willie was on his way to our studios from Baltimore by limousine. That was the good news. The bad news was that I would be spending the first hour of the show solo. I just tried to stay loose and simply go with the flow.

At the beginning of the program, I informed our viewers that Willie Mays had been delayed due to inclement weather. I assured them that he was on his way to the studio. I pointed to the empty chair next to me and said, "He'll be sitting in that chair soon. But I have some great baseball memorabilia to talk about in the meantime. Let's take a look at tonight's lineup." We begin most of our shows on QVC with a preview of the key products that are slated for that hour. As I was going through this preview, I was silently asking God to help Willie's limousine driver to arrive safely and promptly.

One hour into the show, my producer told me, through my earpiece, that Willie was on the phone. I signaled to him to put the call through on the air and I said, "Willie! It's great to hear from you; where are you?" He said he wasn't sure but that his driver said they would probably be at our West Chester Studios within a half hour. He told the viewers to hang on because he was coming!

I thanked him for calling in and looked at my watch. It was 10:10 P.M., and I thought, "Well, at least I'll have him on for the second half of the show."

These situations are always difficult because baseball fans are tuning in to see their baseball hero—in this case, Willie Mays. I was trying to keep everyone's interest up, and since I wanted everyone to stay tuned to QVC, I kept announcing that Willie Mays was on his way and would be sitting in the seat next me very shortly. Inside, I was dying. I kept worrying that we would lose our credibility with the viewers. I wondered if people would lose faith in our ability to bring these legendary sports figures onto our shows. Well, there is an old saying, "the show must go on!" So, I kept talking baseball, presenting products, quoting statistics and glancing at my watch about every two minutes. During the show, I had two callers ask if Willie was really going to be on the show. I kept assuring them that he was on his way and hopefully, they would see him soon.

This show seemed like it lasted for an eternity. At 10:45 P.M., my producer said, "Dan. Guess who's on the line? Willie."

Once again, I took the call on the air and said, "Willie, are you all right?"

He responded, "Oh yes, Dan. As a matter of fact, we are just outside of West Chester and should be there momentarily."

Once again, I thanked him for calling and told him what a pleasure it was going to be to actually talk to him in person. By this time, I was thinking that if he didn't get there soon, he might as well not even bother coming. I wondered if anyone would be watching by the time he finally arrived. When we took a promotional break at 11:00 P.M., "the Say Hey Kid" was still nowhere in sight.

As I opened the third and final hour of Baseball Collectibles without Willie Mays, I decided to just have fun with the situation, so I started to interview the empty chair next to me. I just pretended that Willie was there. I don't know how this played with the audience, but it helped me to deal with the stress I was feeling inside. At the very least, it made my producer laugh.

It was now 11:15 P.M. I had been telling our viewers for two hours and fifteen minutes that Willie Mays was on his way to the studio. I'm not sure that *I* believed it at this point. Guess what? Willie called one more time and said he was just five minutes away. He said he would run into the studio as soon as his limousine driver pulled up in front of the door.

At exactly 11:30 P.M., I looked up and sure enough, Willie was running down the aisle between our phone operators. I think he forgot that he needed a microphone because he was headed directly for the stage. I announced that Willie Mays was indeed "in the house." We went to a promotional spot while they put a microphone on him.

When we came back I said, "Well, better late than never. Mr. Willie Mays is finally here." He seemed to be in pretty good spirits and was very apologetic about being so late. We had less than a half-hour together on QVC, but the conversation was lively and a good number of people dialed in for Willie's autographed merchandise. After the show, Willie and I talked for half an hour. He signed a baseball for me and thanked me for my patience. I told him that I had never been so happy to see anyone in my entire life.

The next time I worked with Willie was in the fall of that same year. He was at the studio a good half-hour before the show and everything went smoothly. In fact, it was so uneventful compared to our first show that I remember very little about it. What I *do* remember is that he showed up early and was pleasant. I think it was one of our better baseball collectibles shows. I was probably so thrilled that he was on time that everything else faded from my memory.

In December of 1993, I put in a proposal to my boss at QVC regarding the San Francisco Giants Fantasy Camp in Scottsdale, Arizona. Most major league baseball teams run fantasy camps in late January and early February for anyone who wants spend around $3,500 to pretend to be a major league baseball player for a week. In my proposal, I mentioned that this would be a great opportunity to get some interviews for our baseball collectibles shows, since many former Giant greats would be in one location for a week. I proposed that they send me to the camp as a player and have a crew come down to document my experience. I outlined how we could tape interviews and have the former big leaguers offer tips on hitting, fielding, running and throwing for the benefit of our younger viewers. We could then run these in every baseball collectibles show. I had fun putting together the proposal, but I never thought anything would come of it.

About a week later, I received a call from the Scoreboard Company asking me if I really wanted to attend the Giants Fantasy Camp. I said, "Absolutely!" They informed me that I was enrolled in the camp in Scottsdale for the week of January 31 through February 6, 1994. I couldn't believe I was actually going to play baseball again. I attended Evangel College in Springfield, Missouri, on a baseball scholarship and played centerfield all four years. I even played some semi-pro ball for a couple of years after college, but I hadn't swung a bat in 12 years. I was really stressed out at this point in my life and playing baseball for a week in sunny Scottsdale, Arizona, sounded like it was just what I needed. I'll tell you all about my experiences at the Fantasy Camp in a later chapter, but here I'll tell you about my encounter with Willie Mays.

As it turned out, it was Willie's agent who made the arrangements for me to attend the Giants Fantasy Camp. Willie was one of the guest instructors, along with Juan Marichal, Orlando Cepeda, Vida Blue and many other former Giants stars. One of the main interviews that I was scheduled to do was Willie Mays.

I ran into Willie on Tuesday afternoon at the lunch area. When I shook his hand and introduced myself he smiled and said he remembered me well. He then started introducing me to everyone, and telling them that I was a great interviewer. When I asked him if we could tape him at some point during the week, he said that it would be no problem. We scheduled it for the next day during the lunch hour.

I showed up with my camera crew the next day ready to videotape an in-depth interview with Willie Mays. This is where the story gets really weird. When I approached Willie about the interview, he acted like he had no idea what I was talking about. I reminded him of the conversation we had had just the day before, and he started to become belligerent. He asked me what I wanted to ask him. I told him I wanted to talk about his baseball career and possibly ask him to comment on some of today's players. He then became angry and said he wouldn't talk about anyone except Willie Mays. I said, "O. K. I'll only ask you about Willie Mays." He then muttered something about how the press always twisted what he said and ended up getting him in trouble. At this point, I tried to calm him down and assured him if he was uncomfortable with anything I asked him that he didn't have to answer and I would simply move on to the next question. To make a long story short, he basically refused to do any kind of an interview with me and really made a scene. I told the crew to stand by. I then told Willie that if he was refusing to do the interview, I had to call Ken Goldin, the president of the Scoreboard Company, and inform him. It was my understanding that Willie was under a contract that required him to do this interview.

Bill Martin, our excellent field producer, had a cellular phone, so I called Ken Goldin. When I explained the situation to Ken he told me to give the phone to Willie. I noticed that Willie had gone inside the locker room, so I walked into the building and found him sitting on a trainer's table chatting with a few of the players. I told him Ken Goldin was on the phone and wanted to speak with him. As I tried to hand him the phone, he began using some pretty foul language and said he didn't want to talk to Ken. I asked Ken if he had heard what Willie said, and he responded that he had. He then told me not to worry about Willie, because he was going to talk to his lawyers.

The rest of the week was like a vacation. Playing baseball made me feel like a kid again. The two pulled hamstring muscles that I took home reminded me that I was not. But more importantly, we were able to get some excellent interviews. Everyone was extremely cooperative, except for Willie Mays.

On Thursday, May 12, 1994, I drove to QVC's studios wondering which Willie was going to show up for our three-hour baseball collectibles show. After what had happened in Scottsdale, I was kind of hoping his plane would be delayed again due to inclement weather. Maybe he just wouldn't show up at all. If he did make it, I had decided that I was not going to meet with him before the show. This is very unusual for me, because I always like to go over the game plan for the show with all of my guests. However, in light of the situation, I figured it would be best to greet him in front of the camera.

Surprisingly, Willie was in a great mood. When I introduced him that evening, he came out smiling, and we went right into the show like we were best friends. About 45 minutes into the show, he mentioned that we had had a small problem down in Scottsdale, but that it was simply a misunderstanding. I couldn't believe my ears. I was never going to bring it up on the air, but the way in which he did it seemed like an apology. After that, the whole show went by without a hitch, and we even spoke for about 15 minutes following the show.

Our paths didn't cross again until September 20, 1995. I received a call about a week earlier from Dave Caputa, who was a representative of the Scoreboard Company at the time. Dave asked if I would be willing to appear for Scoreboard at an arbitration hearing regarding Willie Mays. I was very hesitant to agree, but Dave said they simply wanted me to relate exactly what happened between Willie and me at the Giants Fantasy Camp in 1994. I said that I

151

would appear under the condition that Willie was not there. He assured me that Willie Mays would not be present when I gave my testimony. I also told him that I would need to clear it with my boss at QVC. When I explained the situation to Jack Comstock, Vice President of TV Sales, he said that it would be all right in view of our relationship with the Scoreboard Company. I called Dave back and said that it was on.

A car picked me up early in the morning on Wednesday, September 20, 1995. A gentleman named Robert was driving. Robert used to accompany the various athletes who were under contract with the Scoreboard Company when they came to QVC. He is a super guy, and we had a nice conversation on the way to the hearing, which was being held somewhere in New Jersey. When I walked into the room, I saw the longest conference table I had ever seen. There must have been 25 to 30 people seated around the table. There was one empty seat next to . . . you guessed it, Willie Mays. I couldn't believe it. I was very upset and felt somewhat betrayed. As I sat down, I said hello to Willie and listened to the proceedings.

It wasn't long before the moderator called me forward to testify. Basically, I told the story exactly as it happened. The attorneys for the Scoreboard Company asked me if I thought Willie Mays had behaved in a professional manner. I said that he had not. They asked if he was cooperative, and again I responded in the negative. I have to say that I was probably kind to Willie Mays that day. While I told all of the facts as clearly as I could remember them, I still didn't want to really harm his character in any way. After all, Willie Mays was a sports legend and a member of professional baseball's Hall of Fame. I couldn't believe I had to testify against a childhood hero of mine in this contract dispute.

When I finished my testimony, and the lawyers felt that they had asked me all the necessary questions, I stood up to leave. Before I opened the door to the hallway, I turned around and looked at Willie. He nodded his head toward me as if to say, "It's all right. It's only business." When I got out to the parking lot, I told Robert that it was one of the most unusual experiences of my life. I hated having to testify against Willie Mays with Willie sitting at the table. I knew I would have to work with him again someday.

Someday came about a year later. I was scheduled to do a two-hour show with Willie this time. I decided that I would meet him in the green room and make sure that he harbored no hard feelings. I went into work extra early so that I could get all of my product preparation done before he arrived. Then I waited and waited, and finally went on the air without getting a chance to talk things over with him.

Fortunately, he arrived while I was going through the preview for the show and he came on the set after the first product. We had another great show. Willie gave me a Hall of Fame interview, and we had a chance to talk after the show. I asked him why he became so upset with me at the Giants Fantasy Camp in 1994. He explained that a few weeks before that time, he was at an awards dinner to present Barry Bonds, who is Willie's godson, with his National League MVP award. Barry didn't show up for the dinner, and Willie made a comment that got blown out of proportion in the media. He told me it had caused some problems between Barry and him, so he had become gun-shy of the media. I accepted his answer, and we finally put the incident behind us. I just wish he had explained that at the time. Willie should have known that my job as a host on QVC does not require me to be controversial. Maybe he just didn't realize it at the time.

I remember being 10 years old and imitating Willie Mays' famous "basket catch." He made it look effortless. In fact, he made every aspect of baseball look fun and easy. " The Say Hey Kid" was more than a baseball player: he was a showman and an entertainer. In one of his books, he talks about the fact that all he wanted to do was play baseball forever. I think that he has never been happier than when he was hitting homeruns, stealing bases and making those entertaining basket catches. While I wasn't very happy about our confrontation or having to testify against him, in a way, it helped us form a mutual respect.

Back in the days of those New York street corner discussions about who was the greatest centerfielder in baseball, Willie Mays was nicknamed "The Say Hey Kid." If he saw someone and he couldn't remember their name, he would simply say, "Say, hey!" That's where the nickname comes from. I guess I should look on the bright side of things when it comes to Willie Mays, because, after all that we have been through, he at least knows my name.

Chapter 12

Jim Brown

It had been at least five minutes since anyone had tackled me. I had successfully avoided my classmates through a combination of deceptive moves, quick cuts and pure speed. Three guys, who were much bigger than I, started to close in. "No problem!" I thought to myself. "I'll just fake right, get them leaning and then I'll blow around the left side." I put on the move. They went for it. I cut hard and BOOM! My entire body felt like it was going to crack in two. From the top of my head, running straight down to the bottom of my feet, I felt excruciating pain. I had accelerated right into a steel pole at the end of the tennis court at Jefferson Elementary School in St. Joe, Michigan. I was in pain for several days. I hurt so badly that I didn't play "smear" for about a week.

Recess was really boring without smear. This is a game where you can have as many players as you want. One player begins the game by throwing the football as high in the air as he can. Everybody else then tries to catch it. Whoever catches the ball begins running and *everybody else* tries to tackle him. In other words, the person with the ball gets "smeared."

I was at the peak of my football career. I was faster than everyone else, and they weren't big enough yet to really hurt me when they tackled me. I was fine as long as I avoided that pole at the end of the tennis courts. From 1964 through 1967, my friends and I would not only play smear at recess, but in the fall we would put on our helmets and pads after school and play tackle football up at Dickinson Field until dark. There would usually be anywhere from 10 to 14 of us. We'd always name two captains who would pick sides. Remember that? I was always thrilled and honored if I was picked first. Whenever I got the football I was "on a mission" to get into the opposing team's end zone. To this day, whenever I feel fall in the air toward the end of August, my mind goes back to those games of pick-up football.

I played on the school team through my freshman year. After having my bell rung a few too many times, I decided to stick with baseball and basketball. My mom was very relieved. The one football game in which she watched me play was against Benton Harbor Junior High, during my freshman year. Benton Harbor had a guy who stood 6'5" and weighed about 230 pounds. His name was Anthony Wooden, and he struck fear into my heart in every sport. Well, I received the opening kickoff and I got about 10 yards when suddenly I was hit by Anthony Wooden and a guy who was only about an inch smaller, named Reggie Walker (Reggie's uncle, Chet Walker, starred for several years on the Chicago Bulls in the NBA). My mom covered her eyes as they literally threw me back several yards. When I hit the ground, my body kept rolling backward as if I were doing somersaults. Around that time, I decided that with 90 pounds on my 5-foot 4-inch frame, my chances for an NFL career were not the best.

I picked up with a touch football career many years later, at the age of 25. I was living in Lisle, Illinois, and I hooked up with a team called the Golden Arrows. The Arrows played in a football league that was composed of many former college players. A few had even played in the NFL. While it was called "touch" there was plenty of hitting going on. At the first practice, someone pointed out a guy who was big, fast and strong. He whispered to me, "That's Eddie Dubose. He played running back for the Cleveland Browns with the legendary Jim Brown." I was in awe. Eddie was 43 years old at the time, and was in better shape than anyone else on the team. His body looked like it had been chiseled out of rock.

As I got to know Eddie, I discovered he was a really nice guy, and we became great friends. Eddie loved to barbecue ribs and have the entire team over with their wives or girlfriends. After we had eaten, Eddie would put on the tunes, and everybody would dance the night away and have a great time. I have always loved Motown and rhythm and blues music. Eddie had every great song from that genre. He always used to tell me that white boys couldn't dance. I proved to him that was not entirely true. We used to do spins, splits and dives. In fact, I ripped many a pair of pants in those days doing the splits. If I tried those moves now, I would be in the chiropractor's office the next day. These get-togethers at Eddie's house became known as "sets." Nobody could do a set better than Eddie.

I used to ask Eddie about Jim Brown. He would say, "Jim Brown was a man playing in a league full of boys." Eddie would tell me that Brown could run around tacklers if he wanted to, but he preferred to run through them. Eddie was one of Jim's backups at running back, and because of that he didn't see much playing time.

Jim Brown was born on February 17, 1936, on St. Thomas Island in Georgia. He spent most of his childhood in New York after his mother got a job cleaning houses. He attended Manhassat High School, where he was a superstar athlete in every sport. He earned all-state honors in football, basketball and track. In 1953, he enrolled at Syracuse University where he discovered his talents in yet another sport:

lacrosse. He was an awesome player and was actually inducted into the Lacrosse Hall of Fame. Many people who actually saw him play say he was one of the best lacrosse players ever.

The Cleveland Browns professional football team drafted Jim in the first round in 1957. He quickly made his presence felt by leading the league with 942 yards rushing. He also led the league in rushing touchdowns. At times he seemed unstoppable. In 1963, he rushed for 1,863 yards and in1964, he carried the Browns on his strong shoulders all the way to the NFL Championship. In 1966, after just nine seasons, he suddenly announced his retirement from professional football. At that time, he had rushed for more yards than any player in the history of the National Football League. He totaled 12,312 rushing yards in just 118 games over 9 seasons. He averaged an amazing 5.2 yards per carry. In fact, during the 1963 season alone, his average carry went for 6.4 yards!

When I look at Jim Brown's statistics, I understand why Eddie Dubose used to tell me that Jim Brown was a man playing in a league full of boys. The guy was just tough as nails. To this day, many football fans and experts wonder why he cut his career so short. At the time of his retirement, he announced that he was pursuing a career in acting. He acted for about 11 years. In my mind, his most memorable role was in the movie *The Dirty Dozen.*

At one point, I remember there was a rumor that Jim was thinking of coming out of retirement when his record was about to be broken. He was in his forties at the time, but a lot of people thought he could still play if he really wanted to. Around this time, I distinctly remember watching a live interview with Jim Brown. The interviewer asked him a question that he didn't like, so he simply took off his microphone, got up and walked away. I remember thinking, "Wow! Jim

Brown does not play games. If he doesn't like what you're asking, he'll pull the plug." He is definitely his own man.

When I heard that Jim Brown was going to be appearing with me on a QVC football collectibles show, I was really excited. I absolutely love interviewing the legends. It's a special honor to sit with someone who is considered to be the best there ever was. Jim Brown is that kind of legend. While I was looking forward to his appearance, I still remembered the interview that he walked out on. I definitely didn't want that to happen to me on QVC!

Monday, July 29, 1996, was the date of the show. Jim Brown was punctual, arriving a full half-hour before we were scheduled to go on. He was dressed in a black suit with a black tie. On his head, he wore a tight-fitting green, black and red knit cap. When I introduced myself to him, he was polite but cautious. I sensed that he was sizing me up. I went over the format of the show with him and told him he just had to answer my questions. I explained that I would periodically interject information about the products during the show. He seemed fine with that.

Jim gave me a great interview that night. He seemed to really open up on camera. I began by talking about his lacrosse career and this seemed to loosen him up. His love of lacrosse was evident as he talked about running right up the middle of the field and firing the ball into the net. He told me God had blessed him with the perfect body for lacrosse. It seemed to me that he was usually not given a chance to talk about it in other interviews and he seemed happy that I was genuinely interested.

One of our other topics of conversation that night was the Cleveland Browns. Cleveland lost their beloved Browns when Art Modell moved the team to Baltimore. The city, however, still owned the right to the Browns name. Jim Brown was passionate about bringing the Browns back to

Cleveland. They were scheduled to come back for the 1999 season. I knew I shouldn't bring up the name Art Modell. Browns fans the world over remain incensed with the man and the way he took the team to Baltimore.

For football fans everywhere, the Cleveland Browns are one of the enduring traditions of the NFL. Most people thought the Browns would be in Cleveland forever. Modell's move was so obviously motivated by money that it seemed like any sense of loyalty had gone out the window. I can just imagine what those fans out in the Dawg Pound would be like if Modell ever tried to set foot in that stadium again. Jim Brown, the greatest Cleveland Brown of all time, was leading the charge to bring an NFL team back to Cleveland with the original name. I know Cleveland fans across the country thought it was great that he gave so much time and effort to help restore their beloved Cleveland Browns.

The show could not have gone any better that night. As we were walking off the stage after the show ended, I slapped Jim on the back and said, "Jim, thank you so much for a great show."

He stopped, looked me in the eye and said, "Well Dan, I like you, and believe me, if I didn't like you, we wouldn't have had a good show."

I said, "Jim, I'm awfully glad you like me." Boy, did I mean it. Several of the product coordinators overheard his comments, and they all talked to me about it during the days that followed.

I saw Jim Brown again at Super Bowl XXXII in San Diego. As I took my seat in QualComm Stadium, I looked down my row and there he was about 15 seats away. Eventually he looked my way, and I waved. He waved back, but I'm not sure if he recognized me or not. Because the name of this book is *Best Seat in the House*, I'll tell you that Jim's seat was 15 seats further toward the goal line than mine. Since I was on about the 35-yard line, and Jim was on the 30, I actually had a better seat than Jim Brown! I wouldn't point that out to Jim, though, since I want to stay on his good side.

Many times when people hear that I'm going to have a certain athlete on my show, they will tell me horror stories about how difficult that person is to work with. I remember having Greg Lloyd on QVC the week after he let loose with a string of obscenities on national television. Albert Belle was my guest shortly after he supposedly threw a baseball at a sportscaster. People told me Mike Schmidt was aloof and unfriendly. In every single case, these same athletes gave me an excellent interview. I don't try to get controversial with any of them on QVC. That's not my job.

Of course, I had heard several negatives about Jim Brown before his appearance. He turned out to be an excellent guest. And to tell you the truth, I tried not to be controversial even when I was a sportscaster. I don't blame certain athletes for acting the way they do toward certain sportscasters. I think some people in the media just like to grab attention. They figure the best way to do that is to be controversial and try to present the athletes in a bad light. That's not my style.

If I were going to make somebody mad at me, I definitely wouldn't want it to be Jim Brown. I remember seeing stars after running into that tennis court pole at Jefferson school. If Jim Brown ever hit me, I'm sure I would see the entire galaxy. I would probably be fortunate if I lived to tell about it.

When Jim Brown carried the football in the NFL, he was a man on a mission. To this day he is still looking for worthy missions and causes that he can carry the ball for. In 1990, he founded the Amer-I-Can program, which is a life management course for prison inmates and black youths. Jim received a great deal of recognition for this program. In 1992, he was appointed to the Board of Directors of the Rebuild LA Project. And of course, he was the lead blocker in clearing the way for the triumphant return of the Cleveland Browns.

Whether the game is smear or lacrosse or football, or even helping a charitable organization, Jim Brown is one guy that I'd want on my team. In fact, if we were choosing sides, I'd pick Jim first.

Chapter 13

Hank Aaron

When I was six years old, Kenny Felgner gave me a green t-shirt with bold, white lettering across the front which spelled the word, "Wings." There was a big number 2 on the back. But that's not all, he also gave me a green baseball cap with a white W on the front of the crown. This was my first baseball uniform, and I thought it was the coolest set of duds on the planet. I knew then that I wanted to wear a baseball uniform to work when I grew up.

Two years later, I became an official member of a baseball team. At the age of eight, I was selected to be the batboy for the Reds of the St. Joseph, Michigan, Little League Association. The shirt was just a little big, but the pants were big enough for two of me. My mom bought me another pair in my size, but they didn't match because they didn't have pinstripes like the shirt did. I didn't really mind too much. The important thing was, I had a baseball uniform and I got to sit on the bench and run out and pick up the bat after each player's turn at the plate.

After putting in a full season of running and picking up bats, chasing errant throws, carrying equipment bags and being ordered around by all the players and coaches, I was ready to step up to player status. I can still remember the tryouts for the St. Joseph Minor Leagues for nine-year-old boys.

They pinned a big number on my shirt and told me to catch fly balls, throw, hit and run while a bunch of men with clipboards watched intently. When I got the phone call that the Dodgers had selected me, I was ecstatic! But the best was yet to come.

About the third game of the season, I came up to bat in the bottom of the sixth inning (which was the last inning of the game for nine-year-old boys). My team was down by three runs and the bases were loaded. There were two out and the game was in my hands. My teammates cheered wildly and said things like, "Come on, Wheels, you're the man! You can do it! Hit a homerun!" I became more nervous with every cheer.

I looked down the third base line at my coach, Frank Schnese. He was calm and collected and said, "Wheels, just put the bat on the ball." The pitcher gave me an evil stare and then let it fly. I took a mighty swing, and the ball jumped off my bat and headed for the gap in left centerfield. I began to run as fast as I could. It seemed like the ball kept rolling, so I kept running. When I crossed home plate my entire team jumped on top of me. I had hit a grand slam homerun! Wow!!! To this day, I can remember how excited I was to go home and tell my mom and dad that I had won the game with a grand slam homerun in the last inning. Could life ever get any better? Had I reached the pinnacle of my career at the age of nine?

I played baseball every summer for 15 straight years after that and never hit another grand slam. But every time I came to the plate with the bases loaded, that hope was always there.

The homerun is one of the most exciting events in all of sports. That's why Babe Ruth lives in immortality. He was a big burly guy who lived his life the way he swung his bat: with gusto! Men, women, boys and girls loved to watch him swat the long ball and then trot around the bases on those spindly legs of his. He was exciting to watch even when he struck out because he took such a big swing that he often spun around and fell to the ground when he missed. The fans loved it.

The summer of 1973 was a turning point in my life. I had graduated from high school that spring and spent my summer evenings playing baseball for the St. Joseph American Legion team. Our coach, Mike Winegarden, was the best baseball coach I ever had. He had played in the big leagues for the Chicago White Sox and really ran a first-class operation. We had great-looking "home" and "away" uniforms with our names on the back. We each had two or three of our own personal bats that nobody else was allowed to use. If we showed up for a game and our shoes weren't polished, we were fined five dollars! That was a lot of money in those days; however, it went into a fund that financed our team barbecues. We even took a two-week trip that summer and played baseball in Missouri and Kansas.

One of the coolest things about our Legion baseball team was that we all had great nicknames. Mine had always been "Wheels" because of my last name and the fact that I was pretty fast on the base paths. But there were other nicknames like "Wax," "Howie" and "Leo." My best friend, Mark Ranum, was called "Hank" because he idolized Hank Aaron.

The baseball world said that Hank Aaron snuck up on Babe Ruth's homerun record. Amazingly, he never hit 50 homeruns in a season. However, he hit between 24 and 45 homeruns for 19 seasons in a row! That means he averaged 33 homeruns a year for 19 consecutive years. He also drove in more than 100 runs in a record 13 straight seasons. Of course, he went on to become baseball's all-time power hitting king. His 755 career homeruns make him the greatest homerun hitter of all time. Hank's 2,297 runs batted in rank number one of all time. He also stands on top of the total

165

bases and extra base hit categories. These amazing numbers earned him the nickname "Hammerin' Hank."

The summer of '73 was a big one for Hank Aaron and me. Hank closed in on Babe Ruth's all-time homerun record, and I was awarded the Most Valuable Player award for the St. Joseph, Michigan, American Legion Baseball Team. My season helped me to win a baseball scholarship to Evangel College in Springfield, Missouri, and Hank's onslaught on Ruth's record brought him a great deal of media attention. Sadly, it also brought him all kinds of hate mail and even death threats.

Hank Aaron was a great hero of America's favorite pastime, yet he received death threats. What's wrong with that picture? Well, the same thing that has been wrong with our country since its inception: racism. Ruth's homerun record was among the most cherished in all of sports. Many white people didn't feel that he should lose that record to a black man. While I was having a blast playing a game I loved in Michigan, Hank Aaron was caught in the middle of a storm of controversy. He had to stay in separate hotels from the rest of his team. Special arrangements were made to get him in and out of ballparks. He even encouraged his teammates to stay away from him in the dugout in case some demented fan took aim at him from the stands. And the press, of course, hounded him before and after every game. Amazingly, once Hank was on the playing field, he acted as if he were in the eye of the storm. He remained calm, cool and collected. He never lost his focus and seemed more determined than ever to surpass the Babe.

In the summer of '73, at the age of 39, Hammerin' Hank hit .301, drove in 96 homeruns and slammed 40 homeruns, the most ever by a man his age. When the season ended, his career homerun total stood at 713, just one short of Babe Ruth's record. The hate mail kept pouring in to the Atlanta Braves organization over the winter. Many were calling for his retirement. They just couldn't accept the fact that there would be a new man sitting on the homerun throne, a man whose skin happened to be dark.

The 1974 season opened with yet more controversy for Aaron. The Braves organization wanted him to sit out the first series in Cincinnati so that his record blasts would happen in Atlanta. Bowie Kuhn, the Commissioner of Baseball, and Hank thought he should play. The Hammer went right to work and in his second at-bat on Opening Day, he hit the first homerun ever in Cincinnati's new Riverfront Stadium to tie the Babe with homerun number 714. He then sat out the next game before returning home to Atlanta for a game against the Los Angeles Dodgers.

I remember watching the game on Monday night, April 8, 1974. A bunch of my teammates at Evangel College and I gathered around the television set in the lobby of Krause Hall. Dodger lefty Al Downing delivered a 1-0 fastball to the plate, and Hank launched it into the left field bullpen and into the history books. In his usual manner, Hank jogged around the bases with his head down in a rather emotionless state. Everyone, including the Dodger infielders, congratulated him. When he arrived at home plate, he was greeted by a small mob of people that included his mother. He told me years later that one of the things he remembers most about that moment was that his mother surprised him with her strength. "She hugged my neck so hard that I couldn't breathe!" he said.

Henry Aaron went on to hit another 40 homeruns over the course of the next 2 years to finish with his record total 755 homeruns. He finished his amazing 23-year career in the same city where it all began, Milwaukee, Wisconsin. Four different times, he led the National League in homeruns and runs batted in. He won two batting championships and was named the National League MVP in 1957. On paper these accomplishments seem larger than life, but to Hank they were somewhat hollow victories. What should have been his finest hour instead turned into a horrible ordeal.

I first met the great Henry Aaron on April 8, 1993, which marked the 19th anniversary of his record-breaking shot. I had read his 1991 autobiography entitled, *I Had a Hammer*. In the book, Hank released a lot of the anger and heartache he had harbored over the years. He quoted many of the hate letters that he received during his chase of the Babe. In his years as an executive with the Braves organization, he had pushed hard for the promotion of African-Americans in baseball.

I wasn't sure what to expect when I walked into the green room on that April evening. But the person I met that night was exactly like the ballplayer I had watched. He was polite and unassuming. Hank Aaron is as efficient in his speech as he was on the ballfield. He answered every single question that evening openly and honestly. But he never wasted any words. Hank is not the type of person who talks simply to be heard. He thinks his answers through and delivers a strong, compact answer reminiscent of his swing.

Since a lot of parents like to watch QVC's sports shows with their children, I always like to begin my sports shows by asking the players about their childhood. Hank was born in Mobile, Alabama, on February 5, 1934. He told me he developed his hitting ability by playing stick ball with a broomstick and bottle caps. "We couldn't afford a real baseball and bat so we pitched bottle caps and swung at them with a broomstick," he told me.

At the age of 17, Hank Aaron got on a train for Indianapolis, Indiana, with two sandwiches in a bag, two pairs of pants and two dollars in his pocket. He played two seasons at shortstop with the Indianapolis Clowns of the Negro Leagues before the Braves acquired him in 1952 for $7,500. In fact,

Hank is the last player from the Negro Leagues to play in the major leagues. His hero as a teenager was none other than the great Jackie Robinson, whose fabulous play and courageous stand desegregated major league baseball in 1947. Hank actually desegregated the Braves in 1954, when Bobby Thomson broke a leg in spring training.

I asked him about a strange story I had read that said he actually batted cross-handed early in his career. Hank said it was true. Apparently he batted with his hands reversed on the bat for many years before a coach corrected his hand position. He found it easier to hit the bottle caps with the broomstick that way. That technique probably helped him to develop the powerful wrists and forearms that generated his tremendous bat speed. Even after he un-reversed his hands, Hank possessed an unorthodox swing. While most power hitters hit off their back foot, Hank hit off his front. He was known as a wrist hitter who could wait until the last second before whipping his bat into the ball.

Baseball players are known for their quick wit, which is part of what makes the game so appealing. Some of the greatest quotes in American history have come from baseball players. For example, when Babe Ruth was asked how he felt about the fact that he made more money than the President, he responded that he should since he had had a better year. Well, I love a quote I read by pitcher Curt Simmons about Aaron. He said, "Throwing a fastball by Hank Aaron is like trying to sneak the sun past a rooster."

Another pitcher once described Aaron as "the only hitter I have ever faced who looked as if he were falling asleep between pitches. Unfortunately, he usually woke up in time to hit the next one out of the park."

Hall of Fame pitcher, Don Drysdale, remembered getting a crick in his neck when he turned abruptly to watch an Aaron line drive leave the park at the Los Angeles Coliseum.

"It's bad enough to have him hit any homerun off you—turning and looking and saying to yourself, 'My gosh, how far is that one going to go.' But with the Coliseum homerun, I ended up not only in mental anguish but literally in physical pain."

While most great hitters spend a lot of time studying the science of hitting, Hank Aaron spent most of his time studying pitchers. I'll never forget the first time Hank told me that he would sit in the dugout and put his baseball cap over his face. He looked at the pitcher through one of the tiny vent holes in the cap. "I used to isolate the pitcher by looking at him through that tiny hole. It helped me to completely focus on his motion," he explained. I started to laugh out loud as I pictured baseball's All-Time Homerun King sitting in the dugout with his cap over his face. His teammates must have wondered if Henry was sneaking in little catnaps between innings.

I have had the honor of interviewing most of baseball's greatest hitters. DiMaggio, Mantle, Mays, Schneider, Rose, Williams and Aaron are just a few of the Hall of Fame sluggers I have discussed the art of hitting with. It's a rare treat to hear the inside story on their approach to hitting. Hank told me he always took an educated guess as to what the next pitch would be. For example, he told me he started thinking about Al Downing several days before the historic April 8, 1974, match-up and decided that Downing would not want to hang a curve ball since it broke inside on Hank. This would give him the chance to pull it down the left field line. So Hank disciplined himself to wait for Downing's fastball. When it came, he was ready. "Let's say a pitcher has three good pitches including a fastball, a curve and a slider. What I do after a lot of consideration and studying is to eliminate two of the possibilities. So, by eliminating these two, I convince myself that I'm going to get the pitch I am looking for," he explained.

As of the writing of this book, I have been honored to have worked with Hank Aaron on the anniversary of his record-breaking homerun for the past seven years. If you have ever wondered where Hank is on the anniversary of that momentous occasion, chances are he is spending it on QVC talking baseball with me. On April 8, 1998, Hank and I did the show in front of a live audience in the annex theatre at QVC's Studio Park in West Chester, Pennsylvania. It was interesting to see Hank around a lot of people. He acted, as he always does, in a polite and professional manner. He is definitely not the type who likes to draw attention to himself. I think he is basically a shy person. He likes people a lot, but seems to be more comfortable in a small group as opposed to a large crowd.

After the show, as Hank and I were making our way out of the studio, a woman came up and handed me several pencils with the Cleveland Browns logo on them. She wanted me to give them to Hank because she knew he was a huge Cleveland Browns fan. When I caught up to Hank and handed them to him, I could tell he was touched—he walked back hoping to catch up with the lady to thank her. I was very impressed by his reaction. Hank was genuinely moved by the fact that the woman had brought them as a gift. By the way, when he arrived at the studio that night, he was wearing a Cleveland Browns jacket.

Near the end of the show, I asked Hank if he felt the pressure lift off of him on April 8, 1974, when he touched home plate after homerun number 715. He said, "It was like this incredible burden had been lifted off my shoulders. I felt like I had been locked inside a prison of pressure for the past two years. I didn't realize how bad it was until I visited my daughter in 1973 at her college, and she asked me why the college officials wouldn't allow her to go off campus. That's when it hit me that my chase of Babe's record not only affected me but my entire family as well. Here my daughter couldn't have a normal college experience. That really bothered me."

April 8, 1999, was the 25-year anniversary of Hank's record-breaking homerun in Atlanta. Major League Baseball really did a great job of honoring him. There was a lot of media attention around Hank and on the evening of April 8, there was a huge celebration at Turner Field in Atlanta for the Braves' home game. Baseball's top brass came out to honor Aaron's tremendous achievements and it was all carried on national television.

Hank appeared with me on QVC the evening before, on April 7. We produced a remote broadcast from Frankie's Sports Bar and Grill in Atlanta. It was a really cool setting for the show with a wall of video monitors behind us that flashed Hank's career statistics and showed footage of his historic homerun. The place was packed with base-ball fans who were enthusiastic about the show. QVC's Paul Kelly worked the crowd and fielded questions for Hank from the audience.

Hank was in a private room toward the back of Frankie's before the show started, and in between all the interviews he was doing, we went over the order of the show. Several members of the Atlanta media came by to cover our show—I was even interviewed by a couple different tel-evision stations about Hank. My friend Brian Roland was with me again, and I asked Hank to autograph a baseball for him and for Keelan Wheeler (no relation), a huge fan of Hank's. Hank said, "Dan, I'll do it if they are friends of yours." I really appreciated that.

In July of 1993, I attended my 20-year high school reunion. I was really excited to see many of my high school teammates, especially Mark "Hank" Ranum. I took a special present for him: a Hank Aaron autographed baseball. I had told Hank about Mark and how he idolized him, so he signed a baseball for him, too. I thought Mark was going to cry when I gave it to him. He still has it on display in his office.

When I look at the salaries that professional base-ball players are being paid today, I think it is a shame that the all time Homerun, RBI, Total Bases and Extra Base Hit King never had a contract for more than one year until the final two years of his career. That contract was the largest one Hank ever had. He was paid $240,000 a year. He was the last player from the Negro Leagues to play in the majors, and he was one of the last legends to play who didn't get the huge contracts that even average players are offered today. In fact, the most prolific power hitter in the history of baseball was paid a final salary that barely approaches today's minimum salary for a major league player.

Like Joe DiMaggio, however, Hank Aaron doesn't spend much time looking back. After building his amazing legacy on the playing field, he went on to build the Atlanta Braves farm system into one of baseball's best in his role as corporate vice president in charge of player development. The man is a builder who swings a hammer better than any-one else. And after all these years, I have to say that my buddy "Hammerin' Hank" Ranum was pretty good at picking nick-names—and heroes.

Chapter 14

Brett Favre

When I was 13 years old, I took third place in the Punt, Pass and Kick contest in St. Joe, Michigan. I had always been pretty good at punting and kicking, but that passing part gave me grief. While I had a pretty good arm in baseball, throwing a football never came easily. I always admired guys who could get that perfect spiral on their passes. Since my spirals were more like wobbles, I enjoyed playing wide receiver. I loved using my speed to race past defenders on deep pass routes. It was always a thrill to catch a touchdown pass. But the guy that actually throws the football, with big, mean, hard-hitting linemen rushing in on him, deserves most of the credit. I have tremendous respect for anyone who can play quarterback. It has to be one of the toughest positions to play in all of sports.

Growing up in Michigan, I was a Detroit Lions fan. Greg Landry was a favorite of mine. Of course, during the sixties and seventies there were a lot of excellent quarterbacks in the NFL: guys like Roger Staubach of the Dallas Cowboys, Terry Bradshaw of the Pittsburgh Steelers and, of course, Bart Starr of the Green Bay Packers. When I was a kid, the Green Bay Packers were *the* team. However, in the years that followed it seemed as if the NFL title had left Titletown for good. But in 1997, I sat in the New Orleans Superdome and watched the

Lombardi Trophy return to Green Bay. The Packers' high-powered offense rode the strong arm of Brett Favre and the powerful legs of Desmond Howard to a 35-21 victory over the New England Patriots in Super Bowl XXXI. After the game, I hosted a show from the press box, and QVC's phone lines were jammed as Green Bay fans from all over the country called in.

I was thrilled that Desmond Howard won the Super Bowl MVP. Desmond was the 1991 Heisman Trophy winner from the University of Michigan. He was always an exciting player to watch, but he had a difficult time during his first five seasons in the NFL; 1996-97 was his breakout season. I was also very happy for Brett Favre. After being voted the league's Most Valuable Player following the '95-'96 season, Brett announced to the media that he had become addicted to painkillers. He checked himself into the Meninger Clinic in Topeka, Kansas, and submitted himself to the NFL's substance abuse program. Brett worked hard and overcame the addiction. By the start of the '96 season, he was determined to take his team all the way. Five months later, he had won his second consecutive NFL Most Valuable Player award and the Super Bowl Championship.

I met Brett in 1995 at the *NFL Experience* in Miami, Florida. He was one of my guests during QVC's first-ever football collectibles show from the *NFL Experience*. Brett dresses a lot like I do when I'm away from work. He showed up wearing shorts, a knit shirt and sandals. He was extremely friendly and down-to-earth. In fact, he was only scheduled to be on the show for a half-hour, but my next guest was running late, so I asked him if he would mind sticking around a little longer and he said, "no problem." Brett ended up being on the show for over an hour. The conversation was lively as we discussed his entire career from Hancock North Central High School in Kiln, Mississippi, to Southern Mississippi, to the Atlanta Falcons and, finally, the Green Bay Packers.

As I watched him in Super Bowl XXXI, I was impressed with his confidence and his accuracy. He came out on the Packers' second play from the line of scrimmage, called an audible and hit Andre Rison with a 54-yard touchdown pass. His exhilaration was evident to everyone in the Superdome. He took his helmet off and jumped up and down like a kid who had thrown his first touchdown pass in Pop Warner league. That play symbolizes what I like the most about Brett Favre. He loves to play football, and he doesn't hide his emotions. From that point on, the game was Green Bay's. Of course, Reggie White set a new Super Bowl record with three quarterback sacks, Desmond Howard set several return records, and Antonio Freeman caught the longest touchdown pass in a Super Bowl for 81 yards (thrown by Favre).

By winning his second consecutive Most Valuable Player award following the '96–'97 season, Favre joined Joe Montana as one of only two players ever to win back-to-back league MVP awards. He had thrown for an NFC record 39 touchdowns and had completed his fourth season in a row with over 3,000 yards passing. Brett had come a long way in the two years since I had interviewed him. I wondered if he had changed or if he was still that polite, laid-back guy I had met in Miami. I didn't have to wait long to find out.

The '97 NFL season began with many experts predicting a repeat Super Bowl Championship for the Green Bay Packers. Some actually felt the Pack had a shot at an undefeated season. However, things didn't begin as well as expected for the green and gold. They suffered early losses to Detroit and Philadelphia, and by the middle of October, they found themselves in a three-way tie for first place in the NFC East with Minnesota and Tampa Bay.

I was scheduled to fly to Milwaukee on October 16, 1997, for a two-hour football collectibles show with Brett, to originate from the Brett Favre Steakhouse. I was really

176

looking forward to it because my mom lives just outside of Milwaukee along with my sister, Margie Lou, my brother-in-law, George Baab, and their family. I had scheduled an extra day or two off to spend some time with them.

This particular week was a bye week for the Packers, meaning they didn't have a game the following Sunday. The team was pretty banged up with injuries. Running back Dorsey Levens had a bruised inner rib; wide receiver Robert Brooks had suffered a head injury; nose tackle Gilbert Brown had a bad knee . . . the list went on and on. On Monday October 13, head coach Mike Holmgren announced that he was giving the team the week off. It is pretty unusual for a coach to give his team a week off in the middle of the season, but he felt they just needed a break.

I got a call from the Scoreboard Company on Tuesday telling me that Brett's agent wanted to change the location of the show. Since Holmgren was giving them the week off, Brett wanted to go home to Mississippi. I can't blame him for that, but our crew really had to scramble to find a decent location. By Wednesday, with the help of Brett and his agent, our producer, Rob Anderson, made arrangements for the show to be broadcast from the Old Waverly Golf Club in West Pointe, Mississippi.

I flew into Gulfport, Mississippi, rented a car and drove to West Pointe. I was traveling with Jason Mann, our product coordinator, and Kevin Tully, QVC's Director of Remote Operations at the time. We arrived at the Old Waverly Golf Club around 10:00 P.M. and were very impressed with our accommodations. We shared a three-bedroom condo that overlooked the back nine on the golf course. We were all ravenous from not having eaten since lunch. After driving around West Pointe for about a half-hour we were thrilled to find a McDonald's still open. See—my job isn't all glamour and fine dining!

Around 8:00 the next morning, I was studying for the show, which was to take place in the country club from 7:00 P.M. to 9:00 P.M. that evening. As I mentioned earlier, I really like to have all of my statistics and stories down cold by show time, because I never know which direction the show will take. Live television means it is literally alive and can move in many directions. This is especially true on QVC because we add the extra element of phone calls from the viewers, and you never know what they are going to say. In typical fashion, the product lineup changed a couple of times throughout the course of the day. I spent over an hour on the phone with Ken Goldin, who was the CEO of the Scoreboard Company at the time. He sounded stressed out over the phone, and I sensed that this show was very important to him.

It was a glorious day in Mississippi. The temperatures climbed into the high sixties in the afternoon, so I decided to take my notes out onto the back patio and watch the golfers come down the fairway behind the condo. At one point, I looked up and saw Brett Favre getting out of his golf cart. I watched him walk right up to his ball and take a swing. He made a pretty good shot considering he didn't even take a practice swing. I watched him make his next shot and he did the same thing. I guess Brett likes his game of golf to move along. He doesn't waste time with practice swings. Besides, he's used to things moving at a much quicker pace on the football field.

In his book entitled, *Favre: For the Record*, he talks about having hernia surgery during an off-season. He describes the pain as being so bad that he couldn't play golf for three months. He made it sound like the pain of not being able to play golf was worse than the physical pain from the surgery! It's obvious that he really enjoys the game. In fact, he hosts the Brett Favre Celebrity Golf Tournament every year to benefit charity. His wife, Deanna, is CEO of the Brett Favre Fourward Foundation, which raises money for several different charities.

The staff of the Old Waverly Golf Club was very accommodating to our crew. We had a wonderful meal that evening before the show. They gave Brett and me matching golf shirts to wear that just happened to be the same green as the Green Bay Packers wear. I walked into the clubhouse where our cameras were set up about 6:30 P.M. Brett walked in around 6:45 P.M. and came right up to me, shook my hand and said, "Dan, it's great to see you again!" I asked him if he remembered the last time we had worked together, and he immediately responded, "I sure do. It was 1995 in Miami during the Super Bowl." I was quite surprised, since he does so many radio and television interviews as well as other appearances. I thought either he has a great memory, or his agent is very good at reminding him of things. I honestly believe he has a great memory.

He was very relaxed on this particular evening. It probably worked out better that we did the show in his home state because he seemed very comfortable with the surroundings. He told me he had done a series of commercials for the Old Waverly Golf Club and knew most of the staff personally.

We had a good show that night. I asked him about the current state of the Pack, and he said that his teammates were battered and bruised. However, he was thrilled that coach Holmgren had given them the week off. Brett felt that everyone needed the chance to recuperate physically and mentally. Even though they had two losses at this point, he seemed confident that they were going to return to the Super Bowl, which they did of course, only to lose a close one to John Elway and the Denver Broncos.

One thing that really stands out in my mind about this particular show was that we discussed the importance of parenting at length. As Brett was remembering his early sports career, he talked about his father, who always coached him and his brothers in football and baseball. He felt like his father really guided him throughout his sports career and helped to keep him focused. "I knew I had to work harder than everyone else did because I wasn't the most gifted athlete in the world," he said. "But I was as competitive as anybody," he added.

I think the most important thing he said all night came in his response when I asked him who his role models were growing up. He said that his dad was the most important one by far. "I feel like professional athletes shouldn't be kids' heroes today. I think parents should. Parents need to get more involved with their kids' lives and provide an example for them to follow," he said emphatically. I couldn't agree more.

You can tell that Brett Favre is a good family man. We talked about our daughters when we were off camera. His little girl, Brittany, makes him beam with pride. His wife, Deanna, means the world to him and has been his sweetheart since high school.

My impressions of Brett Favre are all favorable. He is now the only person in the history of the NFL to win three league MVP awards, and he did it three years in a row! He threw for over 3,000 yards in 5 straight seasons and has definitely earned a place in history as one of the best of all time. At the age of 32, he is already a true legend of the game, especially after returning the NFL Championship to Green Bay after 30 years. But all that stuff is on the field, and as I said at the very beginning of this chapter, I admire anyone who can play quarterback, whether it's in a backyard or at the Super Bowl.

To me the most impressive thing about Brett is that he hasn't let all of the success change him. He doesn't try to impress anyone. He is still that fun-loving, easy-going kid from

Kiln, Mississippi. He's extremely likable and brutally honest. I think the way in which he faced his addiction is a testament to that.

This chapter is a tough one to conclude because Brett will still be writing it for years to come on the field. He is improving his game every year, and before it is all over, I think he will rewrite the NFL record books. He's got the intellect, the determination and the heart. But the main reason why I think Brett Favre could possibly go down in history as the best quarterback of all time is that he still loves to play the game. So, don't be surprised to see Brett jumping up and down and head-butting his teammates on his way to another Super Bowl Championship before too long. I'm one person who won't "pass" up the chance to see it.

Chapter 15

San Francisco Giants Fantasy Baseball Camp

The pitcher shook off the sign. I knew he was bringing the fastball. It came in about knee high across the heart of the plate, right where I like it. The ball jumped off my bat into the gap in right centerfield. This one was going to be extra bases. The only problem was, I had two pulled hamstring muscles and a sore left arm. The bases seemed like they were a mile apart, but I gave it everything I had and finally arrived safely at third base with a stand-up triple. The crowd went wild as I gasped for air. I was standing on third base of the Phoenix Firebirds home field. The Firebirds are the Triple A farm club of the San Francisco Giants.

This is what a baseball fantasy camp is all about, and I was enjoying my major league fantasy to the fullest. I was on the best assignment of my career! QVC had sent me to Arizona to videotape interviews and tips with some of the greatest ballplayers ever to don a Giants uniform. And the best part of the assignment was that I got to play baseball all week long in the Arizona sunshine with the other 85 campers enrolled in the San Francisco Giants Fantasy Camp.

Like most boys who grew up in America in the sixties, I dreamed of one day playing in the big leagues. Hour after hour, I practiced pitching a tennis ball into the square that had been etched into the side of Jefferson Elementary

School in St. Joe, Michigan. The square represented a batter's strike zone. We called the game "tenny ball" and it was especially fun when you played one-on-one against a friend. Past the pitcher in the air was a single, past the swing set was a double, past the monkey bars was a triple and if you drove one all the way over the running track in the air it was a HOMERUN! I loved that game. During the summer of 1965, my personal tenny ball record was 53-7 against all comers.

I had been daydreaming about those days on the flight to Arizona for Fantasy Camp when the captain suddenly interrupted with, "Ladies and gentlemen, we are about to start our descent into the Phoenix airport." I had boarded a plane on a cold, snowy Philadelphia morning and landed in a sunny, 70-degree Arizona afternoon. A driver from the camp met me at the airport and took me to one of the nicest hotels I have ever seen.

I attended the opening meeting for the 1994 San Francisco Giants Fantasy Camp later that evening. Juan Marichal, Orlando Cepeda, Vida Blue, Hobie Landreath, Mike McCormick and other former Giant greats were there. Mike Sadek, a former catcher with the Giants' organization, was the general manager in charge of the camp and, as I soon discovered, is one of the funniest people around. Everybody there, including yours truly, was fired up and ready for a week of baseball!

Somehow, I had received a brochure for this camp in my mailbox at QVC in November of 1993. It listed all of the former great Giant ballplayers and coaches who would be running the camp. As I read it, I thought, *Wouldn't it be great to be there to be able to interview all of these legendary ballplayers?* Then I thought, *Wouldn't it be even better if I attended as a camper and got to play baseball and do all of the interviews between games?* The wheels started turning, and before I knew it, I was typing up a proposal for me and a

QVC camera crew to attend. When I submitted it to QVC, I really didn't think I had much of a chance of ever going, but I figured I had nothing to lose by submitting the proposal.

About two weeks later, I received a call from Ken Goldin of the Scoreboard Company asking me if I was serious about wanting to attend the 1994 Giants Fantasy Camp. I said, "Absolutely. I could tape several interviews that we could use in our baseball shows, and I could have the former pros give brief tips for young ballplayers. I think it would add a great deal to our shows." Ken said that he thought he could get me in through Willie Mays's agent. When we hung up, I was excited but I decided I had better not get my hopes too high.

Just before Christmas, I got a call from Sue Schick, who was responsible for all of the schedules of the QVC program hosts at the time. She knew how badly I wanted to go on this trip, so she was very happy to inform me I would be flying to Phoenix on January 30th to play baseball for a week in the sun. I assured her that we would be working very hard down there in that heat. I couldn't believe my good fortune!

I drove straight to a sporting goods store and bought baseball shoes and batting gloves. I got out my fielding glove—which I have had since my junior year in high school—oiled it up and got it ready for action. The very next week, I located an indoor batting cage in the West Chester area and spent a couple of hours trying to get my swing back. After all, I didn't want to embarrass myself in front of the other campers and our camera crew.

After the big welcome meeting on Sunday night, I headed straight for my hotel room to get a good night's rest. I remember thinking that I wanted to play as well as I possibly could. It had been 15 years since I had played in an organized baseball game. This was a dream come true for me, and I wanted to make the most of it.

My alarm went off at 6:30 A.M. I wanted to be one of the first in line at breakfast so I could catch the first bus over to the ballpark. We used the same facility that the San Francisco Giants use for spring training. When I walked into the locker room, I couldn't believe my eyes! Above each full-length wooden locker there was a camper's name. I searched diligently until I found mine. There, hanging in the locker, was a San Francisco Giants uniform with my old number two and my name across the back. I just stared at it for a few moments and then I slowly began putting my uniform on. I went through the same ritual I had gone through every time I put on a baseball uniform during the 16 seasons I played. When I looked in the mirror, I felt like I was 15 years old again. The uniform fit like a glove.

As I walked to the practice field, I reminded myself that I really wasn't 15, I was, in fact, 39. I was going to have to thoroughly stretch out and take it easy the first couple of days. Of course, I had been telling myself to take it easy on the first day of baseball since I was eight years old. While every young boy has every intention of warming up properly that first time out, there is something about the smell of the fresh air, the sound of the ball popping into your glove and the crack of the bat that makes you forget all thoughts of moderation. Baseball season is back! Let's whip it around the horn and hit some fiery blue darts because it's a great day for two! I had that same old feeling again.

We took batting and fielding practice for about an hour, and then we were introduced to a ritual that would be a vital part of our lives every day of camp: Kangaroo Court. This was one of the strangest forms of male bonding I have ever seen. Every day different accusations were brought against various ballplayers and coaches by other ballplayers and coaches. The accused had a chance to defend themselves before a court of judges (made up of the coaches). The judges then decided on the punishment. I had no idea that I would be appearing before the court on a regular basis. Silly as it sounds, it was a great way to bring everyone together, and it always started the day off on a fun note.

The organizers of the camp know the importance of stretching, especially when you are dealing with middle-aged men whose main form of exercise is making the 15-foot walk to the water cooler at work each day. We stretched for about a half-hour every day. After the stretch, we headed off to the field for some instruction in throwing, running, hitting and fielding. I saw a wide range of baseball ability at camp. And I was most impressed with how many former college and minor league players were in attendance. I had played four years of college ball and two years at the semi-pro level, so I felt pretty good going through the drills. In the afternoon, we divided up into teams and played a couple of games while the coaches scouted us. They held a draft that night and selected the teams for the week.

I hit a ground ball to the second baseman my first time at bat. Even though I hadn't sprinted in years, there was something about seeing that ground ball that made me lose all common sense. I ran as fast as I could and beat the throw to first. I had my first base hit, but I also felt something "pop" in my leg as I crossed the bag. I had not even been in camp for a full day, and I already had my first pulled muscle. Fortunately, along with the Giants training facility we also had the Giants training staff. I got to know them well. I started every day with a Jacuzzi and a tape job, and I ended every day with an ice bath.

My team for the week was called "Hobie and Mike's Heroes." Our manager was Hobie Landreath, who was an outstanding catcher for the Giants in the fifties and sixties. We had a great bunch of guys on our team. While we didn't win it all, we were certainly competitive. I was fortunate because

I got to play my favorite position, the one that I had played throughout my entire career, centerfield. While I didn't get to all of the balls that I would have in my younger days, I did have a lot of fun catching what I could. The only time I wasn't in centerfield was when I had to pitch. I am no pitcher, but we definitely had a shortage of hurlers on our team, so one day I had to throw a couple of innings. Even though I tried to bring the heat, I don't think my fastball could have broken a pane of glass ... and after two innings, my arm felt like it was going to fall off.

My locker was located right next to Juan Marichal, the Dominican Dandy himself. He is a very kind and gracious man. It was a real treat to spend time talking with him every day. Juan won twenty games or more in a season six times during his Hall of Fame career with the Giants. He was best known for his trademark, high-kick wind-up. During his playing days in the sixties and early seventies, he generated tremendous velocity on his fastball by kicking his lead leg high above his head during his wind-up. I used to imitate Juan's wind-up and kick back in my tenny ball days.

Mike Sadek, the general manager of the camp, is also a QVC viewer. Every time I stepped up to the plate, I could hear him in the stands yelling, "We're giving it away! Call in quickly!" Mike kept us laughing the entire week. One day as I was slowly walking back toward the locker room from the playing field, he came driving up in a golf cart and said, "Wheels, hop in. I'll give you a ride back!" I was very grateful for his generosity after a long day of baseball. The next day, however, I was brought up on weighty charges in Kangaroo Court. It seems that a player accepting a ride from a coach in a golf cart is one of the most serious crimes you can commit at the Giants Fantasy Camp. By the end of the week, my fines totaled in the millions of dollars. In fact, I was told I hold the distinction of racking up the most fines in the history of this camp. Some of the charges were hilarious. I was fined because my camera crew used a reflector to help fill in some shadows when I was interviewing one of the coaches on the sideline of a field. The court said it reflected some light, which was a distraction to the players on the field. That was a very steep fine as well, because the court said it was "illegally influencing a game of baseball." I had many other charges that were quite humorous. Every time I protested, the court would double or triple my fine.

By the time our QVC camera team arrived, I was "in the groove" of playing baseball again. I had planned it so they would come down on Wednesday of that week. I wanted a few days to get my rhythm back before they began taping. The only problem was that I had pulled both hamstring muscles by the time they arrived, and it was becoming increasingly difficult for me to run. My left arm felt like it was hanging by a string. I got through the week with the help of the Giants' trainers. They did an excellent job of taping me up every day and getting me to the point where I could play.

Our crew did a fantastic job under the direction of producer Bill Martin. The former coaches and players gave us interesting and informative interviews. Some of the guys videotaped great educational segments on the finer points of the game. A few of the Giants' legends shared some really inspirational thoughts about baseball and the game of life. Every former coach and player in camp that week graciously gave of their time and taped segments for *QVC Sports.* There was one exception.

Willie Mays refused to grant us an interview. You'll recall that snafu from my chapter on Willie—but I can honestly say that incident was the only negative thing about the entire week from my perspective. Playing ball again was an absolute blast, and the other players and coaches could not have been any nicer. They were all willing to help us in any way possible. We actually produced over twenty different spots from three days of taping, and we also had enough footage to produce a new open for our QVC baseball shows.

There's something magical for a former ball player—even a college or semi-pro player—in playing with guys from the big leagues, even if just for a week. I had that old feeling of confidence at the plate. I ended up stroking 12 base hits in 24 at-bats for an even .500 batting average. I only committed one error in the field. Admittedly, it wasn't exactly the toughest pitching I have ever faced, but it was good competitive baseball, and it just made me feel great to think that I could still play. After all, that's really the whole point of a fantasy baseball camp.

One of the things that I realized during the camp is how important it is for young athletes to have good coaching. The coaches that I had growing up in St. Joe, Michigan, did their best with the knowledge they had, but during this week, I learned what great coaching was all about. Darrell Evans was a power-hitting third baseman with the Giants and the Detroit Tigers. He spent about 10 minutes with me one day in the batting cage and had me hitting the ball farther than I ever did during my entire playing career. He taught me how to have rhythm in the batter's box: as the pitcher goes back in his wind-up, the batter should be leaning his weight back to generate momentum and bat speed as the pitcher comes forward. I had always stood fairly still in the batter's box and, as a result, had always been more of a "punch hitter." For the first time in my life, I was hitting the ball out of the park during batting practice.

One of the highlights of the week is when the campers get to play the coaches on the second to the last night of camp. There were seven teams of campers, so each team only got to play for two innings. The game was played at the Phoenix Firebirds stadium, which used to be the home of the Giants Triple-A minor league club. The park was beautiful, and it was a thrill to play there. My team only had two hits in our two innings, and I was fortunate enough to have one of them. I hit a sharp line drive into left field off former Giants' pitcher Dave Heaverlo.

Every night during the week, the campers got together for different social events. There were round-table discussions with the former coaches and players where the campers could ask any questions they wanted. One night they held an informal autograph session, and there were a few nights when we all just sat around and relived some of the great plays that had happened that day. Since each team played a double header every day, there was always plenty to discuss. The camp had a video crew of its own to record all of the action. They played the tapes in the hotel lounge just before dinner, so we could all share with each other in the day's victories and defeats.

This week made me realize that one of the things I miss most about playing team sports is the sense of camaraderie that it promotes. I think most guys over 30 really miss that male bonding. I think women tend to do a better job, overall, of staying in touch with their friends. Growing up, I always had plenty of good friends to hang around with. It stayed that way through college and even through most of my twenties. Once I started working at my career more seriously, however, I still had friends, but it became harder to get together with them. When I got married and started a family, I had even less time for my friends. That's just the way life goes, but I think it's really important for men to have close male friends that they can talk to when faced with life's challenges. That's probably what I enjoyed the most about attending the Giants Fantasy Baseball Camp. I made some really good friends.

Saturday night was the final night of camp. They held a big awards banquet, and every camper was acknowledged by his coach for his accomplishments. Each camper received a box of his own personal baseball cards. Professional photographers had taken our pictures in various action poses in our San Francisco Giants uniform. Each player chose the picture that he wanted for the front of his card. The back of the card featured background information, personal statistics and the player's statistics from camp. They look like professional baseball trading cards, and I treasure mine. We also received a videotape featuring our team's highlights from each day of the week. I still have my tape, and I pull it out from time to time and relive that great week of baseball.

When the banquet ended, the 1994 Giants Fantasy Baseball Camp was officially over. I remember feeling as if I were going to cry as I hugged all of my new friends and coaches and said goodbye. It was amazing to me how close we had all become in just one week's time. As I think about it, I realize it was about a lot more than having a great time for a week in the Arizona sun. It was about the common love of a game. It was about belonging to a team. And it was about a lifelong dream that we all shared: the chance to be a big league baseball player.

You're never too old to make your dreams come true. After all, at the age of 39, for one week, I played for the San Francisco Giants in the big leagues.

Chapter 16

Reggie Jackson

Fall is my favorite time of the year. Maybe it's because I was born in October. Or maybe it's because I grew up in Michigan where the trees become emblazoned with the most vibrant colors imaginable. Or just maybe it's because October brings on the biggest baseball event of the year: the World Series. Whatever the reason, I absolutely love the fall, and my favorite month of all is October.

There is one name in all of sports that is forever linked to my favorite month of the year: Reggie Jackson, "Mr. October" himself. Just like the trees, with their golden leaves turning, Reggie loved to end the month in a blaze of glory. While his career batting average of .262 is the lowest of any outfielder in baseball's Hall of Fame, his flair for the dramatic easily ranks number one. In the sixth game of the 1977 World Series against the Los Angeles Dodgers, Jackson hit three homeruns off three consecutive pitches from three different pitchers to clinch the series for the Yankees. If you count his last at-bat in game five, he had a streak of four homers on four swings. The only other player ever to hit three home-runs in a World Series game was Babe Ruth, and he didn't do it consecutively.

Reggie's dramatic moments were not confined to hitting homeruns. In one of the most memorable batter-versus-pitcher confrontations of all time, he struck out swing-ing on a three-two count against Bob Welch of the Dodgers to end game two of the 1978 World Series. There were two run-ners on base, the Yankees were trailing 4-3 and the strikeout came on the ninth pitch of the dual. Jackson later homered off Welch in game 6 of that series, and the Yankees won the championship. He also hit one of the most dramatic home-runs in All-Star Game history when he drove one off the light transformer high above right field at Tiger Stadium in 1971. That could have been the longest homerun ever hit if the transformer hadn't been in the way.

Reggie Jackson is a testament to the fact that the thing that baseball fans come out to see is the homerun. He hit 563 of them in his 21 seasons. That figure places him sixth on the all-time list. But he is number one of all-time in strike-outs with 2,597. In fact, Reggie set or tied six career big league records—all for strikeouts. He also tied the American League record by leading outfielders in errors in five seasons. He tied another American League record once when he com-mitted five errors in a single game. But, in spite of it all, he was easily elected to Baseball's Hall of Fame in his first year of eligibility in 1993.

"Mr. October" is one of two nicknames that belong to Reggie. He called himself "the straw that stirs the drink" and lived up to that name both on and off the field. He was a master at stirring up controversy. His fights with Yankee man-ager Billy Martin are legendary. One time Martin thought Jack-son dogged it on a fly ball, so he pulled him out of the game in the middle of the inning. The two of them got into a heated argument in the dugout. It nearly escalated into a fistfight. On another occasion, Jackson ignored Martin's bunt sign and then disregarded his wishes by bunting on the next pitch. In a rage, Martin threw a clock against his office wall after the game. He suspended Jackson for five games. Reggie got into a fight with Graig Nettles once in a restaurant after a game. And when free agency began in the 1970s, he was *the* free agent.

I didn't know what to expect the first time I worked with Reggie Jackson. I had witnessed all of the above on television, and I had read plenty of other stories that had me on eggshells. A good friend of mine was the target of Reggie's anger one time in Chicago. Dean Anderson was my main camera operator on several shows that I produced during my eight years with WCFC-TV in Chicago. (You read about Dean in the chapter on George Foreman.)

On this occasion, Dean was operating the first-base camera at Comiskey Park when the Yankees were playing the White Sox. Reggie struck out and Dean kept his camera on Reggie as he walked down into the dugout. Reggie yelled at him to take his camera off of him, and when Dean stayed on him, he violently struck the camera with the side of his hand. Dean let go of the camera so that it would spin on the tripod and not absorb the full blow. Needless to say, I considered Reggie to be a volcano that could erupt at any time.

From my research, I knew that Reggie was somewhat of a baseball historian who took pride in his knowledge of the game, so I put in extra hours trying to come up with a few special nuggets of information that I could surprise him with. Sure enough, early on in our first interview, I struck gold when I told him he was the first person ever to steal home successfully in an American League Championship Series. Reggie seemed comfortable with me the rest of the show. Actually, I have to say that he was an excellent guest. He answered my questions intelligently and really kept the discussion lively. That show took place on October 18, 1992.

The next time Reggie came to QVC was on August 14, 1993, the same day that the Yankees retired his number 44 at Yankee Stadium. I figured he would be in a great mood after being honored in front of all of his fans. I figured wrong.

When he walked into the green room that night, I held out my hand to shake his. He ignored my hand and asked, "Where's my pizza?"

His representative had called QVC and insisted that we have warm pizza ready for him when he arrived, which we did. I pointed over to the table where the pizza was and said, "It's right there."

Still not mollified, he demanded to see the product lineup for the evening. As I went over it with him, I explained that we were going to give him about a 10-minute break halfway through the show and then bring him back on for the last 45 minutes. He looked at me incredulously and said, "You're going to use Reggie Jackson to hold the audience over? I don't think so. You had better put all of my products together so that when I'm done I can leave."

At that moment, Dennis Reustle, QVC's Vice President of Programming, walked into the green room. I said, "Well, here's the man you need to talk to right now." I then explained to Dennis that Reggie had a problem with the way the show was programmed, and I walked out of the room. I had enough to worry about before the show without trying to appease Reggie.

Apparently, Dennis was able to work things out because once Reggie was on the air, he was fine. (In his defense, I'm sure he was tired from all of the day's activities, but that should not be a license to be rude.) All in all, this was definitely a memorable evening. About a half-hour into the show, the director went to a few promotional spots on tape. During the breaks, I usually talk to my guests. At one point during the show, I mentioned that I had played baseball in college. During this break, Reggie asked me what college I played for, and I told him Evangel College in Springfield, Missouri. I then remembered that our biggest game ever was when Oklahoma came through one spring break for a scrimmage game. I indicated that we were not on the winning end of the game.

Reggie was tossing his autographed baseball in the air and dropped it. The ball rolled forward on the set toward the monitors, which sat directly below the cameras. He got up from his chair and walked over to the ball and picked it up. As he turned to walk back to his seat, the director punched up my camera and I proceeded to welcome everyone back to the show. Reggie apparently didn't realize that the camera was live, because as he sat down he looked at me and said, "So Dan, did they f---in' drub you or what?"

I looked at him and said, "He's Reggie Jackson everybody and I'm Dan Wheeler and we are *LIVE*!" Reggie's eyes opened the size of half-dollars. We both just rolled on as if nothing had happened. The show was informative and entertaining for sure, but sales were somewhat slow. Afterward, he asked me why I didn't let him know we were on, and I explained that I was talking directly into the camera with the red light on. I couldn't really give him any other signal. He then admitted that he was very tired and probably was not as alert as he should have been.

The following Monday when I walked into QVC, I didn't even make it past the security guards without them asking me if Reggie had really said the "f" word on the air. I explained that he didn't really intend to, but it accidentally slipped out. As I walked down the hall, two more people stopped and asked me about the incident. I went upstairs toward my boss's office and walked past a conference room full of QVC executives. The door was open and as I walked by, Ron Giles, who was the Vice President of Broadcasting at the time, interrupted the meeting and called me in. He asked, "Dan, did Reggie really say the 'f' word?"

Once again, I related the entire story exactly as it happened.

As you are probably aware, profanity is indeed a rarity on QVC. I'm happy to say that it hasn't happened during one of my shows since. This incident, however, created quite a stir—which is fitting for the man who called himself "the straw that stirs the drink."

The next time I saw Reggie was on September 26, 1996. I had decided that after the pizza episode in the green room, I would simply greet him "on the air" with the cameras live. He was in a great mood, as lively as ever—but this time he watched his language, even when the cameras were not on. He was in prime form that night and did a great job of helping me present all of the items in the show, even the ones that didn't have his name on them.

On October 14, 1997, I hosted a two-hour World Series special with Reggie at QVC's Studio Park. When I greeted him backstage, I wasn't sure that it was the same guy. He looked great—Reggie really keeps himself in good shape physically—but there was definitely a different attitude. He was polite and soft-spoken. During the show he was very complimentary of other players, and very modest when it came to discussing his own accomplishments.

Somewhere along the way, when we were discussing collectibles, he told me that he had lost most of his treasured pieces in a fire that had destroyed his home. Apparently, Reggie had lost many items that were irreplaceable in terms of sentimental value. Tragedies like this are never something we hope for in life, but I believe the fire had a profound impact on Reggie Jackson's life. Difficult times can make a person stop and reevaluate everything. I'm not judging what Reggie's life was like before, but I think he had a change of heart. On this particular night, Reggie was one of the nicest people I have ever had the pleasure of working with. There was definitely something different about the man, and I was hoping it would last.

In the spring of 1999, Yankee fans were as excited as ever about a new baseball season. The Yanks had captured the '98 World Series Championship, and they finished with more wins in the regular season and the playoffs than any other team in history. Their record through the World Series was 125-50. *QVC Sports* traveled down to Tampa Bay, which is the Yankees' home for spring training. I hosted a two-hour baseball collectibles show honoring the New York Yankees. My special guests were Reggie Jackson and Darryl Strawberry.

When Reggie first walked in that night, I thought, "Oh no. He's in another one of those foul moods." He was upset because he saw the Salvino Bammer Bears sitting on the table on the stage. These are adorable stuffed bears, and they are officially licensed by Major League Baseball. At the time, they were the only collectible baseball bears that could be shown wearing a team uniform.

Apparently, Reggie had just come out with a line of baseball bears, called "Mr. Octo-Bears." He was threatening not to go on if the Bammer Bears were in the show. Ken Goldin, of Goldin Sports Marketing, Reggie, Reggie's agent and I sat down at a table to work out the situation. It was determined from this meeting that Reggie would go on, but I could not mention Reggie's name during the presentation of the Bammer Bears, nor could I mention the Bammer Bears during Reggie's segment. So "The Straw" was stirring again, but he mellowed before the situation escalated. He calmed down by show time and was actually pretty easy to work with.

"The straw that stirs the drink," the man who used to talk in terms of "the magnitude of me," the man who earned the nickname "Mr. October," starred for both the Oakland A's and the New York Yankees and played with the California Angels. When it was announced in January of 1993 that he had been the only player elected to the Hall of Fame that year, he made it known right away that he wanted his plaque to be emblazoned with the "NY" of the Yankees. He said he always wanted to be right there with all the great Yankees of the past like Babe Ruth, Lou Gehrig, Mickey Mantle and Joe DiMaggio. Now he is.

Reggie Jackson will be remembered by most baseball fans as the man who once hit three consecutive pitches, off three different pitchers out of the ballpark in a World Series game. Like a tree that goes out in a full blaze of glory, Reggie always saved his best for last. I'm hoping that is true of the way he is living his life away from the field. To me that would be the most "stirring" thing of all.

Chapter 17

Bill Russell

This was my final try. If I didn't get it this time, I was hitting the showers. My friend, Jimmy Sullivan, shouted, "You can do it. Really get up this time!" I licked my hand and then wiped the soles of my Chuck Taylor Converse All Stars. The gym floor at St. Joseph Junior High School was always dusty, and I wanted to make sure I had good traction for my takeoff. I started jogging, then picked up speed, leaped and stretched as high as I could! My right hand actually grazed the bottom of the net on a ten-foot basket. "I did it. I got the net!" I screamed. Man, I was on cloud nine that November evening in 1967. I had finally jumped high enough to touch the net on a regulation basketball hoop.

I love basketball. Although I was always the shortest one on the team, nobody loved the game more than I did. I have many memories like the one I just described. I'll never forget lacing up my first pair of Converse All Star basketball shoes. I remember putting on my first basketball uniform, which was about three sizes too big. The first basket I scored, in a junior high game, was a drive right down the middle of the lane against Benton Harbor Junior High in seventh grade. I'll never forget the first points I scored in high school. One of our starting guards, senior Brian Haack, had fouled out. The coach called on me. It was late in a game against the

Buchanan Bucks and we were down by two with about five minutes left. As soon as I touched the ball, I was fouled. I then hit two free throws to tie the game. Near the end of the game, I stole the ball from the point guard for the Bucks, drove the length of the gym and scored a basket to help my team win it. I still have a "highlight film" in my head. In fact, my senior year, my high school team, the St. Joe Bears, beat the Benton Harbor Tigers for the first time in the history of both schools. One of Benton Harbor's starting forwards was a guy named David Adkins. You probably know him better today as the comedian Sinbad.

The summer before my junior year in high school, many people were telling me that I was too short to make the varsity basketball team. St. Joe was a class-A school, which meant that we were in the division with the largest high schools in the state of Michigan. My graduating class had over 330 students, so it was a pretty big school. Whenever I would hear comments about my size, it made me practice all the harder. That summer I played basketball at least four hours a day, everyday. I wore ankle weights to strengthen my legs and spent hours jumping for the rim. By the end of the summer of 1971, I could actually "dunk" a volleyball on a 10-foot rim. Not bad for a kid who was only 5' 7" tall. By my senior year, I grew to my present height of 5'8". I'll never forget how proud I was when the coach handed me my varsity practice uniform. I was one of the first two juniors selected to the team. The other guy was Tom Scheffler, who stood 6' 9" tall and went on to star at Purdue University. Tom played in the NBA for two years and then played professional basketball in Europe.

From the time I was 13 years old until I was 18, basketball was one of the top priorities in my life. When I wasn't practicing or playing in a game, I was watching it on TV. I went wild during March Madness, the NCAA basketball tournament. There's nothing like college hoops because the kids just play their hearts out. When it came to professional basketball, my favorite team was the New York Knicks. They had Walter "Clyde the Glide" Frazier, Earl "The Pearl" Monroe, Dave DeBusschere, Bill Bradley and Willis Reed. Reed used to battle the giants of the league underneath the boards. In the sixties, the giants of the NBA were guys like Nate Thurmond, Wilt "The Stilt" Chamberlain and the incomparable Bill Russell.

Bill Russell was probably the most important cog in the Kelly green machine, the NBA dynasty of the sixties known as the Boston Celtics. Over the span of 13 winters from 1957 to 1969, Boston claimed an incredible 11 world titles. In the battle of the big men, Russell outplayed Wilt "The Stilt" in almost every crucial contest. Many over the years have voted for Wilt Chamberlain as the one of the best players of all time in the NBA. However, neither Chamberlain nor anyone else outplayed Russell in the big games. Big Bill captured five league Most Valuable Player awards in 1958, 1961–63, and 1965. At 6' 9" tall, Russell was a full five inches shorter than Wilt. But his defensive skills and shot blocking ability were unparalleled.

Red Auerbach, the legendary coach of the Boston Celtics, signed Bill Russell in 1956 to what was then considered a huge contract of $20,000 a year. Today, an "average" player in the NBA makes that in a game! During an 82-game season, Michael Jordan made over $400,000 a game near the end of his career. Auerbach's investment paid off immediately as the Celtics, with Russell at center, claimed their first NBA Championship in 1957. In 1958, the St. Louis Hawks defeated the Celtics in the finals. The Celtics then won eight NBA Championships in a row! Auerbach retired as coach after the '65–'66 season and Bill Russell became the first black head coach in the history of the NBA.

When Auerbach moved to the Celtic's front office, Russell became a player/coach. He guided the team to two more championships in 1968 and '69. The '68–'69 Celtics were old men by NBA standards. John "Hondo" Havlicek was the only regular under the age of 30. Russell was 35, but still put his entire heart and soul into playing and coaching. The Celts finished fourth in their division but put it all together in the playoffs and overcame their longtime nemesis Wilt Chamberlain, and the Los Angeles Lakers, 108-106 in the seventh game of the finals in Los Angeles. After this series, Bill decided that 13 seasons and 11 championships were enough. In fact, of those 11 title teams, the only man who had played on all 11 was Bill Russell.

Naturally, I was thrilled when I heard Mr. Russell was going to be my guest on QVC. My mind immediately flashed back to that parquet, wood floor at the Boston Garden. I can still hear that unique rattle sound that the rim made every time the ball struck it. The garden definitely had "dead spots" in the floor. Bill told me that the Celtics knew exactly where they were, and that knowledge gave them a distinct home court advantage. I can still see big Bill Russell going up for a rebound and spinning in mid-air to fire the outlet pass to the likes of Bob Cousy, Sam Jones and John Havlicek.

When I walked up to Bill in the green room on December 17, 1996, he stood up to shake my hand. It seemed as if he kept rising higher and higher as he stood. From my vantage point, 6' 9" looks like the Empire State building. His hands wrapped around mine. At 62 years old, Bill still looked like he was in good shape. His body appeared to be lean and strong. His beard and mustache were now "salt and pepper," with the majority being salt. He actually looked like a professor of basketball.

Bill runs a company called Golden Court 6 by Bill Russell. They manufacture athletic wear. I would assume the

Golden Court stands for his 11 NBA Championships and, of course, his number with the Celtics was 6.

As soon as we began the show, it was obvious that Bill's wit was as sharp as one of his signature outlet passes. I gave him a big introduction and concluded it by saying, "He has been called the greatest defensive player in the history of the NBA. Please welcome to QVC, Mr. Bill Russell."

He looked at me and in a serious tone said, "Well, Dan, I'm afraid some of my teammates would disagree with that statement you just made."

I was surprised and responded by saying, "Really, why do you say that?"

He smiled a sly grin and said, "Well, many of them actually found me quite *offensive!*" He then let out a roar of a laugh and I knew it was going to be a good night.

There is nothing more interesting to me than talking sports with a legendary athlete who is extremely knowledge-able about his or her sport. I can't say that all of the professional athletes I've had on the show were great interviews. As you read in the chapter on Shaquille O'Neal, he enjoyed talking about everything and anything *but* basketball. Bill Russell, on the other hand, really enjoys discussing the finer points of the game. His tremendous knowledge of the sport enabled him to go on to become a successful player and coach. He also knew how to get the most out of the players he had on his team.

It was interesting to talk to Bill about today's play-ers. He said that the game had become much quicker and much more physical than it was during his playing days. I found this comment interesting because when Bill Russell arrived in the NBA, he totally accelerated the pace of the game beyond what it had been. Before Russell's emergence, the big men of the league played a rather slow, plodding game. They used their size to dominate in a thug-like manner. Big Bill was agile both on the floor and in the air.

We talked about Michael Jordan's "explosiveness" in getting up in the air from his dribble. He articulated on Penny Hardaway's complete game and Alonzo Mourning's intimidating style. He had me laughing throughout the show. Bill enjoys finding the humor in every situation. It's one of his most endearing qualities. It's always great to have a guest who enjoys a good laugh. It seems like the legends, the guys who have nothing to prove to anybody, aren't afraid to really let loose with a good laugh from time to time during their interviews.

One of the items we presented that night was a shirt manufactured by Golden Court 6 by Bill Russell. It was an ash gray t-shirt that featured the Boston Celtics logo in embroidery right in the center on the front. Embroidered all the way around the logo were the dates of the Celtics phenomenal 16 NBA championships. Across the bottom of the shirt in Celtic green were the words "NBA Champions." I was able to acquire one of these shirts before the show, so during one of the breaks, I asked Bill if he would sign the shirt for me.

He very firmly said, "I'll sign it after the show."

I said, "That would be great." But I wondered if he would remember. Sure enough, as soon as we signed off, he asked me if I still wanted him to sign the shirt. He gave me a beautiful signature right across the top. That little incident told me a lot about Bill Russell. He has a lot of pride, and he likes to do things on his own terms.

After the show, we walked back to the green room and talked for a few more minutes. He wished me well and said he enjoyed being on QVC. As he took those long strides of his down QVC's hallway, I thought about the amazing strides he took to raise the level of play in the NBA. The fact that he never averaged more than 20 points a game in a season will undoubtedly keep him from gaining the support of the masses as the greatest player of all time. But Bill Russell had the unique ability to make everyone else around him better. Since his teammates helped him bear the offensive load, he was free to concentrate on defense and rebounding. In short, he was probably the greatest team basketball player of all time. He didn't worry about the glamorous aspects of the game as much as he worried about winning. That's why he was the biggest winner ever to step onto an NBA court.

Bill Russell truly stretched himself as far and as high as he could possibly go.

* * *

After working with Bill, I had my driveway widened and I finally did something that I've wanted to do my entire adult life: I put up a basketball hoop. So, Bill, the next time you're in town, feel free to come over to my house for a friendly game of one-on-one. After all, I can still jump high enough to get the net!

Chapter 18

Nolan Ryan

Baseball players have the best nicknames. "Babe," "Big Train," "Yankee Clipper," "The Say Hey Kid" and "The Commerce Comet" are just a few of the really great ones. I have had the privilege of meeting several of the men who answered to these names, but I'll take extra pride telling my grandchildren that I saw the "Von Ryan Express" in action, and that I actually worked with the "Miracle Man" himself: Lynn Nolan Ryan.

Whenever I hear or see the name Nolan Ryan, two words immediately pop into my mind: First Class. I have been in his company on several different occasions over the past five years. He has always been a gentleman to me and— I understand—to every one else that he came in contact with at QVC.

Nolan holds more major league records than any other player in the history of professional baseball. Most people know him as the "All Time No-Hit King." He threw 7 no-hitters during his phenomenal 27-year career. The truly amazing thing about Nolan's accomplishment is that he fired two no-hitters after the age of 40. Number six came on June 11, 1990, at Oakland. His age was 43 years, 4 months and 12 days. With that one, he became the oldest pitcher in history to throw a no-hitter and the only pitcher to throw no-hitters in three different decades. His seventh and final no-hitter came on May 1, 1991. This time Nolan was 44 years, 3 months and 1 day old. His fastball was clocked at 96 miles per hour! He told me that one was extra special because it happened at home in Arlington Stadium with his lovely wife Ruth in attendance.

While Nolan's no-hit accomplishments are tremendous, they are just the tip of the iceberg when it comes to his records. He fired 12 one-hit games during his career, to rank number one on the all-time list in that department. Several times he took no-hitters into the ninth inning, only to lose them with one or two outs to go. He holds the record for career strikeouts with 5,714; single-season strikeouts with 383; most seasons with 100 or more strikeouts, 200 or more strikeouts and 300 or more strikeouts. The list seems endless.

Like Cal Ripken, Jr., Nolan Ryan paved his road to greatness with tons of hard work and consistency. His work ethic is legendary. During his first baseball collectibles show on QVC, I asked him what he did after pitching a game. I was shocked when he said that after conducting his postgame interviews, he headed straight for the locker room where he iced his right arm for 20 to 25 minutes and then hopped onto an exercise bike for half an hour! "I feel the time to begin preparing for my next start is immediately following my last," he told me. In fact, he credits his longevity in baseball to his strict conditioning regimen. Think about it. When most men his age were sitting in their easy chairs watching players who were their sons' age play professional baseball, Nolan was striking them out with a blazing 96-mile-an-hour fastball.

I interviewed Phil Niekro the week before he was inducted into baseball's Hall of Fame. Niekro pitched well into his forties but relied on his lively knuckleball to fool batters. When I mentioned Nolan Ryan, his face filled with admiration. He told me that Nolan threw harder at the age of 45, than he (Niekro) did in his rookie year. Phil, like many other great ballplayers, considers Nolan to be the eighth great wonder of the world.

Several times in this book, I have mentioned Nolan Ryan in the same sentence with Cal Ripken, Jr. I see many similarities in their views on life. Like Cal, Nolan is a dedicated family man. His family has always been his top priority. In fact, he told me that one of his favorite pastimes was playing catch with his kids.

Even though Nolan has retired from playing professional baseball, his life still moves with the speed of his 100-mile-an-hour fastball. In addition to being an executive with the Texas Rangers organization, he is also the owner of two banks and three ranches. His friends and neighbors know him as a true country gentleman. He believes in the old-fashioned values of strong ethics, solid commitment and loyalty. He found the Texas Rangers organization to be loyal and straight with him, but discovered that the California Angels' general manager, Buzzie Bavasi, often seemed just the opposite. He told me he was thrilled to have the chance to end his career at home with the Rangers, not far from his childhood home in Alvin, Texas.

Nolan wore cowboy boots during three of the five interviews I have done with him. They look as natural on him as a pair of baseball cleats. He is not a passive ranch owner. He helps his ranch hands with everything, including turning bulls into steers and delivering calves. You have to appreciate Nolan's old-fashioned work ethic. At QVC, he always shows up early for his scheduled appearances, giving me plenty of time to go over the show's lineup with him and make sure he is comfortable with all of the items we present.

The day before the 1995 All-Star Game at Rangers Stadium in Arlington, Texas, I had scheduled an interview with Nolan in his office. He met the video crew and me in the executive lobby of the stadium. On this day, he wore dress shoes with a very classy, well-tailored gray suit. Several people in the lobby came up to say "hi" to him and a few asked for his autograph. As always, he was very patient and accommodated each request. He then led us onto the elevator and up to his office.

When I walked into his office, I was immediately struck by the incredible view of the field. One wall was a floor-to-ceiling window, offering an aerial look at the entire ball field. This was impressive enough—but then another fact caught my attention. There were absolutely no commendations or awards on any of the walls. I guess I expected to see trophies, plaques, baseballs and other memorabilia. When I asked Nolan about the conspicuous absence of wall hangings, he simply shrugged his shoulders and said that he hadn't gotten around to decorating his office. Knowing the type of guy he is, I think this was a very low priority on his busy agenda: he is definitely not the type to sit around and look at awards and reminders of past accomplishments. He truly lives his life in the here and now. He did say, "I guess I should put something up pretty soon, but decorating is just not my forte."

Our interview that day focused on his retirement from baseball and his future. We rolled Nolan's pre-taped comments into our show later that evening. The actual broadcast originated from a memorabilia store located inside the stadium. My guests for the show were Earl Weaver, the enigmatic manager of the Baltimore Orioles, Giants' slugger Barry Bonds and Raul Mondesi, the hard-hitting outfielder for the Los Angeles Dodgers. We rolled Nolan's comments into the show when we offered his autographed items. The interview went extremely well. As always, Nolan answered all of my questions in an honest and forthright manner. As the crew started breaking down their lighting and camera equipment,

Nolan and I chatted about the All-Star Game, which was coming up the next evening. He was scheduled to throw out the opening pitch, and he told me he was worried about it. I found it hard to believe that the greatest pitcher of all time, a man who had faced countless pressure-filled situations, was nervous about throwing out the opening pitch at an All-Star Game. "I'm worried that I'll throw it in the dirt. I've only played catch with my son, Reese, a couple of times since I retired," he told me. Well, the crew and I laughed, but Nolan had a worried look on his face. He escorted us back down to the main level and we thanked him and went on our way.

I was fortunate enough to attend the game the next night. When I walked into the stadium, it felt like a South American rainforest. The temperature on the field at game time was 112 degrees Fahrenheit! Dallas in July can be sweltering! From my seat, I could see Nolan, who was sitting just beyond the Rangers' dugout. When they introduced him, the place erupted into thunderous applause. When the crowd finally quieted down, Nolan went into his classic wind-up and let go of a "Texas Heater" straight into the dirt to the left of home plate! The Rangers' catcher, Ivan Rodriquez, made a good scoop and the crowd once again erupted as Nolan waved and shook his head in a way that said, "I can't believe I actually threw it in the dirt!" Obviously, the only person it bothered was Nolan.

On September 26, 1998, I worked with Nolan on the 17-year anniversary of his fifth no-hitter. That was the one that made him baseball's All-Time No-Hit King. His investment group had recently purchased the Jackson Generals of the AA Southern Association. His son, Reid, was named the club president. He told me they would be moving the team from Jackson, Mississippi, to Round Rock, Texas, for the 2000 season. Nolan is not only the consummate professional baseball player; he is the consummate businessman.

We presented an interesting piece of memorabilia during this show. It was a plaque containing a limited edition Nolan Ryan autographed baseball and a letter from Nolan. The ball was laser engraved with the name, date and team of each of his 5,714 strikeout victims. All of Nolan's proceeds from each plaque went directly to the Nolan Ryan Foundation to help build the Nolan Ryan Center on the campus of Alvin Community College in Nolan's hometown. The center is designed for continuing education. He told me he had attended this college when he was younger, and that he wanted to give back to the college as a way of saying thanks to the community. People who purchased our plaque had their names engraved on a special contributors' plaque at the center.

On this particular night, Nolan talked about the incredible 1998 baseball season at length. He singled out Cal Ripken, Jr., Sammy Sosa and Mark McGwire for what they had done for the game. He was thrilled that people who normally didn't follow baseball were rushing to open up the sports section of their newspapers every morning. Nolan actually pitched to all three of these guys, as well as the incomparable Roger Maris. All four of these great ballplayers are on Nolan's lifetime list of strikeout victims, but Nolan says that McGwire and Sosa have improved tremendously over the years. "They both used to be very impatient at the plate," he said. He added that Sosa had become a tremendous "bad ball hitter."

Over the years, I have discovered that the greatest athletes of all time, the ones whom I believe truly deserve to be called "legends," are also some of the nicest people I have met. Nolan Ryan is an example of a tremendous athlete who has nothing to prove to anyone except himself. Every time I interview him, he offers fresh insights and engaging conversation. Whether the topic is baseball, business or life in general, he is a man of strong opinions and bedrock values. I believe that he looks back on his baseball career with great satisfaction and absolutely no regrets.

When I look at Nolan Ryan's records, I am struck by the fact that in many categories he is light years ahead of the number two person on the list. For example, his 5,714 strike-outs total 1,578 more than Steve Carlton's career 4,136 strikeouts. Carlton is number two on the all-time strikeout list. Ryan's total went 38 percent beyond what had ever been accomplished before. Sandy Koufax is number two on the all time no-hit list with four. Ryan's 7 represent a 75 percent increase over what anybody else had achieved. He registered over 300 strikeouts in 6 different seasons. Sandy Koufax is also second to Nolan in that department, having done in it in only three seasons.

Only a handful of pitchers have been able to continue pitching at a high level past the age of 35. Phil Niekro pitched until the age of 48; however, as I mentioned earlier, he relied on "junk" pitches. Hoyt Wilhelm and Gaylord Perry also come to mind as junk-ball pitchers who still took the mound well into their forties. Nolan Ryan, however, is the only pitcher whose legendary fastball kept smokin' until his retirement in 1994, at the age of 46.

How do I sum up my impressions of Lynn Nolan Ryan? Everyone can see that he was a fiery competitor on the baseball field, but I have had the privilege to know him as a country gentleman and a dedicated professional whose personal priorities are in the right place. He's a hardworking man who never looks back. His accomplishments and his attitudes are first-class all the way. As I have studied the list of the greatest pitchers of all time, I have come to the conclusion that Nolan Ryan truly belongs in a class all his own.

Chapter 19

The Atlanta Centennial Olympic Games

Once every four years has never been enough for me. I absolutely love watching the Summer Olympic Games. I remember watching practically every televised event from Mexico City in 1968. I can still see Bob Beamon leaping for joy after shattering the world record in the long jump. I'll never forget John Carlos and Tommy "Jet" Smith raising clenched fists during the playing of the National Anthem when they received their gold medals for winning the 4 x 100 meter relay event. And who could ever forget watching "Big George" Foreman wave a tiny American flag around the ring after swinging his way to Olympic gold? There is no better form of live, human drama than the Summer Olympic Games.

Over the years, I have watched the likes of Olga Korbut, Nadia Comaneci, Mark Spitz, Sugar Ray Leonard, Mary Lou Retton, Greg Louganis and Carl Lewis, just to name a few. These athletes pushed their minds, bodies and spirits to amazing heights while the whole world looked on! The Games are as good as it gets, and one of my lifelong goals had always been to attend the Summer Olympic Games in person.

My goal was realized in 1996. Early in the year, I began to hear rumors that *QVC Sports* might be traveling to Atlanta, Georgia, for the Atlanta Centennial Olympic Games. I tried to keep my hopes in check. Around late March, it looked as if we would produce a show from Atlanta covering the opening of Coca-Cola Olympic City in May. This was a big step in the right direction. While it wasn't actually being at the Games, I knew that if things went well, the United States Olympic Committee might be willing to pursue more with QVC. We had offered official Summer Olympic Games merchandise during the countdown to the Games. We presented shows 500 and 100 days before the Atlanta Centennial Olympic Games. Although the excitement level for these shows seemed low, I knew America's interest would grow into a frenzy once summer arrived.

Suzanne Runyan and I were selected to travel to Atlanta to host the show for the opening of Coca-Cola Olympic City. While we were excited about the show, we were even more excited about the possibility of being in Atlanta during the Games in July and August. Not only were these the Summer Olympic Games, but they marked the one hundredth anniversary of the modern Olympic Games, and they were taking place on American soil. What's more, they were the last Summer Olympic Games of the century!

I'll never forget the weekend of May 25, 1996, as long as I live. It had been a very difficult spring for me personally. My father had been battling cancer and Alzheimer's disease since the previous October. I had traveled to South Haven, Michigan, to be with him several times that spring. As I flew to Atlanta, I was praying that I would be able to see him one more time. Since I was scheduled to host a show from Michael Jordan's restaurant in Chicago during the first week in June, I was hoping I could get up to South Haven for a final visit.

When I checked into the hotel in Atlanta, there was a message waiting for me at the front desk. It was from my sister. She wanted me to call right away. I remember running with my luggage trying to get to my room as fast as I could, because I knew it was about Dad.

My sister, Margie Lou, lives just outside of Milwaukee, Wisconsin. She is the calm one in the family and usually handles crises well. Margie told me Dad had taken a turn for the worse and probably wouldn't make it through the weekend. I remember how helpless I felt as I hung up the phone. There I was in Atlanta for our first Olympic Games remote, but all I wanted was to be in South Haven, Michigan, with my dad. I called his wife, Sally. She told me that he had experienced an episode the night before as they were trying to celebrate their anniversary. It seemed like he was getting ready to go, but it was impossible to predict when it would happen.

It never ceases to amaze me how God uses people to help ease our burdens. One of my closest friends is a guy named Brian Roland. Brian and I met in the fall of 1973, in Springfield, Missouri. I was a freshman at Evangel College in Springfield, and Brian was working as an insurance salesman in town. In fact, he sold me a life insurance policy. (It was a whole-life policy that I canceled after graduation when I learned about term insurance. I'm still upset that I let him talk me into it. By the way, he no longer sells insurance.) Our moms had been best friends during the forties and fifties in Cleveland, Ohio. How's that for a coincidence? Brian was working for the Discovery Channel and the Learning Channel at the time. He had been traveling around the world setting up new network operations but "just happened" to be in Atlanta on this particular weekend.

Brian and I went out to dinner that evening. He had lost his father when he was in college. It was a great blessing to me to have such a close friend around at this difficult time. I didn't tell anyone on the QVC crew about my dad, because I didn't want to bring their spirits down. Having a lifelong friend to confide in really helped me make it through the weekend. Brian and I sat in an Italian restaurant in Atlanta that night and talked about our dads for several hours.

The next day QVC produced a two-hour show from Coca-Cola Olympic City. It was an exciting location to work in. Coca-Cola did a superb job of recreating the Olympic experience for the fans. They had a high jump bar that stood as high as the world record, which is well over 7 1/2 feet. When I stood underneath it, I was awed that anyone could defy gravity to such an incredible extent. Bob Beamon's long jump record was marked off on the floor. When I looked at it, I realized he didn't jump in that Mexico City air, he flew! At each location, they showed video footage of the record-breaking event. They even had a mini-track set up for kids to run and jump on. There was a basketball court where you could go one-on-one with Olympian Grant Hill through the magic of interactive video. That same technology allowed fans to climb onto the balance beam with Olympic gold medalist Shannon Miller. My favorite attraction was the 40-yard dash where you raced against seven other fans and world-class sprinter Jackie Joyner-Kersee. One wall was a huge video screen. Jackie ran along on video as if she were in the race. I didn't beat Jackie, but I won my heat. However, I pulled a muscle in my neck doing it. When you're my age, you really shouldn't sprint unless you have stretched out for a minimum of an hour!

The show was a huge success. Suzanne and I had a lot of fun, and everyone—including our producer, Jim Breslin, and QVC's merchandiser for the Atlanta Centennial Olympic Games, Karen Fonner—seemed pleased. My buddy, Brian, was there for the entire show. He definitely helped to keep my spirits up. After the show, I hurried back to the hotel and called Sally. She told me QVC was on the television set in Dad's room all afternoon, so it was like I was there with him. She said he heard my voice and knew it was me.

The next morning while flying back to Philadelphia, I had the distinct feeling that my dad had moved on to his heavenly home. When I arrived at QVC's headquarters, I called my house. "You need to come home right away," Beth said.

"He's gone, isn't he?" I answered. She didn't respond.

My family and I left for Michigan the next morning. I kept wondering if I had done the right thing by staying in Atlanta. You always ask yourself if you did enough. Was I a good enough son? Did he know how much I loved him? I know deep down in my heart that the answer to both of those questions is yes.

My dad and I didn't have the ideal relationship when I was growing up. My parents were divorced when I was 11. I lived with my mom and two of my three sisters. Margie Lou was married by the time they were divorced. My mom is an amazing woman. She went back to school and earned her associates degree shortly after Dad left. She also worked a full-time job. After the divorce, my dad and I spent very little time together. In fact, from the time I was 11 until I was 32, he and I were never together without other people around. One day when I was visiting him in South Haven, Dad, Beth and I were walking on the beach. Beth knew I needed to spend some time alone with him, so she suddenly announced that she was going to run back to the house to use the bathroom. He was stuck. He had to face me now. We ended up walking for miles. When we finally came back to the house, the sun had set over Lake Michigan. It was one of the best days of my life. My dad and I really talked to each other for the first time in 21 years. He finally realized that I wasn't going to judge him for anything he had done. I just wanted to be his friend. From that day on, my dad and I were best friends.

I went to visit him as often as I could, even after I moved to Pennsylvania. We spent many long days together and got to know each other well. Since I have three sisters and no brothers, I realized that all of my life I had this need to spend some quality time with my dad. As a kid, whenever I would visit him at his dentist's office, he would slip me a couple of bucks and say something like, "Here, go buy some baseball cards." I never wanted his money. I wanted his time. Time is the best present any parent can give to a child. It is also the best gift a child can give back to his or her parents as they grow older. Too often people learn this lesson when it's too late. Harry Chapin's song, *The Cat's in the Cradle,* really hits the nail on the head.

When we first arrived in Michigan to make preparations for my dad's funeral, we spent a lot of time looking at old photographs. We put together two montages on poster boards that were placed on easels by his casket at the funeral home for the viewing.

Hundreds of people came to pay their respects. They all enjoyed seeing some of the highlights of Dad's life in pictures. A picture of someone you love is worth more than gold. It's something you're always glad you have.

Once again, I believe that the Lord helped to ease my loss by bringing good friends from my past back into my life when I needed them the most. Several of my best friends came to South Haven to offer their condolences. Mark Schnese, one of my very best friends since childhood, came to the wake with his lovely wife, Marcia and his father, Frank. I was the best man in Mark and Marcia's wedding in 1973. I also had a crush on Marcia in the ninth grade. Since we attended different junior high schools, we sent messages to each other through our French teacher, Miss Drayton, who taught at both schools. We had a great time reminiscing. I have probably seen the Schneses fewer than 10 times over the past 20 years, but I still count them among my dearest friends.

Another great friend of mine is Dr. John Cooke, who now resides in Eustis Springs, Florida. John and I were involved in Bible quizzing through the Youth for Christ organization when we were in junior high and high school. He "just happened" to be visiting his mom in Berrien Springs, Michigan, when he read about my dad in the local paper. He called immediately and asked if he could bring his wife and kids over to visit the night before the wake. We had a wonderful reunion—in spite of the fact that our families got involved in a soccer game, and yours truly went to the emergency room with a sprained ankle. I was slated to be a pallbearer at Dad's funeral, and I was concerned that with the injury I would not be able help carry the casket. But God is good: I was able to attend the wake and fulfill my obligation as a pallbearer without the use of crutches.

The funeral was really a celebration of Dad's life. I delivered a eulogy and made it to the final paragraph before the tears started to well up in my eyes. I talked about how when I was a young child, he used to take me hunting. If we were separated in the woods, he would let me know where he was by whistling like a bobwhite bird. Later, I always knew he was in the gym when I was playing in a high school basketball game, because I could hear his whistle through the noise of the crowd. I closed the eulogy by reciting a poem that he gave to me when I was 11. It's entitled "If" by Rudyard Kipling. I concluded by saying, "I can still hear you whistling, Dad, and I know where you are. I'll keep following the sound until I am out of the woods of this life and with you in heaven."

At the gravesite, one of my father's friends spoke. Near the end of his eulogy he looked at me and said, "Danny, you were the apple of his eye. He was always talking about you. If there was a television set anywhere in sight, he would try to tune it to QVC hoping to catch a glimpse of his son.

You made him very proud." I guess I heard that day what every son hopes to hear.

In a way, getting back to work was therapeutic for me. The summer of '96 was extremely busy. It looked as if we would be going back to Atlanta for several shows during the Centennial Olympic Games. Plans were coming together, and I was really looking forward to being where the world gathered.

But then our family had another scare.

One morning around the Fourth of July, I received a call at 6 A.M. from my sister, Margie Lou. She was concerned about my mom, who had called her a few minutes earlier. Mom rarely cries, so when Margie told me she was crying from a pain in her back, I became alarmed. I phoned her immediately. She was in so much pain she could barely speak. When I heard her crying, I knew something was terribly wrong. I told her I wanted her to get to the hospital right away. She was living with her sister, Betty, at the time. They were caring for their mother, who was 92 years old. I told Mom to give the phone to Betty. When Betty answered, I told her to call her son Rocky and have him take Mom to the hospital right away. Rocky called me about an hour later from the hospital. The doctors already had her in the operating room and were performing angioplasty to clear some badly clogged arteries. They had determined that she had suffered a severe heart attack. I begged the Lord not to take her. Losing my dad was enough for one summer. I don't think I could have handled losing them both.

Mom has had three angioplasty procedures since that time. She now appears to have fully recovered and looks great at 78 years of age. I remember watching her exercise along with Jack LaLanne on his television shows. This was back in the early sixties before fitness became popular. She has always had more energy than anyone I know.

Marjorie Wheeler believes in prayer. She has always prayed daily for her children. I'm convinced that her prayers have kept me safe. She had pictures of all four of her children on the walls of her laundry room. Every day as she would iron and fold clothes, she remembered each of us in prayer. My sisters and I have gained a great deal of strength from those prayers. Parents should never stop praying for their kids even after they grow up, move away and raise their own families. I can't imagine where I would be today if it weren't for those laundry room prayers. I know they are a big reason that I have been blessed with an exciting job that affords me so many great opportunities—like being in Atlanta for the Olympic Games!

The big day finally arrived. Suzanne Runyan and I boarded a plane to Atlanta along with several QVC production people. We arrived early in the afternoon the day before the opening ceremonies. We wanted to get down to the heart of the city on the last day before the Games began. Centennial Park was where all the action was. Since our hotel was located about seven miles north of the city, we hopped a cab. Before long we were where the world wanted to be. First we toured the CNN Studios, which are located in the Omni Hotel. Some QVC viewers even came up and welcomed us to Atlanta while we were waiting for the tour to begin. What a wonderful way to start the afternoon!

After the tour, a lady on the street suddenly came up to us and asked if we would like to watch the U.S. Women's Gymnastics team go through their final public workout. Suzanne and I looked at each other and then asked how much she wanted for the tickets.

"Nothing," she responded. "We can't stay so you might as well use them."

"Are you sure?" I asked.

"Absolutely," she said. "Here they are. Have a great time!"

We couldn't believe she would just give us the tickets, knowing they were worth $22 apiece. We took off running like two kids on their way to Disney World for the first time. The funny thing was, we didn't know where we were going ... but it didn't take us long to find out we needed to go to the Pavilion, and soon we were sitting in this massive complex cheering the U.S. women gymnasts on. We didn't exactly have front-row seats, but we were thrilled to be there anyway. Neither of us had ever attended an Olympic event in person, so this was a treat. The U.S. women put on a phenomenal performance that evening, and everyone there thought Olympic gold would soon be hanging around their necks.

When it comes to television production, QVC's producers, directors and crew members are all gold medalists. We had an excellent location for our two-hour opening ceremonies show. In fact, we were just down the street from Olympic Stadium where the ceremonies took place. Throughout our show, the streets were filled with a variety of people from around the world—what a colorful sight! Suzanne filed some terrific reports that captured the excitement in the streets.

One of the reasons that I have been bragging about our production staff is that they landed this location literally weeks before the start of the Summer Games. Since every television station and network in the world was trying to find a location, it seemed like an impossible task. It usually takes several months of advance work even to think about broadcasting from an Olympic site, but our QVC Team doesn't believe in the word "can't." The show looked great, and we had an overwhelming response from our viewers. QVC's Olympic coverage was off and running at a record pace!

Shortly after the end of the show, Suzanne and I made our way down the street toward the stadium for our chance of a lifetime—being present on opening night of the

Olympic Games. Even though we didn't have tickets for the ceremonies (they were running around $650 apiece), we decided we wanted to hang out with the crowd in the streets and cheer the torchbearer on.

There was plenty of entertainment in the streets. Preachers, singers, actors and, of course, the street vendors were enjoying this very large, receptive audience. We stood among the crowd for hours in that July Atlanta heat. After 2 1/2 hours, somebody in the crowd said they had changed the route! Thousands of people moved from the main street to a side street within a couple of minutes! People were pushing and shoving trying to jockey for position.

This type of a situation can easily lead to crowd panic, and a few times over the course of the Olympic Games, we were suddenly caught in the middle of such a large crowd that it was difficult to move or breathe. It's very frightening to be trapped in the middle of thousands of people.

One night, after a group called Little Feat performed in Centennial Olympic Park, Karen Fonner, Jim Breslin and I became trapped in the crush of the multitude. It came to the point where no one could move even an inch in any direction. People started pushing and shoving, and parents with little children lifted them up on their shoulders so they could breathe. It was terrifying. Karen Fonner was getting extremely claustrophobic and said she had to get out of there immediately. Jim and I looked at each other and then asked, "Where would you like us to go?" Somehow we eventually managed to jump over a gate and take refuge by a tiny snack stand. After about a half-hour, we finally slipped safely out through an alley and onto a side street.

At one point, I really thought somebody was going to get killed. Thank the Lord, there were no fatalities, but there were some injuries. After that experience, I'll always be extremely cautious if I ever see a major crowd forming. It is best to stay in the open spaces on the outskirts.

On opening night, Suzanne and I spent three hours waiting in one huge crowd for the historic Olympic torch to pass by and enter the stadium. After the torch passed, we headed over to Centennial Park where Coca-Cola had set up a giant television screen carrying the coverage from the stadium. I'll never forget watching on the big screen as the torch was carried the final leg to light the Olympic Flame. The torchbearer was Muhammad Ali! The producers of the opening ceremonies managed to keep his identity a secret throughout the weeks leading up to the event. His appearance started things off on a high note, and set the tone for the two weeks that followed.

You could feel the electricity in the air just walking through the city! It seemed like every restaurant in the area had tents set up in the streets with all kinds of food, beverages and entertainment. You knew you were where it was all happening.

"The Macarena" was the big song and dance craze at the time. Suzanne and I learned how to do the moves when we stopped for some barbecued ribs at a tent near Centennial Park. They were playing great music, and everyone was dancing. We enjoyed our ribs and then decided to join the celebration. By the end of the night we had the "Macarena" down. We had a blast dancing, but when our feet began to ache, we decided to start looking for a cab. We had no idea what a difficult task this would be! I am surprised that not one of the major networks covered the cab-hailing competition that happened in Atlanta during the Summer Olympic Games. It took place every night in the downtown area. The fight for a limited number of cabs was fierce. Suzanne and I eventually became "gold medalists" in this event, but that first night we searched for over an hour until we finally flagged one down.

As we were checking out of our hotel the next morning, we ran into QVC host Dan Hughes as he was checking in. Each weekday morning during the *QVC Morning Show*, Dan presented a different Olympic Games t-shirt from Coca Cola Olympic City. This allowed our viewers to enjoy a little bit of the Olympic atmosphere every day. Suzanne and I flew back to Philadelphia and hosted various shows at QVC during the week. I came back on Thursday and did the Friday morning t-shirt presentation on the *Morning Show,* and then I stayed to host the weekend Olympic shows. Dan and I had a running joke: as one would take the other's place in the hotel, the other would remind him to keep the room clean. As one Dan left, another Dan arrived.

The Friday afternoon following the first week of competition, Karen Fonner, QVC's talented buyer for the Atlanta Centennial Olympic Games merchandise, and I visited Centennial Park. We decided to take in the spirit of the games now that the events were in progress. We toured the Nike display (which was like an entire village in itself), then we sampled some Atlanta cuisine and strolled around the park. Centennial Park was built by the city of Atlanta to serve as the central gathering place for the visitors to the Games, and there was always a lot of activity. A tent for trading commemorative pins, fountains that formed the five Olympic rings, broadcast locations, the Swatch building and various entertainment stages were just a few of the attractions located in and around the park. Sometime around mid-afternoon, Karen and I stopped and sat down on a short wall located by the sound booth for the main entertainment stage. We sat there for about 20 minutes and did some serious people watching. This is a wonderful pastime at the Summer Olympic Games because you get the opportunity to watch people from all over the world.

Later that afternoon, we decided to attend the track and field competition, perhaps our only chance to see Michael Johnson run. It was also the last competition for the legendary Carl Lewis. The weather conditions were perfect, so we were looking forward to a great day of sports—but when we arrived at the stadium, we saw the biggest crowd of people yet. It took us 45 minutes just to get inside because of the thorough security checks being performed on every person entering the venue. Although it was time-consuming, I was glad they were doing it. None of us wanted to witness a tragedy in Atlanta like the 1972 Summer Olympic Games in Munich, when several Israeli athletes were killed.

Once inside, we found the events exhilarating. The competition was intense. It was a rare opportunity to watch the fastest men and women in the world go toe-to-toe. Gail Devers, Donovan Bailey and Michael Johnson, in his golden shoes, all sprinted to victory in their individual heats that night.

We decided to leave the stadium around 9:45 P.M., since we were scheduled to produce a big three-hour show beginning at 10:00 A.M. the next morning. We walked for a mile or two before we finally caught a cab in downtown Atlanta, not far from Centennial Park. We arrived at our hotel around 11:00 P.M. I went straight to my room and fell fast asleep. I had asked the front desk to give me a wake-up call at 6:00 A.M., since I needed to be on location by 7:30 A.M. In the middle of the night, my phone rang. Whenever this happens, my body and my pulse shoot straight up. I always figure something terrible has happened when I get a call in the wee hours of the morning. I glanced at my clock. It was 1:30 A.M. When I picked up the phone, I recognized the voice of Jim Breslin, our producer. He asked if I had heard about the bomb.

I said, "Are you joking? What bomb?"

He then broke the news to me that a bomb had exploded earlier that evening in Centennial Park. Several people were injured and at least two people were dead. I turned on my television set and was horrified as I watched the news coverage of the blast. They showed footage of the rock group, Jack Mack and the Heart Attack, playing on the main stage when the explosion interrupted their performance. They then showed people screaming and running frantically around Centennial Park. Total panic had set in. I couldn't believe anyone would commit such a terrible crime in a location where so many innocent people were gathered in the spirit of world unity and good will.

Several QVC personnel gathered in Jim Breslin's room to watch the news. Suddenly it dawned on Karen and me that, earlier that day, we had been sitting right next to the audio booth where the bomb exploded! That really hit home. During the night, it was decided that we should cancel our show the next morning. It would have been inappropriate for us to produce a show offering Olympic merchandise in the midst of this tragedy. Our location at Coca-Cola Olympic City was directly behind the area where the bomb was detonated. In fact, the federal authorities closed down Centennial Park for several days as they investigated and gathered evidence.

Robb Cadigan, QVC's Executive Vice President of Programming and Broadcasting, gave us the directive to stay in Atlanta until they determined when or if we would make up the canceled show. We decided that we would attend some of the events, so we purchased some fairly affordable tickets for women's basketball that afternoon. A group of six of us caught the transit system to the gym where the competition was held. Security was at an all-time high. Everywhere we went we saw local and federal law enforcement agents as well as members of the National Guard. It took about an hour for us to get inside the gym as every person was searched from head to toe. All bags, purses and brief cases were opened and thoroughly searched. It was good to know they were taking every precaution to prevent another tragedy from taking place. Many times when something like this happens, other "copycat" crimes take place. In fact, as we were leaving the competition later that evening, everyone was being evacuated from an area where someone had sandwiched a duffel bag in between two trash cans. The duffel bag was similar to the one that had contained the Centennial Park bomb. Things like this are hard to understand. I guess some people enjoy the feeling of power that comes with inflicting panic on thousands of people.

How sad it was that a few sick people were able to strike such fear into the hearts of so many! I was very impressed with the actions of the Olympic officials and the fans who were determined to go on with the Atlanta Centennial Olympic Games. It seemed as if the majority of the people were saying, "We will not let these foolish actions destroy the Summer Games. They will go on." It may sound melodramatic, but we all felt proud to be involved in the triumph of the human spirit. I have to admit, though, we couldn't help glancing over our shoulders every once in a while that day in Atlanta.

Centennial Park reopened on Wednesday of the following week, and we produced our make-up show on Thursday evening. Several of us visited Centennial Park the day it reopened and saw the special memorial of flowers, cards and pictures that had been erected in the spot where the bombing had occurred. Millions of people stopped by to pay their respects to the two individuals who lost their lives as a result of this tragedy. As I stopped in front of the memorial, I thought about the fact that I had been in this same spot literally hours before the explosion occurred. You always wonder why you were spared when someone else suffers. My heart still goes out to the families of the victims. In retrospect, I believe this tragedy served to solidify Americans in their support of the Summer Olympic Games.

There was a tremendous response to our Thursday evening show. QVC's viewers knew that a portion of the proceeds from all of our sales of Olympic merchandise helped to support America's athletes and the Games. Many of the items we presented completely sold out of our inventory.

After the show, Suzanne and I attended the women's volleyball matches. It was such a treat to watch the very best players in the world compete on the court. They made it look effortless as they fired jump serves over the net and hammered spikes straight down. It was even more exciting to watch a player dig up one of those spikes with a "pancake." (I just couldn't resist using some cool volleyball lingo for the benefit of volleyball aficionados.)

The next morning, I had the joy of rising at 4:45 A.M., in order to be on location at Coca-Cola Olympic City by 6:00 A.M. We went live at 8:00 A.M. with the Olympic t-shirt of the day during the *QVC Morning Show.* The presentation went extremely well. While I was doing our show on one side of the track, Scottie Pippen of the U.S. Men's Basketball Team was being interviewed on the other side. I wanted to say "hello" since he had been my guest on QVC on a couple of occasions. When I was finished, however, I looked over and Scottie and the crew were gone.

After the show, I was interviewed on a radio program that was beamed live to Johannesburg, South Africa. It's quite amazing to think you can talk directly to people on the other side of the planet. The gentleman who interviewed me seemed genuinely interested in QVC and the entire concept of electronic retailing.

We hosted our final Atlanta Centennial Olympic Games show just before the closing ceremonies, and it was the best one of them all. Everyone seemed anxious to have a memory from the One Hundredth Anniversary Games of the Modern Olympics, the last Summer Olympic Games of the

century and the last to be held in America during the twenti-
eth century. After the show, we just had to hang out and celebrate the conclusion of two wonderful weeks of Olympic
competition. People from all over the world were celebrating
and dancing the "Macarena." It seemed like they weren't
ready for the Games to be over.

But finally, it was time for the last heat of the cab-
hailing competition. As I rode through downtown Atlanta on
the way back to my hotel, I couldn't help but think again
about how fortunate I am to have a job that gives me so
many exciting opportunities. It seems like I am always
where the rest of the world (or at least all of my friends)
wants to be. It's not unusual for me to look out my hotel window and see the Goodyear blimp floating by. There's no
doubt about it, being a member of the *QVC Sports* team is a
golden opportunity.

The summer of '96 is one that I will always remember. It was filled with every human emotion. I said goodbye
to my dad as he left this earth and moved on to his heavenly
home. I almost lost my mom to a heart attack, but I watched
her pull through instead. And I watched Americans pull
together to overcome a horrible tragedy in Atlanta. Now, my
Olympic memories are not just those that I have seen on television, but also the ones that I've witnessed in person.

I'll never forget watching Michael Johnson become
the first Olympic athlete to win gold medals in both the 200
and 400 meter events. I'll never forget watching Carl Lewis
win the gold medal in his final Olympic long jump competition. I'll never forget the sick feeling I had as I watched the
news coverage of the bombing in Centennial Olympic Park—
or the pride I felt when I watched Kerri Strug's courageous
vault on a severely sprained ankle to win gold for the U.S.
Women's Gymnastics team. It is all permanently etched in my
mind. Most of all, I'll never forget being in Atlanta to witness

the thrill of victory and the agony of defeat in the actual gyms and stadiums where they occurred.

There is no better stage for human drama than the Summer Olympic Games. While it's great to watch them on television, it's even better watching them from the best seat in the house.

Chapter 20

Emmitt Smith

I stood as straight as I could, then stretched as high as I could. My dad made sure my feet were flat on the floor. He then made the mark on the wall. I turned around, looked and shouted, "Yes! I'm growing!" That little area of wall in our basement on Kingsley Street in St. Joe was filled with lines and dates. I think I made my dad measure me about every other week when I was in grade school.

"The Shortest Kid in the Class" is a distinction I carried until I was in the seventh grade. I mean even the girls were taller than I was. I can still remember how I would get psyched up when they measured us at school. Every time they did it, I was filled with new hope. "Maybe today will be my day," I thought. Just once I wanted to be either taller or heavier than somebody, *anybody* else in my class.

It had been this way for me since I was born. I arrived two weeks early and tipped the scales at five pounds and twelve ounces. My mom said my grandpa told her I was too small and that she should "throw me back." Obviously, grandpa was a fisherman. Mom said I was so tiny that for the first couple weeks of my life they used a man's handkerchief for my diaper.

Little guys learn to be pretty aggressive. That was my approach. I remember lifting weights and standing in front of the mirror for hours flexing my muscles. My dad made me a barbell out of an iron pole and two coffee cans filled with cement. I even had pulleys in my basement that were connected to paint cans filled with cement. We did things in a cost-effective way back then. I used to spend hours down in the makeshift workout room in my basement.

Since I loved sports so much, I learned how to use my quickness and speed to my advantage. Since I didn't have a lot of size and power, this was my only available strategy. Remember I talked about how hard I practiced basketball to disprove the people who said I was too small to make the varsity team? It's all part of the reason I always pull for the little guy. The biblical story of David taking down Goliath is obviously one of my favorites.

I eventually grew to 5' 8". That's not very big, and by NFL standards it is minuscule, if not microscopic. I think that's why I am so impressed with Emmitt Smith. When I stand and talk to Emmitt, we see eye to eye. The big difference is the extra 40 pounds of muscle that Emmitt carries in his arms and legs. He is as strong as an ox. Whenever I see him block those 300-pound-plus linemen in the NFL, I wonder where he gets the courage.

I was very surprised to discover that Emmitt never went through the rituals that I did on school weigh-in and measurement days. He was always very *big* for his age. In fact, the entire time he played youth football, his weight was an issue. Before one game, the coach of the opposing team made him strip down and stand on a scale to make sure he didn't exceed the weight limit for the league. From age 11 on, he played mostly with older kids because he exceeded the weight limit for his age group. That might be one of the reasons why he developed into such an outstanding athlete. When you play against better competition you always get better yourself.

Emmitt grew up in a hotbed of football talent. Florida is well known for turning out football superstars. Guys like Jack Youngblood, Deacon Jones and Deion Sanders, to name just a few, all played high school football in Florida. The Gators and the Seminoles are perennial powerhouses in the major college football arena. Yet, in his four years at Escambia High School, Emmitt was as good a running back as had ever come out of that state. His statistics are mind-boggling. He ran for 8,804 yards, scored 106 touchdowns, gained more than 100 yards in 45 of the 49 games he played, and averaged a superhuman 7.8 yards per carry! But one of the things that makes Emmitt the most proud is that he helped a team, which was 1-9 the year before he arrived, win two state championships.

Emmitt was named the *Parade* Magazine High School Player of the Year following his senior year in high school. Every major college football program came after him. He finally decided on the Florida Gators. Although he didn't start his first two games as a freshman, he still passed the 1,000-yard rushing mark faster than any running back in the history of NCAA football. He ended up leading the SEC with 1,341 yards, 8 100-yard games and an impressive 5.9 yards per carry average his first year.

His sophomore year, however, was a different story. A new offensive coordinator came in, and he stressed the passing game. In the sixth game of the season, Emmitt stretched a ligament in his knee and had to sit out for four weeks. He finished the year with 988 yards, making this the first season dating back to his freshman year in high school that he missed 1,000 yards. Emmitt's junior year was his finest statistically, as he scorched defenses for 1,599 yards, leading the SEC and setting a new Florida record. He rushed for more than 100 yards in 9 of 11 games. His rushing average per carry was 5.6 yards.

In April of 1990, the NFL opened its draft to college juniors for the first time. Florida lost its head coach that same year. Emmitt made the tough choice to leave Florida early and enter the draft. In just 3 seasons, he had established 58 school records. He was the Dallas Cowboys' 17th pick in the first round.

In the fall of 1990, the Cowboys were coming off two horrendous seasons. Their records were 3-13 and 1-15 respectively. Head coach Jimmy Johnson was determined to turn things around, and Emmitt would play an important role in that turnaround. The Cowboys finished with a 7-9 record. Jimmy Johnson was named the NFL Coach of the Year, and Emmitt was named the NFL Rookie of the Year with 937 yards rushing.

One of the things that I discovered about Emmitt the first time I worked with him is that he is extremely goal-oriented. Before every season, he writes down his goals for the year. He looks at his list throughout the season to see how he's doing. Before his rookie campaign, his career goals were

- to be named the Rookie of the Year,
- to lead the NFL in rushing,
- to win the NFL MVP Award and
- to help the Dallas Cowboys win the Super Bowl.

The NFL Rookie of the Year Award was the first of all of his goals to be met. In his second season, at the age of 22, he won his first rushing title with 1,563 yards in the regular season. The Cowboys improved to 11-5 that year and made it to their second game in the playoffs. In just two seasons, Emmitt had already accomplished two of his four original goals.

Emmitt's third year in the NFL brought his second rushing title in a row, as he rushed for over 1,700 yards. His team went on to win the Super Bowl Championship—another goal met.

Year number four in the NFL was probably the sweetest of all for Emmitt. After sitting out the first two weeks of the season due to a contract dispute, Emmitt came back in a big, BIG way. The Cowboys had lost their first two games without him. When Jerry Jones finally came up with a reasonable offer, Mr. Smith came back to lead the 'Boyz to a second straight Super Bowl win. Emmitt captured his third straight rushing title and was named the NFL MVP as well as the Super Bowl MVP. He had accomplished all of his original goals and even added a Super Bowl MVP Award on top of it!

The first time I worked with Emmitt on QVC was February 21, 1995. The San Francisco 49'ers had won Super Bowl XXIX a month earlier. Emmitt had had another awesome year in the NFL, scoring a league high and team record 22 touchdowns. He rushed for 1,484 yards, marking his fourth straight year with over 1,400 yards rushing.

When I first met Emmitt, I was surprised at his size. It is rare for me to be almost as tall as any athlete, let alone a superstar in the NFL. Emmitt is only slightly taller than I am, but his arms and thighs are much larger. Emmitt recalled that as a child, he was bigger than everyone else his age, but by the time he got to high school he had stopped growing, and the other players caught up to him. After high school, many of his critics said he was too small to play football at a major college. After rewriting the record books at Florida, he heard people saying he was too small and too slow to play in the NFL. He told me that while he never had recorded a sizzling time in the 40-yard dash, he had rarely been caught from behind. He always seemed to get into the end zone from 40, 50, 60 or more yards out, so what difference would it make if he got there a tenth of a second faster?

Emmitt is one of those athletes who is actually faster carrying a football with people chasing him than he is just running against a stopwatch. After five outstanding seasons in the NFL, people were no longer saying that he was too small or too slow.

But Emmitt felt like he had to keep proving himself. The contract negotiations with Jerry Jones before the '93 season were really tough on him personally. He recalled how Jones kept trying to low-ball him with the offers. When they finally came to terms, Jones acted like Emmitt had robbed him during the press conference. While it should have been a celebration, Emmitt told me Jones acted like it was a funeral.

At one point during the early part of that season, Jones had made a statement to the press to the effect that Emmitt was a luxury—not a necessity—to the Dallas Cowboys. I remember thinking that this man had no appreciation for what his star running back had done for his organization. He was one of the key reasons why the Cowboys did a complete turnaround from their 1-15 record in 1989.

For a football hero, Emmitt is still a very kind man with a genuinely gentle spirit. For all of the accomplishments this man has in the world of sports, he has kept his ego in check. I have been around a lot of superstars, and I would have to say that Emmitt has a very small ego compared to most. You can talk to him like you would any ordinary person. He is very down-to-earth in that way.

The next time I saw Emmitt was on December 13, 1995. The Cowboys were having a great season and Emmitt was "on fire." I traveled to Irvine, Texas, where we did a live remote from the Cowboys' locker room. When Emmitt walked in, he was in high spirits and acted like he was genuinely happy to see me. You could feel the positive energy just emanating from this guy. We had a wonderful show that night.

The Cowboy cheerleaders were practicing on the field, so a bunch of the guys from the crew and I went down on the field after the show and had our pictures taken with them. Their director gave us videos and calendars. They were all extremely friendly; in fact, the entire organization was very accommodating to all of us from QVC.

The 1995 season was Emmitt's best yet. He set an NFL single-season record for rushing touchdowns and total touchdowns with 25. He was elected to his sixth consecutive Pro Bowl and became the only player in NFL history to rush for over 1,400 yards in 5 straight seasons! He led the NFL in rushing with 1,773, which remains his highest total to date. He was also the fastest ever to reach the 80 career touchdown mark. The Cowboys went on to win Super Bowl XXX in Tempe, Arizona, by defeating the Pittsburgh Steelers 27-17. This was their third Super Bowl victory in four years. It established the Cowboys as the football dynasty of the nineties.

We returned to Dallas the following year for another show with Emmitt on December 3, 1996. Our producer thought we should give this show a different look from the year before, so we did the show on the 50-yard line with a live audience. It sounded like a great idea, but Texas Stadium is open at the top, and in December it can get pretty cool in Dallas. On this particular evening, temperatures dropped into the forties. I had a light jacket on, but Emmitt was wearing only a dress shirt and a vest.

A member of our production team ran out to a nearby department store and bought a space heater, but it really didn't throw off much heat. Fortunately, we were offering an NFL winter jacket that night on the show, so we brought out one of the Cowboys samples for Emmitt to wear. By the end of the show, he was bundled up in the jacket and was wearing Cowboy winter gloves as well. We were both freezing, but I think Emmitt is so used to the warmer climates that he was extra cold. However, he was a real trouper and never complained during the entire two-hour show.

After he had such a spectacular year in 1995, some sports commentators referred to the '96 season as an "off year" for Emmitt. For anyone else, it would have been a *great* year—but the expectations for Mr. Smith run high. He finished up with over 1,200 yards rushing, which was his sixth straight season over 1,000 yards. I remember Emmitt talking about the roller-coaster ride of life in the NFL. He said the fans are great when everything is going your way, but when you get injured and you're going through a tough time, everybody starts saying your career is taking a downward turn.

When I asked him how he remained positive and focused through the tough times, he told me about his faith in the Lord. Emmitt was raised a Baptist in the deep South. As a child, he liked church mainly for the music and the clapping. As he has grown older he has become more aware of the Lord's presence in his life. He told me that he credits Jesus Christ with making his dreams come true. There is no doubt that Emmitt knows the truth behind Philippians 4:13 in the Bible: "I can do all things through Christ who strengthens me."

One of the biggest agents in all of sports is Leigh Steinberg. He threw a party the day before Super Bowl XXXII in San Diego. It took place at the San Diego Zoo. You talk about a bunch of party animals! It was a really nice get-together, and I ran into Emmitt and his girlfriend at the time, Patti. I had a nice talk with both of them that day. We talked about what is really important in life. Emmitt said to me, "You know there is a whole lot more to life than all of this. If I didn't know the Lord none of this would mean much." The '97 season had been a trying one for Emmitt, to say the least. He had to overcome several injuries but still ended up with over 1,000 yards rushing, for the seventh consecutive year. I told him I would be praying for him, and he told me he really appreciated it.

There were several NFL superstars at that party, including Warren Moon, Drew Bledsoe, Ricky Watters, Desmond Howard, Kordell Stewart, Emmitt and others. Emmitt probably maintained the lowest profile of all of them that day. You can tell that he doesn't have anything to prove to anybody, except himself. Nobody expects more from Emmitt Smith than Emmitt Smith. I was also very impressed with Patti, who seemed to have a good handle on her priorities in life. She told me she tries really hard to keep focused on things that have lasting value.

Emmitt's accomplishments on the football field qualify him as one of professional football's legends. He will retire among the top three rushers of all time. He will retire as the all-time leader in rushing touchdowns. He will be among the top three in most touchdowns scored in a career. He is a shoo-in for the football Hall of Fame in Canton, Ohio. He has overcome injuries and even played injured in several key games with great pain.

"Too short. Too small. Too slow." Emmitt has heard them all and he has proved them all wrong. You can measure a person's height and weight, and you can time their speed. But the one thing about an athlete that you can't gauge with a tape measure or a stopwatch is his heart. And in that category Emmitt Smith is a giant. Even in the NFL.

Chapter 21

Ernie Banks

The bell rang, and I shot for the door like a rocket slid on a rail. I used my best moves to get around the onslaught of kids in the hallway and out those big, heavy gray doors on the front of Jefferson Elementary School. I had important business to attend to. You see, I lived in St. Joseph, Michigan, in the days before satellite dishes, cable and Pay-Per-View TV. Fortunately, however, the powerful Chicago television transmitters pushed their broadcast signals all the way across Lake Michigan and into my home. My favorite station growing up was Channel 9, WGN-TV, the home of Chicago Cubs baseball.

On this particular day, the Cubs were playing the Pittsburgh Pirates. I would get to see all of my favorite players, including Roberto Clemente, Willie Stargell, "Sweet Swingin'" Billy Williams and best of all, Mr. Cub himself, Ernie Banks. When I came flying into our family room I went straight for the "on/off" switch (what did we do before remote controls?). As the image began to come into focus, I heard the familiar voice of Cubs announcer Jack Brickhouse say, "Here's the wind-up and the pitch ... There's a sharp drive to left, it's back, back, back and onto Waveland Avenue ... hey, hey Ernie! It's a homerun for Ernie Banks!"

What a combination! Jack Brickhouse and Ernie Banks brought me many an exciting afternoon of baseball from the friendly confines of Wrigley Field on Chicago's near north side. Of course, there were other great players on the Chicago Cubs in the mid-sixties to early seventies. The lineup included second baseman Glenn Beckert, shortstop Don Kessinger, third baseman Ron Santo, catcher Randy Hundley, outfielders Adolpho Phillips, Jim Hickman, Billy Williams and a tremendous pitching staff, including lefty Kenny Holzman, Ted Abernathy and Fergie Jenkins. But my favorite Cub will always be Ernie Banks.

I can still see Ernie at the plate. His trademark was the way he would move his fingers up and down the handle of the bat as if he were playing a flute. He had good rhythm, rocking his body back and forth until he would unleash that powerful swing. The ball would jump off his bat and head over those wonderful ivy vines on Wrigley's outfield walls. What a glorious sight!

I left St. Joseph, Michigan, in the fall of 1973 to begin my freshman year at Evangel College in Springfield, Missouri. While I enjoyed the five years I spent in Springfield, I really missed Cubs baseball. I attended Evangel College for four of those years and spent the fifth working as the sports anchor on KMTC-TV, the ABC affiliate in Springfield. However, in August of 1978, I took a job working in production at WCFC, TV-38 in Chicago. It was great to work in the windy city. The best part of all was catching the "El" train with some of my buddies up to Wrigley Field for an afternoon of Cubs baseball. We were part of the infamous "Bleacher Bums."

It was about this time that I met my wife, Beth. She was working for a relocation company in the Kemper Insurance Building, which was also known as the Civic Opera Building. The television station that I was working for had its studio on the 44th floor, which was the top floor of that building. We actually met riding the train on the way into work. The first day we met, I invited her to the third-floor cafeteria for a bite to eat. When we got through the line to the cashier, I reached into my pockets and discovered they were empty! She thought this was a ploy I had used many times before, but I was actually quite embarrassed! She paid for that first meal, but I made it up to her by taking her to some of Chicago's finest restaurants—whenever I could afford it, which was not often.

On one of those rare occasions, though, we met Ernie Banks! We were waiting for a table at a famous German restaurant. As I looked across the main dining area, I was surprised to see the man himself, Ernie Banks. I just had to go up and say hello and let him know what a huge fan I was. I waited for an opportune time and approached the table. I said, "Mr. Banks, I'm terribly sorry to interrupt you, but I just have to tell you what a huge fan of yours I am. I watched you play for years, and I just wanted to say thanks for all the great memories."

He smiled that familiar smile and said he was glad to meet me. He then surprised me by saying, "Why don't you and your lady friend sit down and join us for a while?" I couldn't believe it! We had a great time sitting and talking with Mr. Cub, Ernie Banks.

I remember Ernie Banks as always being the picture of optimism at a time when the Cubs were never in the pennant chase past July. Every year he would make little rhymes about the Cubs. He used to look into the camera and say, "The Cubs are alive in sixty-five!" or, "The Cubs are great in sixty-eighty" or "The Cubs will shine in sixty-nine!" He was also known for his saying, "What a great day for baseball, let's play two." I was thrilled to discover that he was just as nice in person as he had always seemed on TV.

Twelve years later, on June 21, 1992, I was honored to have Ernie as my guest on a baseball collectibles show on QVC. I remember all of the programs that day had a nostalgic theme, so I interviewed him on this set that looked like a typical malt shop from the early sixties. We had a great time talking baseball, and I shared the story of when I ran into him in that restaurant in Chicago. When I told him the name of the restaurant, he remembered meeting me.

One of our topics of discussion that day was free agency. Ernie said he really missed the way it was when he was playing ball. In those days, players often stayed with the same team for their entire careers. He said that he couldn't imagine ever playing for any team other than the Chicago Cubs. I can't imagine it either—it just wouldn't be right to see Ernie Banks in any other uniform. Even though the Cubs never won a pennant during his playing career, he was as loyal and optimistic as any baseball player ever was.

We reminisced about the good old days of Cubs baseball with Jack Brickhouse, Leo Durocher, Fergie Jenkins, Billy Williams, the ivy vines, the friendly confines and more. I felt like I was a kid again. In fact, I have to admit that there were times during that show when I got so lost in the conversation that I was oblivious to the fact that we were on TV.

After the show, Ernie and I hung out in the green room for about another hour, just reminiscing about Chicago. At one point, he asked me if I enjoyed golf. I said that I did but that I wasn't a very skilled golfer. He then asked me if I wanted to golf with him and Mike Schmidt the next day. When I asked him what kind of a golfer Schmidt was, Ernie said Schmidt could hit a 2-iron about 260 yards straight down the fairway. I said, "Ernie, thanks for the invitation, but I'm afraid I would just slow you guys down!" When he told me the course they were playing, I figured it was a little out of my price range and skill range—it was one of the best courses in the country, and I am a hacker on the golf course. I have a great time, but I could never see paying over $50 in greens fees for an afternoon of frustration.

As our conversation began to wind down, I asked Ernie if he would mind signing a baseball for my daughter, Kirstyn. He signed it, "To Kirstyn, Aim High, Ernie Banks." I shook his hand and thanked him not only for signing the ball but also for being a great hero, a great role model and a great guest on the show.

After he left the green room, I stayed for a few minutes and became lost in thought. My mind was filled with all kinds of memories of watching him play and imitating him on the playground of Jefferson Elementary School. I looked at the baseball he had signed and saw those two words: "Aim High." He certainly had done that during his career. In his early years, he played shortstop before they switched him over to first base. He hit 47 homeruns one season, more than any other shortstop has ever hit. In 13 seasons, he cracked more than 20 homeruns and ended up a member of the immortal 500 Homerun Club with 512 career round-trippers. Ernie won back-to-back MVP awards in 1958 and 1959. In those 2 years, he hit a total of 92 homeruns.

Ernie's Hall of Fame numbers are impressive. But his contributions to baseball go way beyond his statistics. To me, he represents the optimism of the fifties and sixties when America was thriving and baseball was booming. The ballparks of that day were glorious monuments to America's favorite pastime. Players stayed with the same team for their entire careers. They were loyal to their clubs and fans, and the fans were loyal to their teams. And even on those cold, blustery April afternoons in the Windy City, you could always find plenty of warmth in the sunny smile of Mr. Cub, Ernie Banks. As he said, "It's a beautiful day for baseball, let's play two." His eternal optimism is enough to make even today's most jaded fan say, "Hey, hey Ernie!!!!!"

Chapter 22

Other Legends

I didn't get to know each sports legend I encountered well enough to write a chapter on each one, but I thought you would enjoy hearing some of my perceptions and experiences with several other outstanding athletes whose names you'll know—and whom I hope to have the privilege of meeting again some day.

I love to work with people who have a good sense of humor, which is why I am going to begin this chapter with Johnny Bench. This guy loves to have a good time and is a great practical joker. The first time I worked with him was October 6, 1992, when he came to QVC to be my guest on a baseball collectibles show. I like to give my guests a big introduction to establish their place in sports history in the viewer's mind. So, I was talking about many of Bench's accomplishments, including the fact that he was the first catcher to win the National League Rookie of the Year Award in 1968. I then cited some of his records, including the most homeruns ever hit by a catcher and most putouts in a season, which has never been broken. I mentioned his Most Valuable Player Awards in 1970 and 1972. Finally, I said, "And here he is, the greatest catcher in baseball history: Mr. Johnny Bench!" As I turned to shake his hand, I burst out in laughter. While I was going through this big introduction, he had found some catcher's props that were decorating the set, and he put them on behind my back. There he was with a chest protector and face mask on! He simply shook my hand and said how great it was to be on the show, and he never even cracked a smile.

Johnny has appeared with me at least three different times and on every occasion he was in an upbeat, fun-loving mood. He is always an excellent guest, however, and is highly knowledgeable about all facets of the game of baseball. One thing Johnny told me that I'll never forget: the best way for a young player to make it in the major leagues today is as a catcher. Most parents don't want their child to play catcher because it doesn't seem like a very glamorous position. Catching is hard work, and most parents don't want to risk their child's being injured by foul balls. Not only does the catcher have to wear a lot of gear, but also it is tough to be in that crouched stance for an entire game, let alone a double-header. Johnny said that most professional catchers today were converted into catchers from other positions in the minor leagues. He told me that if a kid comes out of high school with a rocket arm and highly developed catching skills, he has a good chance of getting scouted.

The other thing that always stands out in my mind when I hear the name *Johnny Bench* is the size of his hands. He was always known for his large "paws." On his first QVC show, he demonstrated that he can hold eight baseballs in one hand! One thing is for sure. The show is always in very capable hands when Hall-of-Famer Johnny Bench is fielding the questions.

Another great catcher who also happens to be a great guy is Darren Daulton. Darren is a legend in the city of Philadelphia, where he was a leader of the Phillies for most of the '90's. He led the Phillies to the World Series in 1993; however, they lost the Series in heart-breaking fashion to the Toronto Blue Jays. Darren went on to finish his career with the Florida Marlins in 1997. He played an instrumental role in their World Series championship that year and was voted the Comeback Player of the Year in the National League.

I have worked with Darren on several occasions and have discovered that he has a lot of compassion and concern for young people. He often speaks at Christian camps around the country and was involved in producing a project for kids called *Words of Wisdom*. This is an excellent video and audio cassette program that teaches kids good moral values through contemporary music.

The last time I worked with Darren was on June 18, 2000. He appeared with me on QVC selling a product called the Darren Daulton Line Drive Hitter. It's an effective teaching tool for young ball players who want to perfect their swing. In fact, it is so much fun that Darren and I spent about 45 minutes before the show taking turns swinging away on it. He's a terrific guy.

Even Johnny Bench would have had trouble hanging onto the famous knuckleball of Phil Niekro. Phil was my guest on QVC on July 28, 1997, just a few days before he was inducted into baseball's Hall of Fame. I have never had a more humble guest or a more excited guest. After narrowly missing election into the Hall in 1993, '94, '95 and '96, he got the votes he needed in '97. He had tears in his eyes when he described how he felt when he finally got the call from Cooperstown.

Phil Niekro came from a baseball family. His brother, Joe Niekro, was also a fine major league pitcher and his father used to watch both of them play. He had a tough time when they actually pitched against each other in the big leagues. He always rooted for the team in the field.

During the show, Phil and I presented a Nolan Ryan autographed baseball. When he spoke about Nolan Ryan, there was a tone of reverence in his voice. It was obvious that he had a tremendous amount of respect for the man. He told me that he was able to pitch in the major leagues past the age of 40 by relying on his knuckleball, but the thing that amazed him the most about Nolan was that he still overpowered hitters with his fastball in his mid-forties! I'll never forget Phil saying, "He threw harder at 45 than I did when I was 22!"

I just can't say enough nice things about Phil Niekro. He was very kind to everyone at QVC and signed autographs for anyone who asked. After the show, he posed for several pictures with me and several of the QVC production crew. He is one of those guests that are just a joy to be around.

I'm now going to tell you about one of the biggest challenges I ever had on television. Before I became a host on QVC, I was a host on CVN, the Cable Value Network, located in Plymouth, Minnesota. The first sports show I ever hosted at CVN was a baseball show featuring the great Braves slugger, Eddie Mathews. Mathews was an all-star third baseman for the Braves and is also a member of baseball's 500 Homerun Club. Needless to say, I was very excited about doing the show and meeting the legendary Eddie Mathews. When he showed up in the green room before the show, I was a little concerned because I detected the smell of alcohol. He seemed to be in control of his faculties, though, so I figured everything was under control.

The show started out well. The first item we presented was an Eddie Mathews autographed baseball. He fielded all of my questions as smoothly as he had most of the ground balls that were hit his way in the big leagues. The second item we presented was an Eddie Mathews autographed bat. I thought it would be cool if Eddie could show us his batting stance. He grabbed the bat enthusiastically and stood up to go into his stance. Well, I guess the wine he had for dinner hit him on the way up, because he lost his balance and fell. Fortunately, I was backing him up on the play, and I caught him before he went all the way down. We went to a promotional break and I suggested to the producer that they get some coffee into the studio. The rest of the show was fine, and I was nominated for the Golden Glove of electronic retailing that year. I must say that Eddie was a very nice man; I think he probably just stood up too fast.

When I spoke of those legendary New York City street debates of the fifties about who was the greatest center fielder in baseball, you were expecting Mantle and Mays . . . but what about the other great New York centerfielder, Duke Snider? His nickname was "the Silver Fox," and when he retired, he held 10 World Series records. He won league titles in several different offensive categories, including hits, runs batted in and walks. He was the league leader in slugging percentage twice. He hit as many homeruns during the fifties as anybody and retired with a career total of 407.

I worked with Duke on a couple of occasions, but the last time was April 15, 1997, which marked the 50-year anniversary of Jackie Robinson's breaking professional baseball's color barrier. The focus of the show was Robinson, and Duke added marvelous insights into Jackie Robinson, the player and the man. Dave King co-hosted the show with me and afterward we all went to the Sheraton Hotel in Frasier, Pennsylvania, for dinner.

Duke told us a story that I'll never forget about Roy Campanella. He said that since Campy was part African American and part Italian, he had a strong following from both communities. One time during a spring exhibition game, Campy came to the plate and a rather loud African American fan yelled, "Come on Campy, get a hit for our race. Show them what we can do!" The first pitch came in and it was a called strike. The fan continued to yell encouragement. "That's O.K. Campy. You've still got two more. Hit one out of the park for us. Show them what we're made of!" he cried. Campy took a mighty cut and missed.

"Strike two!" the umpire shouted.

Duke had us all on the edge of our seats. He told us the guy started yelling even louder, "O.K. Campy this is it. Now, give that ball a ride and do it for our people all over the world!" Campy took a called third strike over the heart of the plate. As he was walking back to the dugout the fan shouted, "Hey Campy. You stupid Italian, go back to Italy!"

Our entire table broke out in laughter. Duke Snider can still deliver a story with true Hall of Fame form.

In 1979, I hosted and produced a sports segment for a weekly show that aired on channel 38 in Chicago. One of the segments I produced was on the legendary running back for the Chicago Bears, Walter Payton. To this day, he remains the all-time leading rusher in the history of the NFL with 16,726 career yards. At 5 feet 10 inches tall and 210 pounds, he was one of the toughest guys in the league to bring down. Young running backs today should take a lesson from the way Walter kept his legs moving like pistons, even when it seemed he was stopped at the line of scrimmage. Those pumping legs always resulted in a couple of extra yards.

I never understood Walter's nickname, "Sweetness," until I met him in person. He really was a sweetheart of a guy. He was very soft-spoken and polite. During our interview, he told me about the rigorous workout that he put himself through every day of the summer. He always ended his run by climbing a very high hill that was composed of soft dirt. The only way to make it to the top was to pump his legs as hard and as fast as he could. He told me that hill was the key to his tremendously powerful legs. While that was the key to his physical strength, the key to his emotional and spiritual strength was his faith. I'll never forget Walter Payton quoting his favorite passage from the Bible. It is found in Psalm 27, verse 1. It reads, "The Lord is my light and my salvation; Whom shall I fear? The Lord is the strength of my life; Of whom shall

I be afraid?" (New King James Version). As I have often said, the truly great athletes, the ones whom I would label as the true "legends," are also great people. Walter Payton was a prime example. When he passed away in the fall of 1999, the entire world of professional sports mourned the passing of a legendary player and a marvelous human being.

Another legendary running back who is cut from the same cloth as Walter is Herschel Walker. If you combined Herschel's yardage in the USFL with his NFL yardage, he would be the all-time leading rusher in professional football. He began his NFL career with the Dallas Cowboys and then came full circle after stints with the Minnesota Vikings, Philadelphia Eagles and the New York Giants. Did you know he also had a brief career with the U.S. Olympic bobsledding team?

Like Walter Payton, Herschel put himself through a punishing workout and is still in amazing physical condition. At one time in his career, he was doing literally thousands of push-ups and sit-ups each day! He also keeps himself in shape spiritually. When he was with the Philadelphia Eagles, he often went into Philly's toughest neighborhoods with Reggie White to minister to the people there. After one of our shows, he signed an Eagles cap for me, "To Dan, may God bless you! Herschel Walker #34." Here is another tremendous athlete who is also a wonderful human being.

Football is a punishing sport and one of the fiercest hitters of all-time was Ronnie Lott. Ronnie won several Super Bowl rings with the San Francisco 49'ers before wearing the black and silver of the Raiders. Ronnie appeared on QVC three times during the final few years of his career. I was always impressed with his ability on the air and was not at all surprised when he landed a job with *The NFL on Fox*. In fact, I had a lot of fun doing a spoof for their pre-game show in 1996 where I was pretending to offer the infamous Terry award on QVC and nobody was ordering it.

One time when Ronnie was my guest on QVC, my niece, Kim Bellone, was visiting from California. She knew Ronnie very well, because she used to babysit his daughter in the San Francisco area. When she walked into the green room before the show, he looked at her and asked, "What are you doing here?"

She pointed to me and said, "This is my Uncle Dan!" It's a small world.

One of Ronnie's appearances came in the middle of his final season as a pro. I knew the end was near because about halfway through the show, Ronnie stood up to stretch out his knees during a break. It took him a very long time to stand up and he was grimacing in pain. He told me his knees were shot. "It takes me about two hours of stretching before I'm ready to play in a game," he said.

When you are working with professional athletes you always have to stay on your toes. Sometimes they get overbooked; sometimes at an event like the Super Bowl or the All-Star game they have so much going on that one or two appointments fall through the cracks. This happened one time when I was in San Antonio for the 1996 NBA All-Star Game. We were producing a live show right on the river walk in downtown San Antonio. My scheduled guests were Alonzo Mourning, Damon Stoudamire and Dikembe Mutombo.

As I opened the show at 2:00 P.M. San Antonio time, none of my guests had arrived. After about 15 minutes, I began to worry that nobody was going to show up. The main reason the crew and I had traveled over a thousand miles was because it was an easy way to book several basketball stars on one show. Finally, about a half-hour into the show, I noticed that Alonzo had arrived. I had worked with "Zo" before and had a wonderful experience. While he is super intense on the court and one of the fiercest competitors in the NBA, he is just as easygoing and polite away from the game. Our audio director quickly put a microphone on him and escorted him onto the set. While he was only scheduled for a half-hour, he ended up staying on the show for about an hour and 20 minutes.

He really saved the day, because Damon Stoudamire and Dikembe Mutombo were nowhere to be found. In Dikembe's defense, he was a representative for the players' union and a meeting he was involved in ran extra long. His representative called after the show and apologized. I never found out why Damon was a no-show, but he was a phone-in guest on one of my shows not long after that. Thank the Lord Alonzo was so willing to go the extra mile.

Rick Pitino is the type of basketball coach who can always get his players to go the extra mile on the court. In 1997, Rick wrote a book entitled, *Success Is a Choice: Ten Steps to Overachieving in Business and Life*. He appeared with me one evening on QVC to offer the book. I had no idea he was going to be there until about two hours before the show. I was dressed casually that evening so when I heard he was going to be my guest I called home immediately. When my wife Beth answered the phone, I said, "I need a huge favor." I asked her to bring in my dark blue suit with a very sharp tie and my shiniest pair of shoes. Rick Pitino is known to be a sharp dresser, so I wanted to "dress up" to his level. Beth obliged, and I quickly got a copy of his book and started perusing it so that I could conduct a halfway intelligent interview.

When I first met Mr. Pitino, he was talking on his cell phone. The guy is definitely driven and works as hard as anyone I know. He had just coached his Kentucky Wildcats to the 1996 NCAA national championship in basketball, and there were all kinds of rumors floating around that he was going to be coaching an NBA team the next year. Before the show, I was kidding with him about how the Philadelphia 76'ers could sure use his coaching services. The same company that owns QVC, Comcast, owns the 76'ers. As it turns out, the president of the 76'ers had just been with Rick at the Chester County Bookstore in West Chester, and I have my suspicions that they were at QVC that evening as well, trying to woo him into coming to Philadelphia. Rick and I sold 3,000 copies of his book that night. That was the entire number of books that we had in inventory. We did some funny "schtick" to promote his appearance, and he was a great sport. As you probably know, he went on to coach the Boston Celtics later that year.

Everyone knows that Michael Jordan is not only the best basketball player ever, but also a pretty fair golfer. That is not true of every player in the NBA. In the summer of 1997, I was asked to play in a charity golf tournament. As I have mentioned, I am a hacker at best on the golf course, but I really enjoy getting out in the fresh air and swinging the clubs. At one point during the charity tournament, Charles Barkley joined my foursome. We teed off together, and with an easy stroke I drove the ball fairly straight about 200 yards down the fairway. Charles came up and took a mighty cut at the ball, and as he did, his back foot came up off the ground about two feet, and the ball sliced quite severely to the right. He definitely had an unorthodox swing, and I was happy that I out drove Sir Charles. I must say that he was very polite to everyone in the group and signed several autographs along the way.

I worked with one of the greatest golfers of all time one evening on QVC. Gary Player, the man from South Africa who has a slew of major tournament victories on the PGA Tour, came on to demonstrate a special golf club that he was endorsing. The key to the club was the angle and design of the head, which really allowed you to get under the ball. The QVC production crew had set up a giant golf net in the studio for Gary and me to hit balls, demonstrating the lift you could achieve with the club. I'm a lefty, but we were only offering the club in the right-handed model. I'm bad enough golfing left-handed, but the thought of swinging a club from the right side on national television had me greatly concerned.

Gary demonstrated the club beautifully and then suggested that I take a few strokes. My first three shots went almost straight up in the air and actually went over the top of the net. In fact, my second shot took out a couple of our very expensive television lights! I turned to the camera and said, "If I can do that swinging from the wrong side with this club, just think of what it will do for you!" Gary thought it was quite humorous.

Figure skating is one of the most beautiful sports to watch. It combines strength and power with expression and grace. The end result is artistry on ice. One of the very best ever was Michelle Kwan. In January of 1998, Michelle competed at the U.S. National Championships at the Core States Center in Philadelphia. I attended a press conference with Michelle and then interviewed her in the Comcast Sports Network studios, which are located inside the Core States Center. During the press conference, she seemed rather bored with all of the questions about her injuries and her loss at the Nationals in 1996, so I decided to ask a question that would take things in a different direction. I asked her what lessons she had learned after her disappointment at the '96 nationals and how those lessons would help her now.

She lit up as she talked about how she rediscovered the joy of skating. She had been skating since she was seven years old, but somewhere along the way in the midst of all the pressure, she lost her joy for the sport.

I interviewed Michelle one-on-one later that afternoon. She reminisced about being seven years old and going to the skating rink whenever she could. She talked about watching the 1988 Winter Olympic Games on television and dreaming of one day winning an Olympic medal. Her childhood skating heroes were Brian Boitano and Peggy Fleming. She also told me about the good luck charm that she always wears around her neck. It's a necklace that her grandmother gave her, and she never takes it off.

Later that week, Michelle went on to win the Nationals. In Nagano, Japan, at the 1998 Winter Olympic Games, she put on a brilliant performance but narrowly lost the gold medal to Tara Lipinski. I was very impressed with Michelle. She exhibited tremendous grace under pressure. She is wise beyond her years.

Hockey takes place on the ice but most players aren't known for the same type of gracefulness that distinguishes figure skaters. While many members of the National Hockey League are fast and agile on skates, nobody combined those attributes with pure toughness and durability like #9, the legendary Gordie Howe. He is known worldwide as Mr. Hockey and is recognized as the greatest all-around player in history. His remarkable career, which spanned 32 pro seasons, is one of the most amazing in sports history.

After spending 25 consecutive seasons in the NHL with the Detroit Red Wings, he retired for 2 years, only to return to the ice in 1973 with the Houston Aeros of the World Hockey Association. This was after he had established more records than any team athlete in history, including all-time marks for goals, assists, points and games. When his sons, Marty and Mark, signed with the Aeros, it was the first father/son combination ever to play together in a major professional sport. His many accomplishments include 7 Most Valuable Player awards and 6 scoring championships along with playing in an unbelievable 29 All-Star games.

Gordie came to QVC on May 12, 2000. He was my guest on a show called *NHL: Bring the Cup Home*. The show was slated for 9 P.M. eastern time. Gordie showed up at 7:30 P.M. and wanted to spend a good hour with me just talking one on one. I was immediately impressed by how humble and gracious he was. I couldn't believe this was the same guy who made even the toughest of opponents quiver with fear. He told me that the ice had an unusual transforming effect on him. He said, "You know Dan, my family always tells me that I am such a nice person away from the hockey rink. But when I got on the ice, it did something to me."

At 72 years old, he still looked great. I began asking him about different episodes that I had read in his family autobiography, entitled *and . . . HOWE!* (which, incidentally, is a great read). He told me about his most memorable hockey fight. He was still a teenager and it was one of his first encounters as a professional. He got into a brawl with this big, tough veteran. He said the guy just kept cocking his fist back slowly and deliberately and finally exploded into Gordie's chest, knocking him back about 20 feet. He landed on his backside and as the guy came toward him, Gordie started laughing hysterically. The guy decided he wasn't going to mess with anyone who could laugh after being hit that hard. This gives you an idea of how tough Gordie was.

There was one incident when a guy had one of his sons pinned to the ice when they were playing with the Houston Aeros. Gordie said, "I figured I'd let them go for a while, but finally I decided my boy had had enough. I skated up to the guy and told him to get up off of my son. The guy refused and just kept swinging away at him. So, I took these two big fingers of mine and I shoved them up the guy's nose and lifted him up in the air by his nostrils. He started screaming and crying and I told him he should have listened to me the first time."

Gordie told me several great stories that night. At one point I asked him how many stitches he had taken in his face during his career. I nearly fell out of my chair when he responded, "Over 500." He then lifted his pant legs and showed me the scars from his knee surgeries, so I showed him a few of my scars. It reminded me of the scene from the movie *Jaws* where the main actors are out in a boat hunting down the shark, and they begin comparing scars.

After sharing one great story after another, Gordie told me one of his philosophies about the sport of hockey. He said, "I always believed in playing religious hockey. I felt it was better to give than to receive. And, I had a good memory. If they got me, I'd get them back."

I am a big fan of Gordie Howe, especially now that I know he is such a warm, kind and gracious man. He signed a copy of his book to me and posed for a picture with me holding the Stanley Cup. Everybody at QVC fell in love with him. We co-hosted a one-hour show that night in front of a live studio audience. After the show, he stayed and spoke with the audience members for more than half an hour.

Gordie Howe is a very gracious man. He has a genuine love for his wife, Colleen, and all of their children and grandchildren. By the way, Colleen is an amazing woman and is known as Mrs. Hockey. She is recognized as the most influential woman in hockey history and she is the first female manager/agent ever in the sport. All in all, I would have to say that my experience with Gordie Howe ranks right near the top of my career working with the true legends of sports. He is a legendary athlete, a legendary human being and just a very nice man, away from the ice. And I have a feeling that if he wanted to lace up the skates and play again in his seventies, he could still find the back of the net.

Olympic athletes are the most amazing of all to me. They dedicate their lives, year-round, to their sport and then lay it all on the line for one performance in front of the entire world. That is tremendous pressure, and it takes a special kind of person to handle it. Florence Griffith Joyner—or "FloJo," as the world knew her—was at one time known as "the fastest woman in the world." She also made long, colorful fingernails and one-legged tights fashionable. I worked with FloJo and her husband, Al Joyner, who won a gold medal in the triple jump at the 1984 Olympic Games. They were two of the nicest, most giving people I have ever worked with. They did a number of promotional spots for QVC and were excellent guests on one of our countdown to the Centennial Olympic Games shows. They both signed an Olympic hat for me, and FloJo wrote, "Dan, you were the greatest! I'll call you soon! Love FloJo." I never got that phone call. A couple of years later, I heard the shocking news that FloJo had died suddenly. I was deeply saddened for her husband and their little girl, whom they affectionately called "MoJo."

Joe DiMaggio, Mickey Mantle, Billy Martin, Cal Ripken, Sr., Ray Nitschke, and Florence Griffith Joyner were all legends in their sports and in life. We remember them all as heroes of their sports. Each one possessed tremendous energy, strength and a passion for life. Now they are gone. I was honored to have spent a little time with each of them on this earth. May God rest their souls.

These are some of my best memories of the legendary encounters I have had over the years. I guess I'm going to have to think about writing another book one day, because I continue to meet both the legends and the modern-day superstars of sports on QVC.

Chapter 23

Beyond the Legendary Lore

I have saved one of my favorite stories for last. I have told you about my experiences with baseball's most prolific hitter, Hank Aaron, and baseball's all-time "hit king," Pete Rose. I began the book describing one of baseball's most consistent hitters, Joe DiMaggio. Here is a great story about the man whom most experts agree was baseball's best "pure hitter," Ted Williams. They called him "Teddy Ballgame" and "The Splendid Splinter."

Williams was Major League Baseball's last player to hit over .400. He entered the last double-header of the 1941 season hitting .39955, which was rounded off to .400. The manager of the Boston Red Sox at the time was Joe Cronin. He suggested to Williams that he sit out the last two games, so that he wouldn't run the risk of having his average dip below .400. Ted refused and later said, "If I couldn't hit .400 all the way, I didn't deserve it." He went on to crack six hits in eight trips to the plate against Philadelphia and ended the season with a batting average of .406. That is an example of legendary greatness.

Ted appeared as my guest on QVC for a baseball collectibles show on October 17, 1993. I asked him how he thought he could do batting against today's major league pitchers. He calmly responded, "Oh, I think I'd hit about .275."

I was taken aback. I said, "The great Ted Williams,

baseball's last .400 hitter! Do you really think you would only hit .275?"

He said, "Well Dan, you have to remember I'm 74 years old!"

I laughed so hard that I almost fell out of my chair.

As funny as this story is, it reminds us that sooner or later even the legendary athletes slow down. Eventually, there comes a time for even the greatest to hang it up. Their accomplishments live on in the record books, but they don't. Even Pete Rose said that nobody will remember if he was a good person or not, they'll just remember him as the guy who had the most hits. It reminds me of Nadia Comaneci's tarnished Olympic medals and her broken Olympic Wreath. In time, even the greatest accomplishments in the world of sports become distant memories. Somebody always seems to come along to break the records that even the experts say will never be broken.

When you look up the word *legend* in *Webster's New Collegiate Dictionary* you discover that one of the definitions is "a person or thing that inspires legends." Well, I have always been interested in the person who inspires the legend. As I mentioned in the introduction to this book, I have discovered that the greatest of the legendary athletes, for the most part, are great people. They realize that they are blessed with an extraordinary ability or gift. They also work hard to do their very best with their God-given talents.

But they all know that eventually the glory fades. When they are performing their heroics in the spotlight and tens of thousands of fans are chanting their names, they appear almost immortal. But away from the cheers of adoring fans, they're just people like you and me. Alone at night, in the dark, they all have many of the same fears as you and I, regardless of how many trophies, medals or records they own.

I recently had the opportunity to speak to about 900 middle school students in the West Chester, Pennsylvania, area. I was the keynote speaker for a day in which the students were exposed to many different careers. The school brought in a total of 50 professionals from various fields of endeavor. During my talk, I told them that regardless of the occupation they decide on, it is absolutely critical that they choose something they love to do. When you love your job, it's easy to get out of bed in the morning.

I am one of the truly fortunate people in the world who loves his job. I have been blessed with so many tremendous opportunities. How many people get to meet their childhood heroes? I have not only met many of them, but I've had the chance to talk to them at length about their careers and about their lives. While I love discussing any sport, learning about their lives and discovering what really makes them tick is what fascinates me the most. The true legends of sports are the ones who make their teammates better. Michael Jordan is a true legend of basketball not just because he could take anybody on the planet in a game of one-on-one, but because he made everyone around him a better player. That is a special quality that transcends sports. Truly great people make their teammates better, whether that team is at work, home, church or a civic group.

Sports have always been a big part of my life. When I was a kid my mom always knew where to find me: at the ballpark. I wanted to play in the big games. My dreams always included the World Series, the All-Star Games, the Super Bowl and the NBA championships. While I never got to play in any of them, I did get to play in a lot of games through college and even for a few years after. I feel fortunate that I received scholarship money to play baseball in college. When you think about it, millions of kids play in Little League, tens of thousands play in high school, thousands play in college and only hundreds play in the professional ranks. It's really a very small percentage of athletes who make it that far. When you talk about the Hall of Famers and the legends, you are talking about a fraction of a percentage point. It's like a handful of sand compared to the rest of the beach.

Sports are wonderful, and they certainly teach valuable lessons about life. The hard work involved builds character. The performance aspect teaches an athlete about pressure, goals and teamwork. Winning and losing are situations we face every day of our lives. But I think it is important to keep in mind why we play sports.

Many parents and coaches today put too much emphasis on winning. Kids are submitted, in many cases, to entirely too much pressure at a young age. Both of my daughters have played soccer. Kelsey played in an instructional league. She is eight years old and just likes to have fun. Kirstyn, on the other hand, is 14 and is already playing at a high level in both soccer and lacrosse. She has learned a lot about pressure and winning and losing already. Since I tend to be pretty competitive, I have to check myself, all the time, and remind myself why my daughters are playing sports. What lessons am I hoping they both will learn? I hope all of us realize that the *learning* is more important than the *winning*. And in the long run, it is still just a game. The real test comes in the game of life.

The apostle Paul used sports analogies to describe his life in a letter he wrote to Timothy around the year A.D. 67. In the Bible, in 2 Timothy 4 and 7, he writes, "I have fought the good fight, I have finished the race, I have kept the faith" (New International Version). I hope that I can say the same thing at the end of my life.

I told you I have a couple of boxes full of sports trophies in my basement. They are still there. Most of them are badly tarnished, and I'll probably only take them out a couple of times during the rest of my life just to show my kids or my grandkids some day. I'll want them to know that at one time, their old man could play. But mostly it isn't the trophies that make an impression. Rather, the *lessons* I learned playing stay with me.

I have learned more lessons being around the very best athletes who have ever lived. The truly great athletes, the true legends, have learned how to win at the game of life. That is the real reason why I feel so privileged to have met them.

Every year, I continue to visit with great athletes on QVC. While I get to meet the legends from time to time, I also have the opportunity to sit and talk with many of the current superstars of sports. It will be interesting to see which of these athletes will have what it takes to go the distance. Who will continue to perform at the level of greatness day in and day out, year after year? Who will earn the right to be called "a true legend"? Only time will tell. You can keep up with new developments, and find more great untold sports stories, at www.untoldsportsstories.com. In the meantime, I'll leave you with a quote that kind of sums up what sports and life are all about—unfortunately, the author is unknown:

"You win some, you lose some and you even get rained out of some. But you suit up for them all!"

From Joe DiMaggio to Cal Ripken, Jr.; from Joe Namath to Emmitt Smith; from Bill Russell to Penny Hardaway; from big George Foreman to tiny Nadia Comaneci, I have had the tremendous privilege of interviewing some of the greatest athletes of all time. I have observed them and watched how they reacted in various situations. Gold medalists, Hall of Famers and future Hall of Famers have all sat down and talked to me on QVC. I feel very fortunate to have been the one sitting next to them.

I hope you have enjoyed sitting in my seat for a while, the one that I have occupied over the years as I interviewed the heroes and the legends of sports on QVC. I am convinced that it has always been the BEST SEAT IN THE HOUSE.

Magic
Moments
with the
Legends of
Sports

I've always loved sports. Here I am at the age of two trying my hand at golf. Unfortunately, my swing still looks about the same as it did here in 1956!

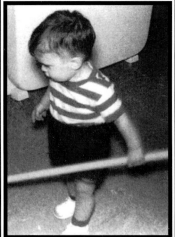

Since golf didn't work out, I immediately took to billiards. We didn't own a pool table, though, so I had to play on the kitchen floor.

This was the pinnacle of my career. "Joltin' Joe" DiMaggio appeared with me on QVC, March 28, 1993.

One of my favorite baseball legends to interview is this guy, Baseball's All Time Hit King, Pete Rose. Here we're on the set of QVC Sports.

Sharing a laugh with Billy Martin and Mickey Mantle at Mickey's Bar and Restaurant in New York City. This photo was taken less than two months before Billy's untimely death.

Two of baseball's all-time great centerfielders. Well, one great centerfielder and a guy who played in college. Mickey Mantle and me in October of 1989.

271

Pete Rose loves telling jokes and pulling pranks in the green room.

Baseball's Ironman and all-around great guy, Cal Ripken, Jr.

Even after retiring from baseball, the All Time No Hit King and Strikeout King still keeps his life moving at the speed of his legendary fast ball.

Nolan Ryan when he was still throwing "Texas Heat" at the age of 45.

Here I am at the 1996 Summer Olympic Games in Atlanta. I am standing within 50 feet of where the bomb exploded later that evening!

IN MEMORIUM:
ALICE HAWTHORNE
U.S.A.

MELIH UZUNYOL
TURKEY

This makeshift memorial was created by visitors to the Atlanta Centennial Olympic Games following the bombing in Centennial Park.

Karen Fonner, QVC's talented buyer, and me standing in front of the fountains at Centennial Park in Atlanta. This picture was taken the afternoon before the bomb exploded, leaving two people dead.

273

I snuck in a quick upper cut on boxing's former World Heavyweight Champ, George Foreman.

Covering the Super Bowl is always a tough assignment. Here I am giving the Green Bay Packer cheerleaders a pre-game pep talk.

Interviewing Super Bowl XXXI Most Valuable Player, Desmond Howard, before Super Bowl XXXII in San Diego.

The halftime show of Super Bowl XXXII was a salute to Motown's 40th Anniversary.

Truly one of the best seats in the house at Super Bowl XXXII. I was in the second section up from the field at the 35-yard line.

The Super Bowl is an entertainment extravaganza from the moment you enter the stadium. I'm enjoying the sights and sounds of Super Bowl XXXII inside QualComm Stadium in San Diego.

The "Say Hey" kid, Willie Mays, and me in February of 1993. This was before I had to testify against my childhood hero at a legal hearing.

It's hard to believe that the legendary Bill Russell was actually considered short for a center in the NBA.

Dwarfed by 2000 NBA Most Valuable Player, Shaquille O'Neal. I have never felt so small in all my life!

Broadway Joe Namath and me before Super Bowl XXXIII in Miami. This was the 30-year anniversary of Joe's guaranteed victory in Super Bowl III.

Mr. Smooth himself, Joe Namath, was a real crowd favorite in Miami in 1999.

I was privileged to have a locker next to the Dominican Dandy, Juan Marichal, when I attended the San Francisco Giants Fantasy Baseball Camp in 1994.

San Francisco Giants '94

Dan Wheeler. CF

Baseball's All Time Home Run and RBI King, Hammerin' Hank Aaron. I have spent the last seven years with Hank on April 8, the anniversary of the night he broke Babe Ruth's career home run record in 1974.

One of my favorite keepsakes is my baseball card from the '94 San Francisco Giants Fantasy Camp. This card is extremely rare and hard to find. The book value is about 10 cents.

Brett Favre was an excellent guest on QVC's very first show from the site of the Super Bowl in Miami in 1995. One of my other guests was late so Brett stayed on for an extra half hour.

Brett Favre and me discussing the Packer's Super Bowl XXXI victory at The Old Waverly Golf Club in West Point, Mississippi, in 1997.

Mr. October himself, Reggie Jackson, is always a "lively" and interesting interview for me.

Perhaps the greatest football player in the history of the game – the legendary Jim Brown.

"Let's Play Two!" One of my childhood heroes, "Mr. Cub," Ernie Banks.

The Biggest Little Man in the NFL – Emmitt Smith. Emmitt is one of the nicest people ever to don an NFL uniform.

279

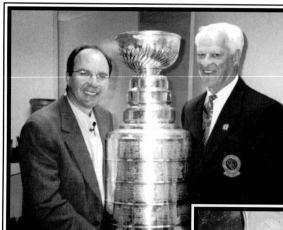

The Stanley Cup is heavy! I'm glad I had one of the toughest and greatest hockey players of all time standing by to help. Gordie Howe and me lifting the cup on May 12, 2000.

I had the wonderful opportunity to interview the Magic Man himself, Earvin Johnson, on June 12, 2000.

Standing six feet nine inches tall, "Magic" Johnson was one of the NBA's tallest point guards ever. Because of his size and agility, he played center and forward at times. His heart and kindness match his size.

Pete Rose says that Mike Schmidt is the best player he ever played with. Here I am with 500 Home Run Club Member Mike Schmidt.

With legendary Brooklyn Dodger slugger, Duke Snider.

Interviewing Sandy Alomar, Jr., the night before the 1997 All Star Game in Cleveland. Sandy hit a game-winning home run for the American League All Stars the next night and was named the MVP of the game.

Entering "the Jake" in Cleveland for Major League Baseball's 1997 All Star Game.

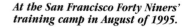

I'm waiting patiently on the bench at Texas Stadium just in case Troy Aikman needs a 40-something backup quarterback.

The author driving to the hoop for his high school varsity basketball team in St. Joseph, Michigan. Notice the flying hair. My hero was "Pistol Pete" Maravich who also had long hair.

After losing all but two games my rookie year in Little League, the Wynn Shuler's Giants went on to claim back-to-back championships in 1964 and 1965 in St. Joe, Michigan. I'm in the second row on the far right.

My QVC Sports partner Dave King and me outside QualComm Stadium in San Diego, California. We were heading inside the house to watch the Denver Broncos and the Green Bay Packers tangle in Super Bowl XXXII on January 25, 1998.

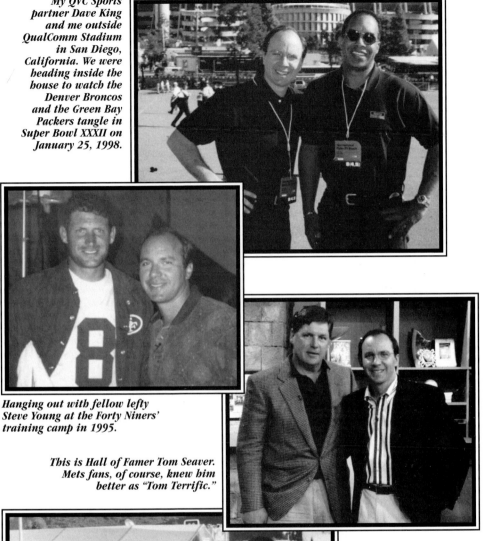

Hanging out with fellow lefty Steve Young at the Forty Niners' training camp in 1995.

This is Hall of Famer Tom Seaver. Mets fans, of course, knew him better as "Tom Terrific."

Legendary running back Marcus Allen and me before Super Bowl XXXII in San Diego.

Reuniting with Nadia Comenici at the 2000 Olympic Games in Sydney, Australia.

Entering Olympic Stadium at Sydney Olympic park for the closing ceremony of the Games of the XXXVII Olympiad.

The entrance to Olympic Stadium in Sydney was especially beautiful after sunset.

Giant Kewpie dolls join the athletes for a colorful goodbye from the Land of Oz in the closing ceremony of the Sydney 2000 Olympic games.

Appendix

Athletes Interviewed by the Author

Baseball

Hank Aaron	Ken Griffey, Sr.
Sandy Alomar, Jr.	Charlie Hayes
Ernie Banks	Tommy Henrich
Albert Belle	Randy Hundley
Johnny Bench	Reggie Jackson
Vida Blue	Chipper Jones
Wade Boggs	David Justice
Barry Bonds	Harmon Killebrew
Bobby Bonds	Ed Kranepool
Orlando Cepeda	Hobie Landreth
Roberto Clemente, Jr.	Bill Laskey
Darren Daulton	Jim Leyritz
Joe DiMaggio	Mickey Mantle
Lenny Dykstra	Juan Marichal
Darryl Evans	Billy Martin
Robert Feller	Eddie Mathews
Cecil Fielder	Willie Mays
Rollie Fingers	Mike McCormick
Carlton Fisk	Raul Mondesi
Whitey Ford	Joe Morgan
Tommy Greene	Phil Niekro
Ken Griffey, Jr.	Fritz Peterson

Cal Ripken, Jr.   Tom Seaver
Cal Ripken, Sr.   Gary Sheffield
Phil Rizzuto   Ozzie Smith
Brooks Robinson   Duke Snider
Frank Robinson   Darryl Strawberry
Alex Rodriguez   Bruce Sutter
Pete Rose   Earl Weaver
Nolan Ryan   Bernie Williams
Mike Sadek   Ted Williams
Mike Schmidt   Mark Wohlers

Basketball

Randy Brown   Alonzo Mourning
Judd Buechler   Dikembe Mutombo
Terry Cummings   Shaquille O'Neal
Chuck Daly, coach   Scottie Pippen
Anfernee Hardaway   Rick Pitino, coach
Ron Harper   Bill Russell
Juwan Howard   John Starks
Jimmy Jackson   Damon Stoudamire
Magic Johnson   Reggie Theus
Christian Laettner   Rasheed Wallace
Jamal Mashburn   Charlie Ward
Antonio McDyess   Chris Webber
Oliver Miller   Bill Wennington

Football

Troy Aikman   Kevin Brown
Marcus Allen   Kerry Collins
Drew Bledsoe   Roger Craig
Jim Brown   Randal Cunningham
Larry Brown   Trent Dilfer

Tony Dorsett	Ken Norton, Jr.
John Elway	Jay Novacek
Vince Evans	Terrell Owens
Marshall Faulk	Neil O'Donnell
Brett Favre	Walter Payton
Doug Flutie	Drew Pearson
William Floyd	Rodney Peete
Antonio Freeman	Jerry Rice
Bob Griese	Tony Rice
Jack Ham	Jason Sehorn
Franco Harris	Rashaan Salaam
Desmond Howard	Emmitt Smith
Paul Hornung	Neil Smith
Brad Johnson	Rod Smith
Michael Irvin	Kordell Stewart
Deacon Jones	Lawrence Taylor
Greg Lloyd	Joe Theissman
Howie Long	Jessie Tuggle
Ronnie Lott	Herschel Walker
Mike Mamula	Ricky Watters
Joe Montana	Randy White
Joe Namath	Kevin Williams
Ray Nitschke	Steve Young

Boxing

George Foreman

Figure Skating

Tai Babilonia	Randy Gardner
Peggy Fleming	Michelle Kwan

Golf

Gary Player

Gymnastics

Nadia Comenici   Bart Conner
Cathy Rigby

Hockey

Mike Bossy   Gordie Howe

Auto Racing

Geoff Bodine   Ward Burton   Dale Jarrett
"Big Daddy" Don Garlits

Track and Field

Bruce Jenner   Al Joyner   Florence Griffith Joyner

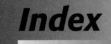

Index